Art
Fundamentals
Theory and
Practice

Art
Fundamentals
Theory and
Practice

Third Edition by
Otto G. Ocvirk, Robert O. Bone,
Robert E. Stinson, Philip R. Wigg

School of Art / Bowling Green State University, Bowling Green, Ohio

WM. C. BROWN COMPANY, PUBLISHERS / DUBUQUE, IOWA

Contents

Black and White Illustrations

Color Illustrations

Number following artist and Plate Title refers to page number preceding location in text.

Preface

A worthwhile book is always written out of an assumed need and on the basis of what it intends to do about it. A book on art instruction, perhaps more than any other kind, should be equally realistic about what it cannot do. Beyond a certain point, the more one attempts to be "systematic" in this instruction, the more one misses the essential value of art. One cannot legislate feelings or emotions, and art is nothing if it lacks these qualities. One cannot prescribe personality, and art is always stamped with the honest imprint of its author.

Art instruction, therefore, narrows down to a few simple procedures which are deceptively complex in their application. It always succeeds or fails with the sensitivity of the student and his capacity for work. A person who would teach art well must learn to live with the knowledge that this student sensitivity feeds on the enthusiasm exhibited by the teacher. An atmosphere of creative excitement is always the most important step toward meaningful art instruction.

Beyond this, instruction in art must function elastically; it should always be presented on as personal a basis as possible, but it should also insure that personal experiences add up to those factors which are fundamental in art expression. In short, there should be some system to the instruction but the "system" should be kept within tolerances which permit discovery. There must always be a point at which the student may take over.

This book is an effort to fulfill the need for such a cautious system of instruction. It is not a "How-to-do-it" book; it contains no rules, formulas, or guarantees. In art such things are not possible; it is, however, predicated on certain principles which are presumed to be of such a fundamental nature as to encompass a wide range of expression. These principles are those which underlie every work of art, historical and contemporary, and can hardly claim to be original with the authors. Their search was not for novelty but for a sound but supple method of guidance which will encourage the development of understanding and ability. One should always be aware that most of the original thinking in this field is in the art, not on it.

Thinking and feeling are the two prerequisites to the successful use of the problems in this book; they are meant to be sensed and understood, not mechanically repeated. None of the problems, individually, is of any great importance, nor is the resultant work likely to be of surpassing beauty. But each exercise represents a problem which eventually appears in the total art form. Once the problem has been experienced, it is easier to recognize it as such and find its answer.

The best use of the recommended creative exercises can be made only if the text has been read before and after their execution. If the work is being done in a class, the chapters may very well serve as a basis for lecture and/or discussion. Text presentation has been deliberately kept at a reasonably challenging level (despite the fact that the book deals with the elementary phases of art) in the belief that this approach provides stimulation for a greater range of abilities.

Organization on the basis of art elements is a method which evolved out of the instructional experiences of the authors. Any book on art must break down *form* in some way in order to illustrate and instruct, and division into the elements of art structure of *line, shape, value, texture,* and *color* has the advantage that these elements, universal and unchanging, are unlikely to be challenged in their interpretation. The one disadvantage of this division is the one which is recognized as being a potential threat in any course of study—the possibility that the student may fail to make a final integration of the concepts illustrated by this breakdown. If an instructor is present, it is his responsibility to see that any learning developing out of the study of any *one* art element should find application in any future work.

The use of this book should be accompanied by studies of reproductions, and, even more, of original works of art. No text of this kind is able to provide ample quantity and quality of illustration. Those which were here selected were chosen because they were considered the most obvious examples of points brought up in the text. Most of them are good works of art, but certainly not of uniformly high quality in everyone's judgment. Their use here does not suggest a sweeping endorsement of their value. One of the interesting things about art is that there is rarely, if ever, an art work which is wholly good or wholly bad. An illustration used to depict an admirable quality of one sort might very well be used to show an unfortunate lapse in some other respect. Use the pictures with discrimination and judgment or even as the focus of healthy debate.

Terminology is included in the book solely for the establishment of a common basis of communication between those using it. It is impossible to find universal agreement among art people on terms, their significance, or their interpretation. A glance at other art books will confirm that words, definitions, and emphases vary. Consistency seems to be the important thing here; use of the book will be more profitable if its vocabulary is used consistently. It has been said that Georges Braque once remarked that he wanted his students to paint in his style as long as they studied with him; only in this way did he feel that they could understand each other. Anyone who has taught art understands the wisdom and the danger in this remark; but the danger is avoided if the "style" or "method" is understood as being only a temporary expedient. In a sense, this book may be considered a "temporary expedient." It is *temporary* in the sense that anyone who would become an artist must go far beyond it; it is *expedient* because it is hoped that its composition will expedite the development of sound attitudes.

Acknowledgments

With this, the third edition of ART FUNDAMENTALS, we find that the number of contributors has increased significantly, as has our sense of obligation. We take this opportunity to thank them publicly, and hope that they find some additional measure of reward in the favor with which past editions have been received.

The greatest contributions continue to be made by the Museum of Modern Art, New York City, and the National Gallery, Washington, D.C. Every degree of cooperation is appreciated, but we must give special thanks to the Toledo Museum of Art, the Cleveland Museum of Art, the Detroit Institute of Art, and the Art Institute of Chicago.

New in the book are a number of works from the Owens-Corning Collection. The Owens-Corning Fiberglas Corporation has been immensely helpful in making this collection available to us.

Both Willard Wankelman and the representatives of our publisher have conspired to infect us with the sense of desperate urgency every author must feel before embarking on another revision.

Once again the wives have resignedly donned their "widow's weeds" during our long absences from the hearth.

Chapter 1 / Introduction

One of the familiar characteristics of our times is ceaseless and often violent change. The promise and threat of this change are sensed by us all. We sometimes wish we could make time stand still so that we could experience the comfort and security that we think might come with absolute values, standards by which we could, with certainty, isolate the good from the bad. Yet, in so wishing we know that we delude ourselves; we all as human beings share in the desire for progress. Few, if any of us, would be content to revert to the discomforts of an earlier age, and none of us would be happy to live in that age if it meant the surrender of our individuality. It is individuality which produces all that we value, which creates progress, which, in short, is change. If we are to honor individuality, we must honor its expression; this is often easy to do when expression comes in the form of a product clearly usable. It is not so easy for us to value expression in its pure form as art, particularly when in this form individuality is undisguised and speaks as it must in many ways.

Since change is such an obvious factor in our society, and since change is magnified in art by the search for individual expression, the newcomer to art may ask if there is any genuinely reliable standard to guide him through the hazards of shifting historical styles and seemingly contradictory theories. The less diligent of us might be content to stand pat insofar as art matters are concerned; indeed, this may seem the easiest path, although in the end, the least satisfying. It is always easier to argue against things than to learn what they are all about. Any learning (or expansion of outlook) calls for discarding old and comfortable standards, a sacrifice which in art frequently involves many of our cherished opinions. The learner in art must be willing to concede the possible validity of many unfamiliar forms of individual expression; this means that the learner must place his own taste on trial.

We cannot deny that personal taste is always influential in forming art judgments, but we would certainly be remiss in not investigating the origins of this taste. Personal preference without benefit of experience cannot legitimately pose as criticism in art or in any other field. We may argue our feelings by saying that "one man's meat is another man's poison," but in saying this we must remember that this cliché deals with exceptions to the rule. In *general* meat is nourishing and poison is quite the opposite; so that, although individual reaction may vary, there is still an essential difference btween meat and poison as far as most of us are concerned. In art one may say "that's bad" or "that's good," but it is prudent to question whether one is speaking from the stand point of purely personal reaction and, if so, whether this constitutes an acceptable evaluation. If the critic is seriously pressed on this point, he is less likely to make snap judgment.

Why must an immediate reaction to a work of art be regarded with suspicion? In making a decision, one invariably calls into play all those past experiences which might have any relationship to the problem at hand. Whether we like it or not, these experiences cannot be translated into concrete, verifiable material in the field of art. An engineer, on the contrary, faced with a professional problem in building a bridge is able to convert experience into mathematical forms which will substantiate his judgment. On the other hand, a problem in art judgment which is compounded of feelings and understanding is less factual and more general in nature. The solution therefore lies in large part with one's intuition. This does not mean that a decision cannot be justified, but it does mean that the defense is more difficult than the prosecution. The novice in art, lacking the benefit of experience, has no course than to let his feelings rule his judgment. Lacking a basis for comparison and evaluation, he is frequently led out on a limb. He forms his opinion in a twinkling, instinctively; the concepts produced by his limited background quickly jell into positive or negative attitudes.

In view of the subconscious nature of the art experience, our critic might find some difficulty in accounting for his seemingly automatic reactions. He could say that a work is "pretty," but what does that say, and must it be the end of the argument? Is the prettiness incapable of description or analysis? Are there principles by means of which this elusive quality can be argued or illustrated, or must the sensation of prettiness be confined to the individual observer? He may say that the work reminds him of something which he had found pleasurable, but this seems to indicate that his experience of beauty was not available to others lacking the advantage of the experience by which he judged the work. Does this mean that the quality of a work varies according to the person viewing it, or is it possible that there are qualities which could make it meaningful to people having little in common?

These are some of the disturbing questions which can arise when one becomes aware that passive acceptance of inherited attitudes can thwart new experience and understanding. By taking things for granted, by failing to realize that art necessarily takes many forms, one erects a screen, a fixed concept or petrified viewpoint, which seals off enjoyment. A solidified concept develops steadily and frequently unconsciously; for instance, once we are accustomed to an environment, we perform our duties with a regularity which in time becomes automatic routine. The pattern of such activities is soon taken for granted to the extent that it may be a real discovery to find that others may have an entirely different approach to the same tasks. Our standards of morality similarly become built in. We are some-

times shocked to find that moral codes in other societies frequently contradict our own. It would take little effort however to establish that, in the long run, evolving economies and human relationships result in gradual but very definite moral changes in our own culture. As an example, we need only mention the contrast between mid-Victorian and contemporary attitudes.

Art expression also changes steadily according to traceable reasons, but it is often more difficult to understand because we do not live consciously with art as we do with the restraints of society. Unless art changes with the times, it loses most of its meaning, for it exists only to reflect our life and our opinion of the world. Unfortunately, for many of us taste in art undergoes no evolution but remains where it was when we received our first (too often least or last) exposure to art as a child at the height of our formative period, through the taste of our parents, the environment of the school room, and the general preferences of the times. From this point on, our idea of art is likely to undergo little revision unless an extraordinary interest in the subject motivates us toward more active observation or participation. True, we are often confronted with advertising and illustrational art, but such work is usually limited by the necessity of its commercial application.

In view of the foregoing, it is little wonder that confusion, embarrassment, or defiance is often exhibited when one is faced with a serious work. Genuine art is unlimited in its mode of expression; it generally sells no product but its own quality; it tells no obvious story but inclines one toward general attitudes of thought; it exhibits its art elements simply for the excitement their relationships afford. It does not limit itself to superficial appearances, but tries to reveal that which lies deeper, and takes delight in pure adventure and invention.

If we further examine the characteristics of serious art, we discover that basically they are nonpractical in nature and obviously ask us to divorce ourselves from practical matters in order to enjoy them. In an age of automation and technical emphasis, it is difficult to imagine anything as an end in itself rather than as a means to an end. This, however, was our childhood view of things; as children, we were surprised and delighted by those things which we now think of as commonplace. We were not at all concerned with the function of the objects we encountered, but enjoyed them as things unique and marvelous in their own right. Our concepts were not fixed but constantly developing, and every moment of life was an adventure. The true art enthusiast must recapture some of this impractical awe if art is to be meaningful to him. He must remind himself that one does not enjoy a sunset by counting dust particles and measuring light rays, that indeed a scientist's factual description of a sunset forfeits much of the beauty of poetic description—beauty founded on eloquence, selectivity, and exaggeration.

Thus we see that, whereas facts may play a part in art, there is really little excuse for judging a work of art purely on the basis of accuracy. One would probably be willing to concede that a true-false examination is a poor basis for the grading of a painting; more effective evaluation would be a review of its effect on one's private feelings. When an artist works, he is moved by impressions rather than by specific things. The artist's reaction is general rather than precise, and to judge his product by any other standard is to miss his intention. The true critic is also affected more by impression than by fact; if he saw an area of green on a canvas, he would not immediately concern himself with its identification as trees, grass, or water, but would be much more interested in the emotional feelings provoked by that particular green in its interplay with the other color areas.

Growth of understanding and enjoyment is possible in art, as it is in other fields, *provided* that the individual has the interest and resolution to make full use of his powers of observation and introspection. It is foolish to speak of the artistic to one who has no ambition for sensing it, nor any intention of taking the time to view works of art again and again. The faculties of judgment must be enlarged and kept fresh by constant practice. Happily, the opportunities for this practice are present every day. Art infiltrates every phase of life; we must often choose wallpaper, carpeting, interior and exterior color, and all the other fixtures and furnishings which play a part in our domestic environment. Our choice is generally made on the basis of whatever feeling we have for the principles of design, and we may sometimes feel frustration because we know that our selective faculties have lain dormant, undeveloped by any of the educative processes by which our capabilities in other areas have developed.

Fundamentally, the principles through which we design and furnish our homes are the very ones which underlie all phases of creative expression. The more closely we can keep to open recognition of these principles, the more sound will be the style created by our discrimination. The terms *fad* and *fashion* refer to temporary trends which are misapplication or misinterpretation of the underlying nature of design, but *style* in the best sense of the word refers to a quality which is enduring because it is not icing on the cake, but the cake itself. No doubt all of us have at times become nearsighted victims of fashions or fads whose extreme popularity while in vogue aids their infiltration into the intimacies of our lives. Yet, given the perspective of a few years, we may be appalled to find that the presumed stylishness was, in fact, a breach of good taste. The garish and synthetic character of many of the fashions of past periods, for example, is obvious to most of us now, but the delusion of the people of that time was virtually complete, much to our current amusement.

Art, being human in origin, has never been exempt from the dictates of fashion. It was nonconformity to fashion which led his contemporaries, and indeed people for many years later, to overlook Rembrandt as a significant artist. It was the fashionableness of devotion to classical art which for centuries caused men to classify art of the medieval period as Gothic or barbaric. Our own private fixation of concept is but a faint reflection of the paralysis of vision which may affect cultures and populations for generations. Of course, one cannot and should not shut his eyes to the present nor fail to be a part of it. But it is possible to develop vision which looks through the encrustations of fashion, fad, and temporary prejudice into the bone and marrow of formal structure, the ultimate gauge of soundness in art. Genuine quality does not, therefore, necessarily subtend popular or personal bias. The minor roots of art are imbedded in temporary preference, but the fundamental roots are those which force down through all eras of art and their attendant phraseologies.

We could, for want of a better term, call these formal roots the *Core of Universality* in this book because attention to form epitomizes those art products which survive time through generations of fluctuating taste. Form is also universal in the sense that it rises above geographical boundaries and makes the works of various cultures meaningful to each other despite the fact that they may be largely alien in other respects. We may consider ourselves fortunate that we are living in an age which through research and widespread reproduction makes the output of all the peoples of the earth, past and present, accessible to us. This puts us in a favorable position to detect the common qualities of those works of art which have retained their significance. Invariably the same qualities are detectable, although they are, as would be expected in works of any depth, difficult to analyze or describe.

The development of the formal qualities of a work of art takes place in the feelings of the artist, and only through the use of our feelings are we able to perceive these qualities. Perception or intuition can be sharpened and refined by an explanation of the principles of pictorial organization and, even more, by practice in their use. Ideally this practice is sought through exercises of increasing ambition (as in this book) and through constant and critical probing of the works of art of all historical periods. Some gifted individuals possess an inherent responsiveness to form which may shorten this educative process, or even render it unnecessary. But most of us can best find this new vision when our interest is tied to some systematic method of search and guid-

ance. This is true because the fundamental properties of art are those which are most effectively concealed from the inexperienced observer. In fact, many beginning art students are highly skeptical of the existence of some of the qualities which the instructor may read into works of art. This is not surprising; the experience always lies *within* the observer, and the instructor has no tangible evidence of its presence except by developing the insight of his students. In this sense, art could be compared to religion—faith must often come before understanding. If the beginner is willing to accept on faith some of the basic premises of this book, he can well expect an enlarged understanding of the nature of art. This should not be interpreted as saying that this understanding will be final or that an artist will be created. Artists are those who learn to make use of their growing understanding through trial and error. As soon as they begin to feel that they know everything about art, they cease to be *artists*. Mistakes are to be expected in art as in any learning process; it is the eventual *recognition of error* which guarantees development, and recognition occurs only at the highest intensity of one's thoughts and feelings.

Chapter 2/The Nature of Art

Definitions:

Abstract, abstraction: A term given to forms created by the artist but usually derived from objects actually observed or experienced. It usually involves a simplification and/or rearrangement of natural objects to meet needs of artistic organization or expression. Sometimes there is so little resemblance to the original object that the shapes seem to have no relationship to anything ever experienced in the natural environment.

Academic: A term applied to any kind of art which stresses the use of accepted rules for technique and form organization. It represents the exact opposite of the original approach which results in a vital, individual style of expression.

Content: The essential meaning, significance, or aesthetic value of an art form. It refers to the sensory, psychological or emotional properties which one tends to feel in a work of art as opposed to the perception of mere descriptive aspects.

Craftsmanship: Aptitude, skill, or manual dexterity in the use of tools and materials.

Form: The arbitrary organization or inventive arrangement of all of the visual elements according to principles which will develop an organic unity in the total work of art.

Media, mediums: The materials and tools used by the artist to create the visual elements perceived by the viewer of the work of art.

Naturalism: The approach to art in which all forms used by the artist are essentially descriptive representation of things visually experienced. True naturalism contains no interpretation introduced by the artist for expressive purposes. "The complete recording of the visual effects of nature is a physical impossibility, and naturalistic style thus becomes a matter of degree."

Nonobjective: An approach to art in which the visual signs are entirely imaginative and do not derive from anything ever seen by the artist. The shapes, their organization, and their treatment by the artist are entirely personalized and consequently not associated by the observer with any previously experienced natural form.

Optical perception: A way of seeing in which the mind seems to have no other function than the natural one of providing the physical sensation of recognition of form. "Conceptual perception, on the other hand, refers to the artist's imagination and creative vision."

Realism: A form of expression which retains the basic impression of visual reality but, in addition, attempts to relate and interpret the universal meanings which lie underneath the surface appearance of natural form.

Representation: A manner of expression by the artist in which the subject matter is naturalistically presented so that the visual elements seen by the observer are reminiscent of actual forms previously perceived.

Style: The specific artistic character and dominant form trends noted in art movements or during specific periods of history. It may also mean the artist's expressive use of the media to give his work an individual character.

Subject matter: This term in a descriptive style of art refers to the persons or things represented as well as the artist's experience which serve as his inspiration. In abstract or nonobjective forms of art it refers merely to the basic character of all the visual signs employed by the artist. In this case the subject matter has little to do with anything experienced in the natural environment.

Technique: The manner and skill with which the artist employs his tools and materials to achieve a predetermined expressive effect. The ways of using the media can have an effect on the aesthetic quality of the artist's total concept.

MEANING OF "ART"

Art has meant different things to different people at different times. The term as we use it today probably derives from the Renaissance words arti and arte. Arti was the designation for the craft guilds of the fourteenth, fifteenth, and sixteenth centuries to which the artists were closely tied by the traditions of their calling. Art, the word for craftsmanship, implied a knowledge of materials used by the artist, such as the chemical nature of his pigments and their interaction with one another, as well as the grounds on which a painter applied those pigments. Arte or craftsmanship also implied skillful handling of those materials in the sense of producing images more or less like those of nature, but certainly not in the sense of imitating the exact appearance of nature. Art in the Renaissance thus served both as a technical and an interpretive record of human experience; it has continued to fulfill this function down to the present time, although more meagerly at some times than at others. In the nineteenth century, emphasis was often placed on the technical aspects of art, but in the hands of the greatest masters it always remained interpretive.

Art deals with visual signs to convey ideas, moods, or generalized emotional experiences. It may be called a language of visual signs. Unlike the language of words, however, art is not meant to be informative. Information is the province of symbols, as in the words of literature or the numbers of mathematics. Sometimes in the interpretation of ideas or moods, however, the artist may employ visual symbols, but the meaning of such symbols is embodied in the forms or images which the artist creates, just as are the ideas, moods, or experiences he conveys.

Since art is not intended to convey facts or information, the appreciation of art (by which we mean understanding of art) may be enhanced when the observer attempts to grasp the meaning of works of art through intuition or instinct.

Although the observer may realize that the language of words and that of visual signs as used in art are disparate, he may not recognize the varied problems of understanding and explaining art that arise. The limitations of the printed or spoken word in fully explaining art must be accepted as the natural inability of one medium to replace another. We have all felt the frustration which accompanies our attempt to describe a moving experience to a friend. We are soon convinced that the only description lies in the experience itself. Nonetheless, for education in a better understanding of art, the medium of words has to be used in order to attempt to explain the nature of art and the ideas presented by the works of art.

Unfortunately, the most moving experiences are usually those which are least expressible no matter how much we may wish to share them. The sensations of experience vary according to the senses which are stimulated, and since certain major divisions of art developed around each of these senses, we may assume that certain qualities exist which make these means separate and unique.

MAJOR FORMS OF ART

The means which are most frequently used to convey human feelings are prose, poetry, music, the dance, the cinema, the theater, and the plastic and graphic arts. Subdivisions of the last two groups include painting, prints, drawing, sculpture, ceramics, and architecture. Each of these divisions fulfills a specific need and therefore has its own province or expression. For example, one cannot very successfully paint a picture of a novel, describe a melody, or dance a poem. There have always been attempts to extend the limits of art, but they have been successful only insofar as they have respected the particular properties of the medium of translation.

The opera, the theater, and the cinema are fields in which other arts are often introduced. They are rarely equally successful in all departments. Each medium contains its own problems; hence with so many demands to be met, it is obvious that concessions must be made. As an analogy, the building of a house requires the sacrifice of some structural strength for lighting and visibility, of living space for storage, of utility for beauty, and so forth; each house represents a series of compromises according to the determinants of site, climate, taste of the architect, owner, and builder, and finances available. The house which loses least in the inevitable series of compromises is, in the end, the most organically successful design. This is equally true of the composite art divisions.

There have been periods in which one or several of the media or art forms have enjoyed unusual interest. The people of the Italian Ren-

Fig. 1. SPRING (PRIMAVERA) (1455) by Sandro Botticelli. This is an excellent example of an early Italian Renaissance work of art whose subject, while based on classical mythology, also infers a Christian theme. Venus, for example, is not only *classical* in concept, but also symbolizes the Virgin Mary. The three part composition, which was of Roman origin, may be said to symbolize the Christian Trinity; the classically derived dancing nymphs may be reinterpreted as representations of Christian angels.
Courtesy Alinari-Art Reference Bureau, Uffizi Gallery, Florence

aissance made art the measure of all things, and their lives were motivated by its enjoyment. Accomplishments in other fields were measured by their "artfulness," even to the extent that war itself became a work of art (Machiavelli). Though each of the arts found its enthusiastic audience, the epicenter of the arts lay in painting and sculpture. Here, as elsewhere, the themes depicted were usually of religious origin, the subject matter of greatest interest to the people. But interest in the subject was equalled by enthusiasm for the revolutionary concepts of *form* which derived from classical examples and which had been largely ignored during the intervening years (fig. 1). The transition from medieval to Renaissance style, based on the Graeco-Roman style of antiquity, produced remarkable *form-consciousness* in the populace and introduced a period of history unique in its agreement on the value of art and its aesthetics. However, the advances which marked this revised outlook

eventually became ends in themselves, leading to emphasis on scale and technical facility. In addition, the alliance of art with the growth of scientific method at times produced a "scientific art" which was cold and calculated, a product of conformity to standardized rules.

NARRATION AND DESCRIPTION IN ART

The layman continues to assume that an art work should be recognizable or tell a story in a visually descriptive manner. It is true that some great works of art in the past have often told stories, but there is no obligation on the part of artists to narrate, since narration is not directly a part of their medium. Even when artists have chosen to narrate, their pictorial story may be visualized in many ways, due to the nature of artistically expressed form.

Fig. 2. THE NUT GATHERERS (ca. 1870) by Adolphe William Bouguereau. An abandonment of *form* as a means of expression in which the *subject matter* is saturated with sentimentality and is essentially descriptive in nature.
Courtesy the Detroit Institute of Arts. Gift of Mrs. William E. Scripps

In the nineteenth century, when the influence of poetry and prose reached its zenith, art often became a handmaiden of literature and, aided by science, attempted factual interpretation of romantic and allegorical writing. There was marked abandonment of *form* as an expressive agent in its own right, while the favored subject matter was saturated with emotion and sentimentality. The role of art became to *narrate* and *describe,* as though one attempted to give the feeling of battle by counting the troops and weapons or tried to express mother love by taking an inventory of nursery equipment. In short, artists had de-emphasized the essential ingredient of art and made it a second-rate translator of other media (fig. 2).

Art must, in its way, narrate and describe to some degree, for its is a medium developed out of man's need for a particular type of communication. However, art is at its best when its *form* communicates directly, with *subject matter* and *symbols* playing subordinate roles. The mechanics of art reception are quite different from those of other media. An art work does not flow in

time; it does not involve physical anticipation as in turning the pages of a book or in listening for the next measure of music. The complete unity of a painting registers in a moment. The totality of the work can be taken in with one hard look, although this is hardly the recommended procedure for real appreciation. Hence, art does not lend itself wholeheartedly to the recitation of action in sequence form as does literature which is unfolding in its presentation. Narration is more properly a *by-product* of the artist's search.

ILLUSION AND REALITY IN ART

Similarly, art is by its very nature more a matter of illusion than are the other forms of expression, music excepted. Action is never really present in paint or stone, and the actual human body plays no part in its expression as in the theater or dance. Although the artist activates his tools in the creation of a work of art, in the work itself such activity has become static and but a reminder of past activity. Such a reminder of past activity may be stimulating in a manner somewhat like that of the present movement in the theater and the dance, but it is illusive and not real. Because of this gulf between art and objective reality, there seems little excuse for forcing art into a completely realistic or descriptive role. All media employ calculated deceits which help to create the unrealistic or imaginative atmosphere which is the unique value and appeal of the arts.

We certainly do not go to a play because we expect duplication of everyday life. Instead we presumably hope to be transported into a situation which through the imagination and perception of the artist exalts and comes to grips with the fundamental forces of life. The make-believe deception in a theatrical production is purposely emphasized by our isolation from the stage—from the unnatural postures and diction of the actors, the exaggerated costumes, and the countless other stratagems. Unreality is sought in varied ways in the other arts, serving always to draw man out of himself into a world of separate, yet meaningfully related, existence. Despite all this evidence of admittedly premeditated and justifiable guile, there are those who would miscast art in the role of a mirror reflecting the everyday world. Imagination, invention, daring are ignored in favor of routine, rules and rote, and unremitting slavishness to visual details, which even photography avoids through manipulation of focus and timing. Art which places chief emphasis on accuracy of description is essentially repetitive rather than creative.

Reality as it has been used here is a term of convenience for identification of the most common and superficial sensations of life. Even in this sense one could extend the description by pointing out that variations in physical and mental makeup among individuals create differences of sensation among those individuals and, thus, varying ideas of reality. Art, of course, constitutes an outlet for differences of opinion. Genuine reality for each of us is defined by our most personal experiences and interest, producing a specialized outlook. As we progress in our studies in any field, we experience a change of mind about the truly important factors in that area. As we dig more deeply into the fields of the intellect and the subconscious, we become aware that more basic realities underlie the appearances of commonplace experience.

It is this reality of broader and deeper understanding which marks the work of the true creator. Einstein shared the conventional patterns of life with the rest of us, but his perception revealed relationships which have helped to reshape our view of the world and our place in it. Between the world of convention and the world of perception there can be little doubt as to which for Einstein was the truer reality. Beethoven was very little different from the rest of us anatomically, but inwardly he sensed revolutionary sounds which in an abstract way expressed the experiences and hopes of the human race. This to Beethoven was the true reality, not the payment of rent, the eating of meals, the reading of the evening newspaper. These two men and all those of equal significance contributed a fundamental theory of reality as discovered and transmitted through the medium in which they worked. Our society, receiving this creativity, gradually and often unconsciously experiences a parallel change in its own point of view. Creative men alter the frame of reference through which we see the things about us.

SPECIAL NATURE OF ARTISTIC EXPERIENCE

In reference to the foregoing, works of art may be called unique *form experiences* intended to evoke sensation in the observer. They are unique because they are different from objects and incidents of everyday association, even though the artist may have used such objects or incidents as subjects. One should see a work of art from the special frame of reference of aesthetic or artistic experience. When looking at a piece of sculpture, for example, we have a special attitude which is not present when we see an ordinary chair. Both forms stand on all sides surrounded by space, but the chair is seen as having a special function. On the other hand, the sculptural form is intended to arouse subtle emotional states having nothing to do with use in the observer.

This very uniqueness sets works of art apart from functional or commonplace objects of everyday use; yet most people fail to make a distinction in regard to art. When they want to know what a painting is "about," they have the same attitude toward the painting as toward any ordinary object of use. Of course, a chair, let us say, may be not only of practical usefulness but also a work of art. When this is true, the dimensions of *meaning* and *significance* are added to the usual commonplace meaning of practical use.

With the distinction of this added uniqueness in mind, the observer should be able to approach works of visual art as he would poetry, as opposed to a scientific treatise, or as he would a symphony or jazz concert, as opposed to a commercial jingle on television.

Thus, we may call a painting or sculpture the objectification, record, or expression of an artist's experiences during the age and place in which he lives (fig. 3). In this way, a work of art is different from a product of an industrial designer or architect which includes also the practical association engendered by its form. Again, a work of art may be defined as a kind of autobiography of an artist's attitude in *line, value, shape, texture,* and *color* which the uninitiated observer must learn to read.

The mind determines how and what we see, and mental activity is necessary before the subtle qualities or characterful nuances of painting or sculpture are discernible. This is similar to the way in which training through experience is needed to hear the handsome inflections of metric rhyme in poetry or the melodic counterpart of music.

Fig. 3. MCSORLEY'S BAR (1912) by John Sloan. The sensitive artist communicates to us the special aura of the period in which he lived. As an early Egyptian recorded the character of life on the Nile, so John Sloan has transmitted the life style of the United States in the early twentieth century

Courtesy the Detroit Institute of Arts. Gift of the Founders' Society

The province of the artist is to enlarge our comprehension of the world or universe, to widen our imaginative horizons, and to enrich our sensory enjoyment of all things. In order to do this, the artist is obliged to create new forms by the *selection, rearrangement,* or *exaggeration (distortion)* of the forms he sees or experiences in his environment. It is this environmental influence that causes the artist to reflect the time and place of his endeavours.

Twentieth-century artists may be credited with reasserting this creative principle, which is fundamental to the visual arts. This principle was largely neglected during the nineteen century when rapid scientific, industrial, and geographic expansion caused both artists and the public to think of art as a kind of science or mechanically learned skill. When the invention of the camera in the nineteenth century gradually obviated the representation of nature as a primary goal, artists began to reassert this principle.[1] They realized that there was no such thing as a "correct procedure" for originality, and that there was no basic "right" or "wrong" way to create. Artists began to see that the most *effective* art form was the most *unique* form, and by its very uniqueness it was most communicative of the ideas and feelings of the artist.

On the other hand, the public still tends to think of art in nineteenth-century terms. A surprisingly large number of persons apparently believe that art should *imitate* nature, and that the best artists are those who make the most faithful duplication. A large part of the art of this century has little resemblance to nature forms; however, the backward-thinking layman seems to assume that the artist has either not achieved the skills necessary to duplicate nature, or that he is merely seeking notoriety by sensational images. Since art is not a science or a technical performance in which the main aim is the surface description of objects, the sympathetic student must realize the nature and function of art before he can understand the goals he should try to achieve in studio performance.

The student must reorient himself away from a type of art that has as its highest aim the descriptive or factual rendition of subject matter. After practicing with the devices which may be found by analyzing works of art, the student may eventually find that these become instinctive tools of expression. Then, like most present-day professional artists (who are concerned with what people feel and think—their tragedies, hopes, joys, and aspirations), the student may be able to conceive or imagine form in an original way.

COMPONENTS OF A WORK OF ART

In order to approach art from the angle of expressing *meanings* and *ideas,* the student will first need to know something of the ingredients or components which make up a work of art. These ingredients are the *subject matter,* the *form,* and the *content* or *meaning* of a work.

Subject Matter

There is nearly always *subject matter* in a work of art. This is true even when the form style is *abstract* (subject matter is limited insofar as it may be based on perceivable objects from nature). *Subject matter* in *abstract* art may lie more in the realm of ideas or of intellectual concepts which are abstruse rather than that of material objects or facts (*see* plate 20). However, even in works of art which may be more obviously based on a representation of perceivable objects, the *subject matter* or object used is not of importance in itself to the artist. Subjects which the artist uses are merely a *stimulus to creativity* (plate 1). It is the artist's initial response to *subject matter* and the way thereafter in which he presents the subject that are of importance. In addition, the artist during the course of giving *form* to his subject may reinterpret its character; thus, the final form of the work of art may be far removed, in terms of what the observer sees, from the *original* subject or even from the original *response* of the artist to that subject.

The most significant problem in creating a work of art is not what one uses as a subject, therefore, but how one interprets a subject in order to achieve character. The how of works of art involves the other ingredients of the art product—*form* and *content.* These are the most important components of a work of art.

Form

By *form* we mean the totality of the work of art. *Form* is the organization (design) of all elements which make up the work of art. An-

---

1. The term *representation* really means to *re-present,* as opposed to the direct presentation of meaning desirable in art forms.

other way of defining this term is as follows: the use made of the *visual devices* available to the artist. The visual devices or *elements* of *form*, as we tend to call them, are: *lines, shapes, values* (*varied lights* and *darks*), *textures,* and *colors.* The use to which the artist puts these elements determines the final appearance of his work of art (plate 2).

Principles of Organization

Use of the *elements* concerns the particular physical and psychological relationships between *visual devices* which in some way seem to affect us in their own right; that is, each element individually seems to have *intrinsic* (*inbuilt*) effects which are multiplied and made richer in their impact upon us when used in combinations.

The physical relationships of the elements are founded upon traditional, nearly universal, *principles,* called generally the *principles of organization* or of *design,* or as at times in the past, *rules of composition* (i.e., *balance, rhythm, domination, harmony,* etc.). Some artists use these principles more consciously or logically than others, but all artists can be said to have at least instinctive sensitivity to the value of *organization.* These *principles of organization* are discussed in more detail later in the text; they should be regarded as guides, not as dogmatic rules, else the expressive quotient of *form* may be lost and the work may become *academic.* Nevertheless, throughout the history of art, it is in the area of basic principles by which works of art are given order that men have most often agreed lies the locus of beauty in art. Thus beauty, an abstract concept, becomes tangible and universal in terms of *form organization* in art; hence terms like *beauty of form* or *formal beauty* are often applied to great works of art.

Media and Technique

Form-ordering is concerned not only with the *visual devices* and principles of relating the said devices, but also with the *materials* (*media*) (i.e., pigments, inks, graphite) and the *tools* (i.e., brushes, pens, pencils) used by the artist, and with the manner (*technique*) in which these are used. *Technique* in painting, drawing, and printmaking also has to bring into artistic consideration the support, ground, or surface on which the artist applies his materials. While this is also true of the *spatial arts* of sculpture, architecture,

and three-dimensional design where materials are more directly a part of artistic execution, it does not seem to be such a separate consideration as with the two-dimensional arts.

Organic Unity—Form Organization

The real *feeling* of a work of art cannot be exposed by a breakdown of its parts. However, for the purpose of illustration and instruction we are often compelled to isolate the elements composing the *form* of the work. One could make a comparison with the parts of a radio and the parts or *elements of form* in a painting. If we should break down the radio and spread all the parts before us so that we were forced to examine each one separately, the form of the radio, as well as its meaning and function, would be lost to us. We could then put these parts together in such a way that a completely new device had been created. This contrivance would have the form of something not then recognizable (because it is outside human experience) nor even graced by a name. It would certainly not be the *form* of a radio, despite the presence of all the *parts* needed to make a radio. The device obviously would not fit our idea of *radio form* until all the parts were once again assigned their original position. Once reassembled, the radio would work just as a competent art form works, although the elusive property of life, in a work of art as in a human body, is impossible to define effectively. This difficulty stems from the fact that we can recognize life when all the parts are working, but we do not know what has been lost when they cease to work; life, like electricity, remains a mystery to us.

The anatomical parts of a painting which the artist manipulates are the *elements of form* previously listed. The artist hopes to assemble these in such a way that they will work together to create a meaningful *organic or living unity.* The result may be a hybrid work (similar to the device mentioned in the radio analogy) which functions only as a series of parts, and which consequently has no *unity of meaning and function* (fig. 4). On the other hand, he may be successful in creating a work in which each of the parts is vital, not by itself but in the general functioning of the work as a whole. In such an ideal development, the total organization or *form* cannot be conceived when any one of its parts is missing. With such a work, an entity is created which, like the radio, has a separate and distinct

Fig. 4. SUMMER by Giuseppe Archimboldi. This engaging work, a forerunner of Surrealism, utilizes parts related only by classification and the common image they create; they do not, however, create any *formal* unity.
Courtesy Kunsthistorisches Museum Vienna, Austria and Art Reference Bureau

personality but, unlike the radio, is incapable of being named or classified, except according to a broad category. A radio would not ordinarily be confused with a chair, for each has its own characteristic distribution of *form* in which all those things have been eliminated that do not serve their particular utility. So it is with a distinguished work of art: every part aids in the purpose of expression. The painting as an entity is inconceivable without those parts, and we can therefore say that it demonstrates perfect *unity* or total *form organization*. We could go farther and say that, although there are many identical radios of a particular model, every work of art has qualities which tend to make it unlike any previously created; in the best sense of the word it is truly original.

In the studio the suggestions offered in this book should be used in a way to emphasize the practice and observation of the potentialities for *form-building* and the psychological or *expressive* impact.

Content or Meaning

When we begin to analyze *why* form affects us emotionally or expressively or stimulates the intellectual activity of the observer, we are concerned with *content* or *form-meaning*, the third component of a work of art. This component is the one in which the *quality* or *significance* of a work of art seems to reside. We may define *content* as the final statement, mood, or spectator experience with the work of art. It can also be called the *significance* of the *art form*; the kinds of emotions, intellectual activity or associations we make between art objects and our subconscious or conscious experiences seem to arise out of an *art form* and are completely inseparable from it except for purposes of discussion. In other words, *content*, is the essential *meaning* of *form*. As Frank J. Mather points out: "Meaning and Form are merely two aspects of the same thing—a form containing and conveying a meaning cast in a form in order that it may be expressed."[2]

If we consider for a moment the present-day abstract approach to form by many artists, wherein the form is decorative or patterned, there seems to be little if any *meaning*. However, there *is* meaning because there is no *form*, artistic or otherwise, which in some way does not have *meaning* for someone. In *abstract* art, it may be the unobvious but direct meaning inherent in visual relationship, such as a black line set off against colored shapes of varied contours (plate 3). Abstract artists obviously must find much that is pleasurable in such artistic arrangements, and the *form-conscious* observer may also feel this kind of *enjoyment-meaning* present in a well-organized relationship of artistic elements.

Abstraction

Sheldon Cheney says "Abstraction is an idea stripped of its concrete accompaniments, an *essense* or *summary*."[3] However, everyone abstracts from environment, the experiences that are of value to him, and they are not necessarily concrete if they lie within the realm of intuition or imagination. In art, if one takes away only a few of the surface effects from what is usually considered real or tangible, he is abstracting in a limited way. The artist who draws a tree as closely as he can to the optical appearance of an actual tree is still abstracting his idea of "tree" in order to put it down in the graphic signs of art. In art terminology, however, we usually reserve the term *abstract art* for a type of form arrangement in which the *concept* of relating artistic devices (or *formal elements*) is more important

than any indication of the perceivable objects which the artist may have seen in nature and used as *subject matter*.

Nonobjective Art

There are some artists who use *motifs* entirely from within themselves, rather than observe them in nature. Such artists begin with *form*, such as areas of color or line and value, and arrive at artistic conclusions with these elements alone. Such artists have been called *nonobjective* since they never resort to the use of natural objects, believing them inconsequential in artistic expression. Artists of this persuasion feel natural objects are unimportant as subjects because they believe the work of art should live on its own merits (fig. 5).

Within these generally inclusive terms of *abstract* and *nonobjective* art, many diverse form concepts have developed over the years since 1910–1911. Perhaps the style in art called Abstract-Expressionism should be mentioned as an extension of *abstract* and *nonobjective* art. It seems that artists interested in this style have often abandoned the predilection for geometric planes of *abstract* and *nonobjective* art in favor of emotional freedom and amorphous shapes.

Form-meaning

Despite the fact that the terms *abstract* and *nonobjective* tend to bring to mind that "nothing is perceivable in such works," and in view of the preceding explanation that concepts or ideas are manifest in such works (and are equally valid as subject matter along with natural objects), one can see that it is not true that such works have no content. *Content* or *meaning* lies in the *form* and is effective in so far as the observer is conversant with *form-meaning*.

There is little doubt, however, that public vision has been conditioned to read form representationally, in much the same sense that a snapshot represents nature in an optical manner. Of course, as suggested earlier, photography also may be handled less in this optical or mechanical manner and more in an artistic fashion. Such images will probably not appeal too much to

2. Frank J. Mather, *Concerning Beauty* (Princeton: Princeton University Press, 1935), p. 128.

3. Sheldon Cheney, *Expressionism in Art* (New York: Liveright Publishing Corp, 1934), p. 80.

Fig. 5. CUBI VII, MARCH 8 (1963) (welded steel) by David Smith. Smith was rarely concerned with likeness to natural objects. Instead, he used nonobjective forms and tried to give them a life of their own through the animation created by his sense of arrangement.

Courtesy the Art Institute of Chicago. Grant J. Pick Purchase Fund

the object-minded person, but may get a certain acceptance for their technological value. Such individuals tend to look for similarly descriptive values in art and are only happy when *natural-appearing* objects that provide an obvious basis of recognition are produced.

With sufficient experience in looking at works of art, however, most individuals will eventually begin to realize that no particular emphasis on visual description of objects is needed; for them painting and sculpture may be optically understandable and yet have character above and beyond ordinary description. Almost anyone can sense the universal quality of serenity in a Cézanne landscape. (*see* plate 15); or the impassioned response to objects and life expressed by Van Gogh (plate 4). Van Gogh has depicted the quality of nature as a living, stimulating force in such a way as to make his painting a vital expression in its own right. This is made possible through the swirling shapes, the direct clash of colors, and the heavily pigmented surface. The

meaning of "city" in the painting by Charles Demuth (plate 5) should be apparent in his machinelike shapes and movement-tensions, all of which are a part of his *form concept.*

Aesthetic Experience

Previously in this chapter it was mentioned that the quality or significance of a work of art lies in our interpretation of the *content*. We called this the *aesthetic* value of the work of art. Experiencing a work of art when it is enjoyable, persuasive, stimulating, disturbing, or otherwise evocative of our senses is an *aesthetic* or artistic experience. This is meaningful and of value to us because it is *really* what we hope to experience when we look at works of art. Obvious recognition of common, everyday items carried over into art cannot make this much of an artistic experience, and hence, not *meaningful* in the deepest sense as art. It merely has some small element of value on an associational basis, but once we have identified the object, we are done

Fig. 6. HOUSE BY THE RAILROAD (1925) by Edward Hopper. The passive serenity of this painting has character above and beyond ordinary description.
Collection, the Museum of Modern Art, New York. Given anonymously

with the form and forget it. Works of art are *meaningful* when they seem to remain a *part of us* after we have left them. If we are inclined to come back and see them again, we have had a worthwhile experience that does not terminate at the instant we have seen but one aspect. It is not enough, therefore, that art form be merely associated with natural objects or natural forms. A good work of art must be seen by the observer as well as the artist with *aptness,* power of expression, and flexibility (fig. 6).

When a work of art represents natural objects, many people continue to assume that it is meant to tell a visual story, but let us remember from our earlier discussion of this point that narration is really the province of literature. What the observer must learn to look for in works of art are not specifically recognizable associations with objects, stories, or events in life, but a general *expression* of general experiences provided by the artist in new forms—and, thus, with uncommon *meaning* or aesthetic significance.

It is perhaps interesting to note at this point that the *naturalist* style of the 1870s and 1880s in France, which the layman has tended to maintain as his "norm of vision" down to the midtwentieth century, was at its time a *new form* of art based on the science-centering of culture resulting from the Industrial Revolution. As a new *form of art* with unfamiliar meaning for its time, *Naturalism* was largely rejected or neglected by the public in about the same manner as most people today react to present-day art.

Having now studied the main points of theory dealing with the *nature of art,* let us move on to a study of the chapters on the *form elements* and their possibilities and then attempt to put into practice the suggestions offered. It should be understood that other than further theoretical discussion, as in this chapter, the studio teacher cannot really teach the *subject matter, form,* and *content* of works of art, but can only expose the student to *experiences* in the area of these components.

Plate 1. BEDROOM AT ARLES (1889) by Vincent van Gogh. The subjects or objects used are not of importance in themselves to artists, as in the case of still-life objects which are often used by artists as subjects. The subject is merely a **stimulus** to creativity, but what makes this van Gogh of value and unique from other paintings, his own, or those by other artists, is the presentation.

Courtesy The Art Institute of Chicago.

Plate 2. WINTER (RETURN OF THE HUNTERS) (1565) by Pieter Brueghel. The visual devices of line direction, spotting of light and dark areas, of rhythmic repetition of similar shape patterns, and the sense of spatial indication all contribute to the total pictorial organization which is called FORM.

Courtesy, Alinari Art Reference Bureau, Kunsthistorisches Museum, Vienna.

Plate 3. PANEL (3) (1914) by Wassily Kandinsky.
In **abstract** art there **is** CONTENT, but it may be
the unobvious form meaning inherent in a visual
relationship, such as a black line, or lines
set-off against colored shapes of varied contours.

**Plate 4. THE STARRY NIGHT (1889) by Vincent
van Gogh.** Van Gogh's impassioned response to
life can be seen in his swirling shapes, intensity
of colors and heavily pigmented surfaces.

Plate 5. AND THE HOME OF THE BRAVE (1963) by Charles Demuth. Sharpness, hardness, and impersonality are among the factors Demuth has chosen to specify in interpreting an urban situation.

Chapter 3/Form

Definitions:

Approximate symmetry: The use of forms which are similar on either side of a vertical axis. They may give a feeling of the exactness of equal relationship but are sufficiently varied to prevent visual monotony.

Asymetrical balance: A form of balance attained when the visual units on either side of a vertical axis are not identical but are placed in positions within the pictorial field so as to create a "felt" equilibrium of the total form concept.

Balance: A feeling of equality in weight, attention, or attraction of the various visual elements within the pictorial field as a means of accomplishing organic unity.

Dominance: The principle of visual organization which suggests that certain elements should assume more importance than others in the same composition. It contributes to organic unity by emphasizing the fact that there is one main feature and that other elements are subordinate to it. The principle applies in both representational and non-representational work.

Elements of art: The basic visual signs as they are combined into optical units which are used by the artist to communicate or express his creative ideas. The combination of the basic elements of line, shape, value, texture, and color represent the visual language of the artist.

Harmony: The unity of all of the visual elements of a composition achieved by the repetition of the same characteristics or those which are similar in nature.

Motif: A visual element or a combination of elements which is repeated often enough in a composition to make it the dominating feature of the artist's expression. Similar to theme or melody in a musical composition.

Negative areas: The unoccupied or empty space left after the positive shapes have been laid down by the artist. However, because these areas have boundaries, they also function as shapes in the total pictorial structure.

Pattern: The obvious emphasis on certain visual form relationships and certain directional movements within the visual field. It also refers to the repetition of elements or the combinations of elements in a readily recognized systematic organization.

Picture Frame: The outermost limits or boundary of the picture plane.

Picture Plane: The actual flat surface on which the artist executes his pictorial image. In some cases it acts merely as a transparent plane of reference to establish the illusion of forms existing in a three-dimensional space.

Positive Shapes: The enclosed areas which represent the initial selection of shapes planned by the artist. They may suggest recognizable objects or merely be planned nonrepresentational shapes.

Repetition: The use of the same visual element a number of times in the same composition. It may accomplish a dominance of one visual idea, a feeling of harmonious relationship, an obviously planned pattern, or a rhythmic movement.

Rhythm: A continuance, a flow, or a feeling of movement achieved by repetition of regulated visual units; the use of measured accents.

Symmetrical balance: A form of balance achieved by the use of identical compositional units on either side of a vertical axis within the confining pictorial space.

Unity: The whole or total effect of a work of art which results from the combination of all of its component parts, including the assigned ratio between harmony and variety."

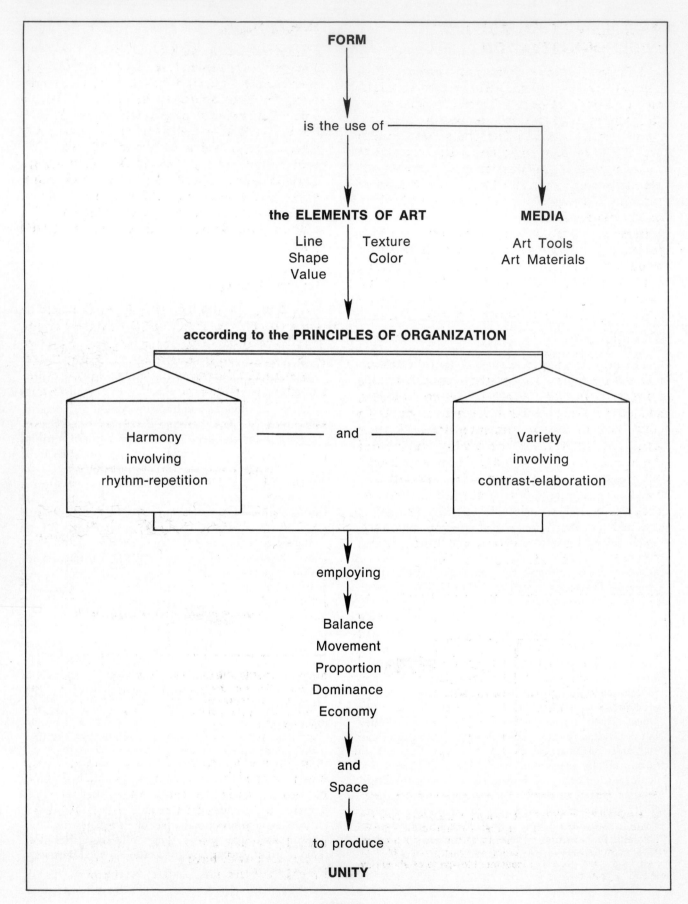

FORM

is the use of

the **ELEMENTS OF ART**

Line   Texture
Shape   Color
Value

MEDIA

Art Tools
Art Materials

according to the PRINCIPLES OF ORGANIZATION

Harmony

involving

rhythm-repetition

——— and ———

Variety

involving

contrast-elaboration

employing

Balance

Movement

Proportion

Dominance

Economy

and

Space

to produce

UNITY

Fig. 7.

PRELIMINARY FACTORS OF FORM ORGANIZATION

In a completed work of art, there are three components, common denominators which change only in emphasis. These components are so interwoven that to isolate any one of them would mean total disorder. The whole work of art is always more important than any one of its components. In this chapter emphasis is placed on the component *form* in order to theorize and investigate some of the physical principles of visual order.

In seeing images, one takes part in *visual forming* (or ordering): In this act, the eye and mind organize visual differences by integrating optical units into a unified whole. The mind instinctively tries to create order out of chaos. This order adds equilibrium to human visual experience which would otherwise be confusing and garbled.

The artist is a visual former with a plan. With his materials, he arranges the *elements for his form-structure: lines, shapes, values, textures,* and *colors.* The elements he uses need to be controlled, organized, and integrated. This the artist manages through the binding qualities of the *principles of organization: harmony, variety, balance, movement, proportion, dominance, economy,* and *space.* The sum total of these, assuming the success of his plan and its execution, equal *unity.* Unity in this instance means *oneness,* an organization of parts which fit into the order of a whole and become vital to it.

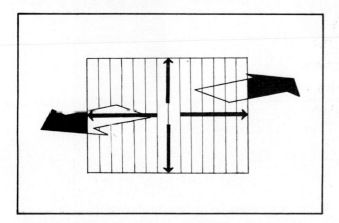

Fig. 8. PICTURE PLANE. Movement may take place on a flat surface as indicated by the vertical and horizontal arrows. The vertical lines represent an imaginary plane through which a picture is seen. The artist may also give the illusion of advancing and receding movement in space as shown by the two large arrows.

Picture Plane

There are many ways to begin a work of art. However, it is generally accepted that the picturemaker must begin with a flat surface. To the artist, the flat surface is the *picture plane* on which he executes his pictorial image (fig. 8). The flat surface further represents an imaginary plane through which his picture is seen. This plane establishes by comparative relationships all other lines, planes, directions, and movements in the space on, behind, and in front of it. In this instance, the picture plane is used as a basis for judging two- and three-dimensional space.

Picture Frame

A picture is limited entirely to the *picture frame* which, by definition, is described as the outermost limits or the boundary of the *picture plane* (fig. 9). The picture frame should be clearly established at the beginning of a pictorial organization; once its shape and proportion are defined,

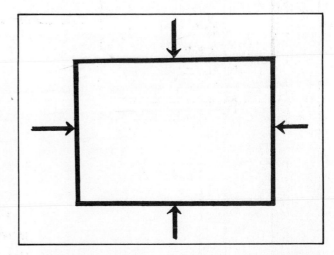

Fig. 9. PICTURE FRAME. The picture frame represents the outermost limits or the boundary of the picture plane. These limits may be represented by the edges of the canvas or paper in which the artist works or the margin drawn within these edges.

all of the art elements and their employment will be influenced by it. The first problem for the pictorial artist is to organize the elements of art within the picture frame on the picture plane.

The proportions and shapes of picture frames used by artists are varied. Squares, triangles, circles, and ovals have been used as frame shapes by artists of the past, but the most popular is the rectangular frame which in its varying proportions offers the artist an interesting two-dimensional space variety (plates 6 and 7). Many artists select the outside proportions of their pictures on the basis of geometric, mathematical formulas. These rules suggest dividing surface areas into odd proportions of two to three or three to five rather than into equal relationships. The results are pleasing visual and mathematical spatial arrangements. After the picture frame has been established, the *elements of art,* their direction and movement, should be in harmonious relation to this shape; otherwise they will interrupt the mainstream of *pictorial unity.*

Positive-Negative

All of the surface areas in a picture should contribute to total unity. Those areas which represent the initial selection of the artist in terms of recognizable objects or nonrepresentational shapes are generally called *positive areas* (fig. 10). Unoccupied spaces are termed *negative areas* (fig. 11). The negative areas are just as important to total picture unity as are the positive units which are tangible and more explicitly laid

Fig. 12. KEY (student work). The maximum contrast of pure black and pure white create equality of values; being equal in strength, the positive shapes (the keys) and the negative shapes (the spaces between them) are often confused in an optical illusion.

down. Further, negative areas might be considered that portion of the picture plane which continues to show through after the positive units have been placed in a framed area (fig. 12).

Fig. 10.

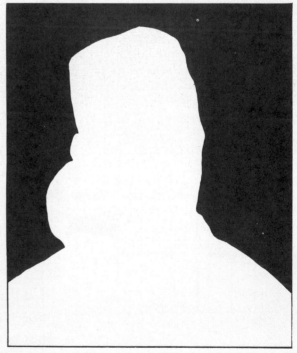

Fig. 11.

POPE INNOCENT X (ca. 1650) by Diego Velazquez. The subject in this painting represents a *positive* shape which has been enhanced by careful consideration of the *negative* areas or the surrounding space. The dark area in figure 11 indicates the *negative* shape and the white area the *positive* shape.

Traditionally, foreground positions were considered positive and background spaces negative (plate 8).

The term *positive-negative* is important to the student who is investigating art organization since the beginner usually directs his attention to positive object units and neglects the surrounding spaces. The resulting pictures are generally overcrowded, busy, and confusing.

PRINCIPLES OF ORGANIZATION

The reader should be reminded, once again, that the *principles of organization* are only guides for seeing for the beginning student. They are *not* laws having only one interpretation or application. The principles of organization may help in finding certain pictorial solutions for *unity*, but they are not ends in themselves, and following them will not always guarantee the best results. Art works are created by personal interpretation and should be judged as total visual expressions.

Harmony and Variety

The artist can now set about organizing the elements of art in his plan. First, he must know what the controlling factors are in organizing.

Organization in art consists of developing a *unified* whole out of diverse units. This is done by relating contrasts through certain similar means. To explain further, an artist might use in his picture two opposing kinds of lines, vertical and horizontal. Since both the horizontal and vertical lines are already straight, this likeness of *type* would relate them. It would seem here that harmonious means are necessary to hold contrasts together. Unity and organization in art are dependent upon dualism—balance between harmony and variety. This balance does not have to be of equal proportions; harmony might outweigh variety, or variety might outweigh harmony (plates 9 and 10).

Harmony

Rhythm and *repetition* act as agents for creating order out of forces which are otherwise in opposition. They relate picture parts. After reconciliation between the forces in opposition has been effected, *harmony* on a picture surface re-sults. Harmony is a necessary ingredient of *unity*; likewise rhythm and repetition are essential to harmony.

Rhythm

Rhythm is the continuance, or flow, which is affected by reiterating and measuring related, similar, or equal parts. It is recurrence, a measure such as meter, tempo, or beat. Walking, running, dancing, woodchopping, and hammering are human activities having recurring measures.

In art if particular parts are recalled in a rhythmical way, a work will be seen as a whole. *Rhythm* in this instance has the effect of giving both *unity* and *balance* to a work of art.

Rhythm exists in many different ways on a picture surface. It may be *simple,* as when it repeats only one type of measure, it may be *composite* of two or more recurring measures which exist simultaneously, or it may be a complex variation which recalls a particular accent in a usual way. José Clemente Orozco charges his pictures with obvious rhythmical order (plate 11). He uses several rhythmical measures simultaneously to create a geometric unity. He welds his pictures together by repeating shape directions and edges, value differences, and color modifications.

Motif. In music, rhythm may be associated with a theme which is repeated with simple variation throughout a score. The *motif* of a work of art is perhaps the equivalent of the *theme* in music. It might be described as a composite of several rhythmical measures, or it may be looked on as a picture within a picture. A motif may be *objective* when it borrows from nature, or it may be *invented*, drawing its inspiration from configurations found in the art elements, their direction or space.

Rhythm is not a single part; it is an order in the whole work. A motif in a picture, for example, is only one accent in a *system* of accents and pauses. Once the beat of this system is felt in an art work, visual organization will be formed (fig. 13).

Pattern. A pattern in a work of art is used to establish harmonious relationship of parts, usually similar or repetitive in character. It will lead the eye in a movement from one element to another or from one accent to another. The handling and placement of a line, shape, value, texture, or color will guide the underlying pictorial structure which is called pattern.

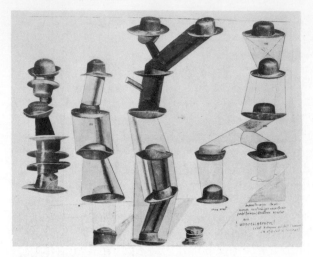

Fig. 13. THE HAT MAKES THE MAN (1920) by Max Ernst. *Motif:* the hats in this picture represent strong *accents, motifs,* in a system of accents and pauses. Notice the variety of style, size, and shape contour within the repetitive order. Collection, the Museum of Modern Art, New York. Purchase

Rhythms, repetitions, and their alternating pauses are systems which aid in the creation of pattern. The elements of art are interwoven with rhythmical repetitions, beats, which pulsate in movement from one picture part to another to create order, or unity. Pattern is generally two-dimensional or *decorative* in character, and it emphasizes the unifying qualities of form (fig. 14).

Repetition

Repetition and rhythm are inseparable. Rhythm is the *result* of repetition. Repetition is a method used to reemphasize visual units again and again in a marked pattern. It is an easy way to bind the work together, to achieve unity. By its insistence, repetition demands attention or emphasis, and it allows pause for examination.

Repetition does not always mean exact *duplication,* but it does mean similarity or *near-likeness.* Slight variations of a simple repetition will add absorbing interest to pattern which might otherwise be tiring (plate 12).

Variety

Harmony is the counterweight of variety. It is the other side of organization essential to unity. With *harmony,* the artist binds the picture parts together into one whole; with *variety,* he adds interest to this total form. Here, interest refers to the ability of a work of art to hold the attention of a viewer. If the creator combines visual forces which are all equal on a picture surface, he will find balance, but it will be static, lifeless, and without tension. By adding variation to his picture forces, the artist attaches essential ingredients (i.e., diversion or change) for enduring attention.

Fig. 14. PATTERNS: TREES (student work). Although the subject is "trees," the distinctive pictorial characteristic of this work is the pattern produced by the tree relationships, a pattern which is repeated, though not identically, in all areas of the work, thus creating a unifying effect.

Contrast and Elaboration

The artist controls and uses variety in two ways. *First,* he finds variety in opposition or *contrast,* and he reconciles the visual differences to create unity. *Second,* the artist *elaborates* upon forces which are equal in quality and strength; he does not work spontaneously, but he reworks picture areas persistently until a satisfactory solution is reached. The picture grows as the artist works. Surfaces become rich with interesting and subtle material changes, the theme develops dramatic strength, and the ensuing form attaches purposeful meaning.

Variations add vibration to static picture surfaces. As in music, the contrasting forces act as modulators in changing the pitch or the vibrating qualities of a pictorial pattern. If the contrast is increased, the pitch is raised; as the differences are brought into close accord, the pitch is lowered. The pitch that sets the contrast in order adds dynamic vitality to pictorial organization.

Balance

Balance is so fundamental to unity that it is impossible to present the problems of organization without giving it consideration. At the simplest level, balance suggests the gravitational equilibrium of a single unit in space or of pairs symmetrically arranged with respect to a central axis or point. Perhaps the balancing of pairs can be best illustrated by a weighing scale. Visually, the scale is associated with an apparatus for weighing which has a beam poised on a central pivot (the fulcrum) so as to move freely, with a pan on each end. When such a scale is used, balance is achieved, not through an actual physical weighing process, but through visual judgment by the observer based upon his past experiences and his knowledge of certain principles of physics. In this type of scale, the forces are balanced left and right or *horizontally* with respect to the supporting crossline. In the illustration of the horizontal balance scale, a line of one physical dimension balances or counterbalances a line with the same (or equal) physical characteristics. Other examples point out the balance between lines, shapes, and values which have been modified and varied. In the second type of weighing scale, forces are balanced *vertically.* The third illustrated weighing device points out not only horizontal and vertical balance, but also balance of forces which are distributed around a center point. This is a *radial* weighing scale (fig. 15).

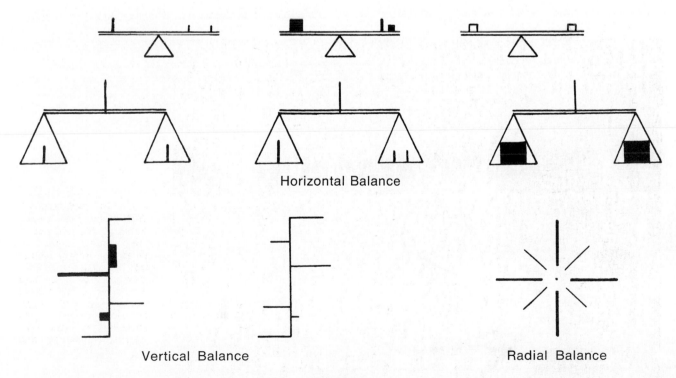

Horizontal Balance

Vertical Balance

Radial Balance

Fig. 15.

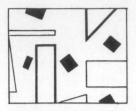

Fig. 16. Balance in all directions, horizontal, vertical, radial, and diagonal.

In picturemaking, balance refers to the felt optical equilibrium between all parts of the work. The artist balances forces horizontally, vertically, radially, and diagonally in all directions and positions (fig. 16).

Several *factors,* when combined with the elements, contribute to balance in a work of art. These factors or variables are *position* or placement, *size, proportion, quality,* and *direction* of the elements. Of these factors, *position* plays the

lead role. If two shapes of equal physical qualities are placed near the bottom of a picture frame, the work will appear bottom-heavy or out of balance with the large upper space. Such shapes should be placed in positions which will contribute to the *total balance* of all the involved picture parts. Similarly, the other factors can put a pictorial arrangement in or out of balance according to their use.

In seeking balance, one should recognize that the elements of art represent "moments of force." The eye as it travels over the picture surface pauses momentarily for significant picture parts which are contrasting in character. These contrasts represent moving and directional forces which must counterbalance one another so that *controlled tension* results. In the painting *Handball* by Ben Shahn, the moments of force are felt in tension which exists between the two figures in the foreground and the num-

Fig. 17. HANDBALL (1939) by Ben Shahn.   Collection, the Museum of Modern Art, New York. Abby Aldrich Rockefeller Fund

Fig. 18. LAKE GEORGE WINDOW (1929) by Georgia O'Keeffe. The window, its moldings, and its shutters are equally distributed on either side of an imaginary vertical axis in mirrorlike repetition. Georgia O'Keeffe has balanced this painting symmetrically.

Collection, the Museum of Modern Art, New York. Acquired through the Richard D. Brixley Bequest

Fig. 19. AMERICAN GOTHIC (1930) by Grant Wood. The two figures in this picture create repetitious relationships so that their *vertical axis* is optically felt. This may be termed *approximate symmetry.*

Courtesy the Art Institute of Chicago

ber 1 which has been placed on the top of the wall (fig. 17). These forces together support one another. The problem of visual balance has resulted in two basic types of organization, symmetrical and asymmetrical.

Symmetrical (Formal) Balance

The beginner will find that *symmetry* is the simplest and most obvious type of balance. In pure symmetry, identical *optical units* (or forces) are *equally* distributed on either side of a vertical axis or axes in mirrorlike repetition (fig. 18). Because of its identical repetition, the effect of pure symmetrical balance is usually static, lifeless. It is simply too monotonous for prolonged audience attention. However, by its use, *unity* is easily attained.

Approximate symmetry. The severe monotony of pure symmetry in pictorial arrangements is often relieved by a method which is sometimes called approximate symmetry (fig .19). Here, the

two sides of a picture are varied to hold audience attention, but they are similar enough to make repetitious relationships and their vertical axis optically felt.

Radial balance. This is another type of pictorial arrangement which, through repetitive association, belongs to the family of symmetry. In radial balance two or more forces identical in strength and character are distributed around a center point. The balance of rotating forces creates visual circular movement on the picture surface, thus adding a new dimension to an otherwise static symmetrical balance. Although pure radial balance opposes identical forces, interesting varieties can be created by means of spatial, numerical, and directional modification. In spite of such modifications, the principle of repetition must be stressed, and the results create a decorative allover effect. Radial balance is chiefly used to make commercial decorative patterns.

Asymmetrical (Occult) Balance

Asymmetrical balance means visual control of contrasts through felt equilibrium between parts of a picture. For example, felt balance might be achieved between a small area of strong color and a large empty space. Particular parts may be contrasting, provided that they contribute to the allover balance of the total picture. There are no rules for achieving asymmetrical balance; there is no center point and no dividing axis. If, however, the artist can feel, judge, or estimate the opposing forces and their tensions so that they balance each other in total concept, vital, dynamic, and expressive organization on the picture plane will result. A picture balanced by contradictory forces, for instance, black and white, blue and orange, shape and space, impels further investigation of these relationships and thus becomes an inquiring and interesting visual experience (plates 13 and 14).

Movement

A picture surface is static; its parts do not move. Thus any animation in a work must come from an illusion created by the artist through placement and configuration of the picture parts. The written word is read from side to side, but a visual image can be read in a variety of directions. The directions are created by the artist out of a need for a means to bind the various parts together in rhythmic, legible, and logical sequence. The movement should assure that all areas of the picture plane are exploited, that is, that there are no dead spots. This goal is realized by directing shapes and lines toward each other in a not always obvious manner so that the spectator is unconsciously swept along major and secondary visual channels. The movement should be self-renewing, constantly drawing attention back into the format (figs. 20 and 21).

Proportion

Since *proportion* deals with the ratio of one part to another, it must fall under the heading "principles of organization." Ratio implies comparison and is expressed in *size, number, position,* and *space.* In a picture, the relation of one size to another is always important. The artist tends to use sizes which seem to balance, are similar, and seem related by comparison. If he uses a large shape beside a small one, it will seem

uncomfortable and out of scale. A shape should fit properly in its position and space; if it feels comfortable, it should be kept. Fitting requires personal judgment by the creator since there are no rules for presenting the right size or the correct proportion (*see* plate 63 and fig. 201). Here, once again, the artist must rely on harmony and variety for judging and evaluating the parts of his organization.

Dominance

Any work of art which strives for interest must exhibit differences which emphasize the

Fig. 20.

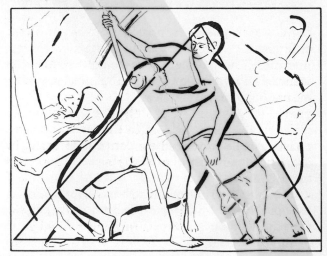

Fig. 21. VENUS AND ADONIS (ca. 1522–24) by Titian. The movement in this painting was planned by Titian to carry the spectator's eye along guided visual paths. These were created (as is indicated by the accented lines in the diagram) by emphasizing the figure contours and the light values. The triangular shape made by the main figures serves as a pivotal motif around which secondary movements circulate.
Courtesy National Gallery of Art, Washington, D.C. Widener Collection

Fig. 22. UNTITLED by Fiorini. The factor of contrast affects dominance in both figurative and nonobjective works. In this instance its darkness and slight angularity and value contrast emphasize the pipelike shape, and the white shape stands out through value alone.

Courtesy Bowling Green State University. School of Art Print Collection

degrees of importance of its various parts. These differences are according to medium and need. A musical piece, for example, could utilize crescendo; a dramatic production, a spotlight. The means by which differences can be achieved are many, and if we substitute the term *contrast* for *difference,* we can see that in the visual arts emphasis can be produced by *contrast* in scale, in character, and in any of the physical properties of the elements.

Obviously, it is the intention of the artist to use contrast to call attention to the significant parts of the work, thus making them dominant. A work which neglects *dominance* implies that everything is of equal importance; thus, it not only fails to communicate, but also creates a confusing visual image in which no direction is given the viewer. In a sense, all parts are important because the secondary ones produce the norm against which the dominant parts are contrasted.

In dealing with dominance, the artist has two problems; first he must see that each part has the necessary *degree* of importance, and, second, he must incorporate these parts with their varying degrees of importance into the rhythmic movement and balance of the work. In doing this, he often finds that he must use different methods to achieve dominance; one significant area might derive importance from its change in value, whereas another might rely on its busy or exciting shape (fig. 22 and plate 15).

The star system in the entertainment field; the hierarchy of political, ecclesiastical, and civic organizations; the atomic system, the solar system, and the galaxy—all are witness to the basic order created by variations in dominance.

Economy

Often in the beginning of a creation the parts are complicated, too important, and confusing. The result is disorganization or visual turmoil. Generally, these parts can be brought into agreement by *economically* sacrificing certain particulars and relating each part to the whole picture. Economy of expression is vital to unity. A picture should be composed in a simple, direct manner. There are no rules for achieving economy. If a part works in an organization with respect to the whole, it should be kept; if it disrupts the unity, it should be reworked and reevaluated in a purposeful manner. Economy is often associated with the term *abstraction,* which by its very definition includes simplicity of means (fig .23). The modern artist often sacrifices, abstracts so to speak, particular details in order to strengthen the organizing conclusions of his picture (plate 16).

Fig. 23. OWL (student work). The artist has economized by eliminating everything from the owl but those things deemed absolutely necessary for recognition.

Space

The problems of *space* in art organization are of such great magnitude that an entire chapter is devoted to them later in this text. It will suffice to mention here that space when used in a work of art should be *consistent*. There is nothing by way of comparison that can throw a picture so "out of kilter" as a jumbled spatial representation. If an artist begins his picture with one kind of spatial representation, he should continue to use the same qualities in the succeeding stages of his work. It is almost a necessity for an artist to preplan his space. This early planning will contribute immeasurably to the unity in any work of art.

SUMMARY

Unity in art results from practicing, knowing, and selecting the right visual devices and using the best principles to relate them to each other. An understanding of the principles of form-structure is fundamental to art education. The investigation discussed in the previous chapters are only an intellectual beginning for seeing some of the vast possibilities in the creative art realm. By studying the principles of form organization, the beginner will gain an understanding that later will help him find *intuitive* and *creative* experience.

The group of art elements *line, shape, value, texture,* and *color* cannot exist exclusively in themselves. Often these art elements constantly overlap as they borrow from one another to become visible or more expressive.

Due to the fact that the art elements each have intrinsic appeal, they are discussed separately in the following five chapters for the purpose of individual study. When two, three, or all of the elements are used in one picture, they are separated only for the purpose of discussion. In reality, the artist must consider these elements together as contributing factors to one complete statement, the whole art work.

FORM PROBLEMS

Preliminary problems to create understanding of *form* may be worked using simple basic shapes to emphasize the idea that the relationships to the elements to the space which they occupy create the *form unity*. Repeating simple shapes in different ways demonstrates the various principles indicated in this chapter. To emphasize the importance of the relationship between the elements and the picture frame, some problems may be done in horizontal areas, some in vertical areas, and some within squares.

Problem 1

On a background draw a frame shape about 9 x 12 inches in size. Within this area, arrange 6 to 9 one-inch squares cut from a dark-colored piece of paper. Since these shapes are all the same size and color, it will be necessary to make the arrangement interesting by variety in their spacing. Balance within the space should be informal in character in order to create greater interest. There will be tension or attraction between the shapes, depending upon how close they are to each other. If they are placed too close to the edge, they will exhibit greater attraction to the outside of the frame shape. This is a simple problem in trying to balance harmony with variety.

This problem may be varied by working with a vertical, as well as a horizontal, frame shape.

Using a square frame shape such as 10 by 10 inches also requires a different type of arrangement. In the different arrangements, keep the square shapes parallel to the edges of the frame.

Problem 2

This experiment is a continuation of Problem 1 but attempts to create greater variety. Use squares of varying sizes but still cut from one color of paper. The number of shapes used will vary according to the sizes used. Informal balance should be used to create greater interest. Remember that the negative shapes of the background area are just as important as the positive shapes (squares).

Problem 3

Contrast and elaboration can be achieved in a format similar to Problems 1 and 2 by using two different kinds of shapes. For example, triangles could be combined with the squares for additional interest. When this is done, one of the two kinds of shapes used should be dominant either through size or number. Another way of creating the desired contrast is through the use of two different colors. Again, a kind of unity would be achieved by making one color dominant over the other.

Problem 4

Several diverse motifs may achieve unity of total form by allowing some shapes to touch or overlap. Cut some circles and rectangles of varying sizes from two different colors of paper and arrange them so that some shapes overlap others. Make one kind of shape dominate over the other or one color dominate over the other. Remember that you are striving to make enough similarities for harmony and enough differences for contrast and elaboration. Also keep in mind that there should be a feeling of equilibrium throughout the entire pattern.

Where forms are overlapped, there will be a sense of space within the frame shape. Consequently, instead of the shapes seeming to be on one plane, they will give the illusion of moving back and forth in space. In order to keep the unity of the picture plane, do not allow too much of this back-and-forth movement.

Problem 5

An experiment with a different type of overlap makes an interesting problem and at the same time demonstrates some things about shape relationship. Again, use two simple geometric shapes such as circles and triangles or circles and squares. Make patterns for these by cutting them out of heavy paper. One of these shapes could be made in two different sizes to create variety. Fill a frame shape by drawing around these patterns, allowing the shapes to overlap so that one shape is seen through another. This kind of transparent overlap not only helps to relate the shapes themselves, but also creates new shapes, thus adding to the total interest of the pattern. Fill in the areas of the shapes or background with a dark value, leaving other areas white.

Problem 6

As lines are drawn across a frame shape, not only are linear rhythms immediately created,

but also shapes that have relationship to each other. This matter of space-breaking is the artist's primary problem in creating form unity. Using mechanical instruments such as a compass for curved lines and a ruler for straight lines break up a frame shape into smaller areas. As the lines are parallel, they will create shape harmony; as they oppose each other, they will give contrast for a more interesting expression. You may use curved lines only, created with a compass or combine them with straight lines created with a ruler. Make the lines solid black by using drawing ink. Some of the resulting areas (positive or negative) can then be filled in with solid black. Variation in the size of areas results in interesting proportional relationships (fig. 24 and 25).

Fig. 24.

Fig. 25.

Problem 7

Using a square frame shape, create a pattern by repeating a basic motif. Use an ordinary tool or a kitchen appliance as a basic shape. If it is too complicated, simplify the shape by leaving out small unnecessary details. Cut out the shape as a silhouette and use it as a pattern which you can draw around. The entire shape does not have to show, but may be cut by the edges of the square. The positive shape will always be the same, but the negative shapes of the background will have considerable variety. Some of these negative shapes will be simple, but others will exhibit considerable variety. Make the negative areas black and leave the positive shapes white. It is also possible to use a few lines for textural interest or to add interesting detail (fig. 26).

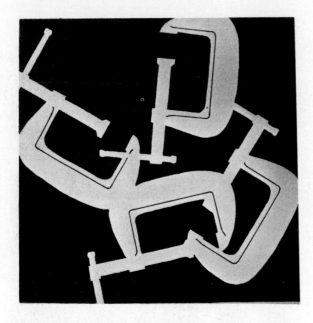

Fig. 26.

Chapter 4/Line

Definitions:

Calligraphy: The use of flowing rhythmical lines which intrigue the eye as they enrich surfaces. Calligraphy is highly personal in nature similar to the individual qualities found in handwriting.

Contour: A line which creates a boundary separating an area of space from its surrounding background.

Decorative: The quality which emphasizes the two-dimensional nature of any of the visual elements. Decoration enriches a surface without denying the essential flatness of its nature.

Line: The path of a moving point, that is, a mark made by a tool or instrument as it is drawn across a surface. It is usually made visible by the fact that it contrasts in value with the surface on which it is drawn.

Mass: A three-dimensional form or body which stands out from the space surrounding it because of difference in color, value, or texture. The physical bulk of a solid body of material.

Plastic: A quality which emphasizes the three-dimensional nature of shape or mass. On a two-dimensional surface, plasticity is always an illusion created by the use of the visual elements in special ways.

LINE IS THE ELEMENTARY MEANS OF VISUAL COMMUNICATION

Line is a graphic device made to function symbolically in artistic and literary expression. Its expression may be employed on *subjective* and *objective* levels. Objectively it may describe simple measurements and surface characteristics. Subjectively it may be modified to suggest many emotional states and responses (fig. 27). Linear designs in the form of ideograms and alphabetical letters are used by man as a basic means of

Fig. 27. TWO NUDES from La Belle Chair by Volti. The artist's response to the idea of human figure is reflected in his use of line as an interpretive instrument.

Courtesy Bowling Green State University. School of Art Print Collection communication. The artist similarly uses line but in a more broadly communicative manner. Line seems to be fundamental in such expression, and since the *elements of art structure* are to be studied separately, it seems appropriate to begin with *line*.

Line, as such, does not exist in nature; it is a man-made invention, an *abstraction*, developed as an agent for the *simplification* of statements of visual fact and for *symbolizing* graphic ideas (fig. 28). Nature contains only *mass*, the measurements of which are conveniently demonstrated in art by the use of line as *contour*.

Line operates on elastic terms in the visual field symbolizing an *edge* as on a piece of sculpture (*see* fig. 156), a *meeting of areas* where textural or color differences do not blend, a *contour* as it defines a drawn shape; *plastic* insofar as it suggests space, or *calligraphic* as it enriches a surface (plate 17 and fig. 30). The line may perform several of these functions at the same time. Its wide application ranges into the creation of *value* and *texture*, illustrating the impossibility of making a completely arbitrary and final distinction between the elements of art structure (fig. 29). However, it is possible to recognize and analyze the linear components of a work of art.

Fig. 29. SELF PORTRAIT by James Steg. This engraving illustrates the wide application of line; a *meeting* of *areas* where texture and values change (contrast between crosshatching pattern of background and the white of hair), *contour* as it defines the edge of the face, and *enrichment* of the *surface as seen* in many areas throughout the print.
Courtesy of the artist

Fig. 28. THREE MUSICIANS (1944) by Fernand Léger. Léger used line in an *abstract* manner to *simplify* complex forms which exist in nature as *masses*.

Collection, the Museum of Modern Art, New York. Mrs. Simon Guggenheim Fund

Plate 6. THE VIRGIN WITH SAINT INÉS AND SAINT TECLA (c. 1576-80) by El Greco. The rectangular frame shape, by its proportions, offers to the artist a pleasing and interesting spatial arrangement. Here, El Greco has elongated his main shapes to repeat and harmonize with the vertical character of the picture frame.

Courtesy The National Gallery of Art, Washington, D.C. Widener Collection.

Plate 7. THE ADORATION OF THE MAGI by Fra Angelico and Fra Filippo Lippi. The artists have used figures and architecture, the elements of art, their directions and movements in harmonious relation to a circular picture frame.

Courtesy The National Gallery of Art, Washington, D.C. Samuel H. Kress Collection.

Plate 8. A GIRL WITH A WATERING CAN by Auguste Renoir. Since the figure is located in the **foreground** of Renoir's painting, it is considered a **positive** unit. Traditionally, the surrounding **background** areas are considered negative space.

Courtesy The National Gallery of Art. Washington. D.C. Chester Dale Collection.

Plate 9. FISH MAGIC (1925) by Paul Klee. In this painting by Paul Klee, the object shapes through their repetition and transitional variation create harmonious relationships. Variety in **size** and **treatment** create contrasting notes which are balanced by the repetition of color and shape character.

Courtesy Philadelphia Museum of Art: The Louise and Walter Arensberg Collection.

Plate 10. LAC LARANGE IV (1969) by Frank Stella. Stella has harmonized the painting through his insistent use of the curve; variety is provided by contrasting colors and shape sizes.

Plate 11. ZAPATISTAS (1931) by José Clemente Orozco. Rhythm: A continuous **movement** is suggested as the Zapatistas cross the picture surface from right to left. In passing, these figures form a **repetitious beat;** as their shapes, leaning in the same direction, create a **rhythmic order.**

Plate 12. NUMBER 1 (1951) by Ad Reinhardt. The visual units in Reinhardt's painting are rectangular modules. The repetition of this motif creates harmony, and the variety develops out of the subtle differences in scale and color.

Courtesy The Toledo Museum of Art, Toledo, Ohio.

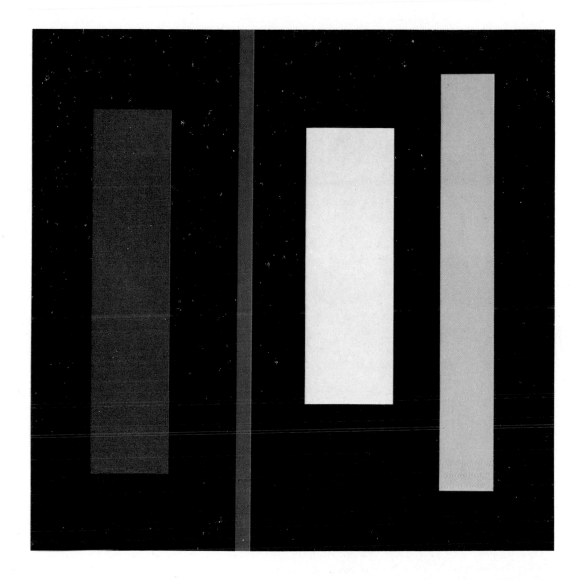

Plate 13. FIRST THEME (1962) by Burgoyne Diller. The contradictory forces of similar shapes with differing color and size are weighed by the observer's instincts and intuition, arriving at an asymmetrical balance.

Courtesy The Art Institute of Chicago.

Plate 14. FAMILY OF SALTIMBANQUES (1905) by Picasso. Asymmetrical balance: a "felt" balance is achieved through a juxtaposition of the varying shapes and a continuing distribution of similar values and colors.

Courtesy The National Gallery of Art, Washington, D.C. Chester Dale Collection.

Plate 15. CHESTNUT TREES AT JAS DE BOUFFAN (1885-87) by Paul Cezanne. Dominance: Although some of the trees in this work are stronger than others, they are collectively seen as an individual unit which dominates the other parts. The dominance is achieved by size, dark value, and complex relationships. Secondary areas take their place in the dominance scale largely through reduced values and color strengths as they recede in space (atmospheric perspective).

Courtesy The Minneapolis Institute of Arts.

Plate 16. THE LOVERS (1923) by Pablo Picasso. Economy: Pablo Picasso has simplified the complex qualities of the surface structures of his two figures. He has reduced the representation of his lovers to contour lines and flat color renderings. Here, Picasso has abstracted (used economical means) the two lovers in order to strengthen the expressive bond between them.

Courtesy The National Gallery of Art, Washington, D.C. Chester Dale Collection.

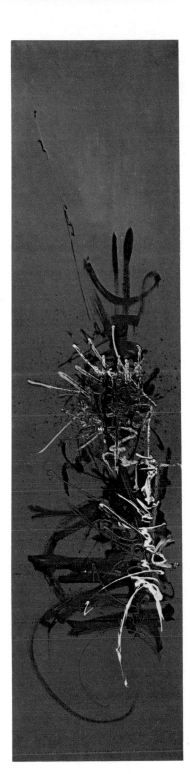

Plate 17. MONTJOIE SAINT DENIS! (1954) by Georges Mathieu. The use of red, yellow, dark blue (primary colors) and white in these calligraphic lines serves to produce a forceful, strong, emotional effect.

Collection, The Museum of Modern Art, New York. Gift of Mr. and Mrs. Harold Kaye.

Plate 18. TRIO by Steve Magada. Line may be admired for its own sake. Steve Magada has exploited this appeal by creating a picture in which the linear effects are dominant.

Courtesy Steve Magada.

Plate 19. THE DREAM (1910) by Henri Rousseau. Rousseau has used groupings of lines in a decorative manner to stimulate the feeling of the textural **pattern** in jungle growth.

Collection, The Museum of Modern Art, New York. Gift of Nelson A. Rockefeller.

PHYSICAL CHARACTERISTICS OF LINES

The *physical* properties of line are *measure, type, direction, location,* and *character.*

Measure

Measure refers to the length and width of line. A line may be of any length or shortness and breadth or narrowness. There are an infinite number of combinations of long and short or thick and thin lines which, according to their use, may divide or unify the *pictorial area.*

Type

Any line is by its own nature a particular type. If the line continues in only *one* direction, it will be straight; if *gradual changes* of direction occur, it will be curved; if those changes are sudden and abrupt, an *angular* line will be created. In adding this dimension to that of *measure,* we find that long or short, thick or thin lines can be straight, angular, or curved. The straight line in its continuity ultimately becomes *repetitious* and, depending on its length, either rigid or brittle. The curved line may curve to form an arc, reverse its curve to become wavy, or continue turning within itself to produce a spiral. The alterations of movement becomes *visually entertaining* and physically stimulating if *rhythmical* (*see* fig. 30). A curved line is inherently graceful and, to a degree, unstable. The abrupt changes of direction in an angular line create excitement and/or confusion (fig. 31). Our eyes frequently find difficulty in adapting themselves to its unexpected deviations of direction. Hence, the angular line is one which is full of challenging interest.

Fig. 30. ACTOR AS A MONKEY SHOWMAN by Torii Kiyonobu. The alterations of movement in the *curved lines* of this Japanese print are visually entertaining as well as calligraphic because of their subtle rhythmical quality.

Courtesy the Metropolitan Museum of Art, New York. Rogers Fund 1936

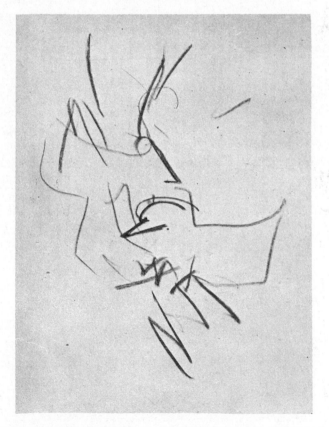

Fig. 31. COCK FIGHT (Student Work). The abrupt changes of direction in the *angular lines* of the student drawing of a *Cock Fight* create the excitement and tension of the combat.

Direction

A further complication of line is its *basic direction,* one which may exist irrespective of the component movements *within* the line. That is, a line may be a *zigzag type* but take a generally *curved direction.* Thus the *line type* may be contradicted or flattered by its *basic movement.* A generally horizontal direction could indicate serenity and perfect stability, whereas a diagonal direction would probably imply agitation and motion. A vertical line generally speaks of such things as poise and aspiration. Line's direction is most important, for in a large measure it controls the movements of our eyes while viewing a picture. This movement may bring about continuity of relationships among the various elements and their properties.

Location

The control exercised over the foregoing line properties may be enhanced or diminished by the *location* of the line. According to its placement, a line may serve to *unify* or *divide* and *balance* or *unbalance* a pictorial area. A diagonal line may be soaring or plunging, depending upon its high or low position relative to the frame. The various attributes of line may act in concert toward one goal or may be serving separate roles of expression and design. It is obvious, therefore, that a fully developed work may recognize and utilize all physical factors, although it is also possible that less than the total number may be successfully used. This is true largely because of the dual role of these properties. For instance, *unity* in a work may be achieved by *repetition* of line length while *variety* is being created by *difference* in its width, medium, or other properties.

Character

Along with *measure, type, direction,* and *location,* line possesses *character,* a term largely related to the *medium* with which it is created. Different media or medium conditions may be used to create greater interest. Monotony could result from the consistent use of lines of the same character unless the unity so gained was balanced by the variation of other physical properties. The nature of the drawing instrument is important in determining the *emotional quality* of the line. One can easily see the different *expressive* qualities inherent in the soft, blurred lines of *chalk* as opposed to the precise and firm lines of *pen* and *ink* (fig. 32). Other instruments, *brush, burin, stick, fingers,* and so forth, all contain distinctive expressive capabilities which may be exploited by the artist. The artist is the real master of the situation, and it is his ability, experience, intention, and mental and physical condition that will determine the effectiveness of *line character.* According to the artist one may find lines of uniformity or accent, certainty or indecision, tension or relaxation.

Fig. 32. LINE CHARACTER (student work). A number of tools and media are found in this one drawing: brush and ink, pen and ink, chalk, pencil, matchstick, and ink. The variety of materials and their manipulation by the artist give expressive qualities to each individual figure.

Fig. 33. VIOLINIST.

EXPRESSIVE QUALITY (student work). A number of qualities can be created by the manner in which the artist varies *line character.* The idea of *violinist* is expressed in one of these line groupings; the other represents an abstract concept of an *orchestra leader.*

Fig. 34. ORCHESTRA LEADER (student work).

EXPRESSIVE PROPERTIES OF LINE

The *qualities* of line may be described by general states of feeling—gay, somber, tired, energetic, brittle, alive, and the like. However, in a work of art, as in the human mind, such feelings are rarely so clearly defined. There are an infinite number of conditions of varying subtleties which may be communicated by the artist (figs. 33 and 34). The recognition of these qualities by the spectator is a matter of feeling, which means that he must be receptive and perceptive and have his own reservoir of experiences.

One can enlarge quite extensively on the many uses of line in a work of art. Through the factors of *composition* and *expression*, individ-

ual lines come to life as they play their various roles. Some lines are dominant and some subordinate, but all are of supreme importance in a work of art. Although lines may be admired separately, their real beauty lies in the *relationships* which they help to establish, the *form* created. This form may be *representational* or *nonrepresentational*, but the recognition and the enjoyment of the work on the *abstract* level is of first importance. Primary preoccupation with subject identification will materially reduce the appreciation of the truly expressive art qualities.

LINE AS RELATED TO THE OTHER ART ELEMENTS

There are other physical properties of line which are so closely involved with the other art elements that they should be studied in terms of those relationships. Line may possess *color, value,* and *texture,* and it may create *shape.* Some of these factors are essential to the very creation of line, while others may be introduced as needed. These properties may be thought of separately, but nevertheless they cooperate to give line an intrinsic appeal, meaning that line may be admired for its own sake (plate 18). Artists often exploit this appeal by creating pictures in which the linear effects are dominant, the others subordinate.

Line and Shape

In creating *shape,* line serves as a continuous *edge* of a figure, object, or mass. A line which describes an area in this manner is called *contour* (fig. 35). *Contour* may further operate as a separation between *shapes, values, textures,* and *colors.*

A series of closely placed lines create *textures* and *toned areas.* The relationships of the ends of these *linear areas* establish boundaries that transpose them into *shapes.*

Line and Value

The contrast in light and dark which a line exhibits against its background is termed *value.* Every line must demonstrate this quality in order to remain visible. This *value* may be the result of mixture or pressure, depending on the *medium* being used. *Groups* of single lines create areas which show *value* differences (fig. 36). Parallel lines, hatchings, and so forth, are included in such groups (fig. 37).

Fig. 35. A *contour* drawing when made without looking at the paper may create unexpected distortions which add *expressive* quality to the line produced.

Fig. 36. RUBENS SERIES by Philip R. Wigg. Pressure, proximity, and concentration of lines can be used to create varying values.
Courtesy of the Artist

Fig. 37. HOUSE WITH CLARK SIGN by Glenn Felch. Values may be created by varying the spaces between the lines; the parallel quality of the lines also injects a degree of harmony.
Courtesy of the Artist

Line and Texture

When groups of lines such as those mentioned combine to produce a flat or two-dimensional effect, *pattern* results (plate 19). If, however, the result is one which stimulates our sensation of touch by suggesting degrees of roughness or smoothness, the effect may be termed *texture*. *Texture* also resides within the character of various *media* and *tools* and gives them their distinctive qualities (fig. 38). Each tool possesses the *textural properties* of its structure and use, and these in turn may be enhanced or diminished by the manner of handling. Brushes of a hard bristle, for instance, can make either sharp or rough lines, depending on hand pressure, *amount* of medium carried, and *quality* of execution. Brushes with soft hairs can produce smooth lines if loaded with thin paint and thick blotted lines if loaded with heavy paint. Other *tools* and *media* similarly produce variations of *line* in terms of the factors mentioned.

Line and Color

The introduction of *color* to a line adds a vast creative potential. Color may serve to *accent* or neutralize other line properites; a hard line combined with an *intense* color will produce a forceful or even harsh effect. This effect could be considerably overcome were the identical line created in a more gentle color. *Color* has become identified with various emotional states and may be used by the artist to indicate them. For instance, red might symbolize passion or anger, yellow could suggest cowardice or warmth, and so forth (*see* plate 17).

SPATIAL CHARACTERISTICS OF LINE

All of the physical properties of line contain *spatial* ingredients which are subject to control by the artist. Mere position within a prescribed area suggests *space*. *Value contrast* may cause lines to advance and recede (fig. 39). An individual line which has varied *values* throughout

Fig. 38. OWLS (woodcut) (student work). If it is respected, each medium creates its own characteristic imprint.

Fig. 39. (1919) PORTRAIT OF MAX JACOB by Juan Gris. Line can add *spatial dimension* to representative drawing. The accent and modulation of line used to describe this figure helps to give it a *plastic* quality.

Collection, the Museum of Modern Art, New York. Gift of James Thrall Soby

Fig. 40. THE CITY (1951) by Maria Helena Vieira da Silva. The spatial illusion, of such obvious importance in this example, is largely the product of the physical properties of its lines strengthened by value shapes.
Courtesy the Toledo Museum of Art

its length may appear to writhe and twist in space. As in general *warm* colors *advance* and *cool* colors *recede*, the *spatial properties* of colored lines are obvious. Every factor which produces *line* has something to say about its location in space (fig. 40). The artist's job is to use these factors to create *spatial order*.

LINE AND REPRESENTATION

Line creates *representation* on both *abstract* and *realistic* levels. In general, we have dealt primarily with abstract definitions, but it is easy to see that the application may be simultaneously observed in a material context. For example, we have mentioned the *advancing-receding* qualities of value in a line; if this particular line was one which had been drawn to represent the *contours* of a piece of drapery, we could see that *value contrast* might describe the relative *spatial* position of the folds of the drapery (fig. 41). A linear portrait of a person may utilize line properties to suggest more than its mere physical presence. It may contain much information on the character of the sitter. The artist may state this satirically or sympathetically. Thus, line in representation has many implications both objective and subjective. All are the direct result of the manipulation of the *physical properties* by the artist.

Fig. 41. (student work). The *plastic* quality of a shape may be produced by lines which move across and within the form as well as on the edge or *contour*.

In their role of signifying ideas and conveying feelings, lines move and live, pulsating with significant emotions. In art, line becomes a means for transcribing the *graphic language* of ideas and emotions. It describes the edges or *contours* of shapes, it diagrams silhouettes, it encompasses spaces and areas—all done in such a way as to convey meaning.

Line is not used *extensively* to express deep emotion and experience in this manner. Often, it is used for planning *utilitarian* objects: the line drawings of a building prepared by an architect or the drawings of a bridge made by an engineer; the lines drawn on maps to represent rivers, roads, or contours; or the lines drawn on paper to represent words. Such use of line is primarily utilitarian, a convenient way of communicating ideas to another person. Whichever the emphasis, *expression* of human emotions or *communication* of factual materials, line is an important *plastic element* at the disposal of the artist.

LINE PROBLEMS

Problem 1

Line has infinite variety according to the medium used and the manipulation of that medium by the artist.

Cover a whole sheet of paper with lines using every medium which you have available. Strive for variety by manipulating the medium in every conceivable way.

Problem 2

Lines may vary as to direction and position.

In frame shapes, create four interesting line patterns. One should be composed of vertical and horizontal lines only, one of diagonal lines, one of curved lines, and one of a combination of lines of all directions. Vary the length, thickness, spacing, and color of the lines so as to make the pattern interesting.

Problem 3

Lines may be balanced symmetrically or they may be balanced asymmetrically. When lines are paired equally on either side of a vertical axis, they are balanced symmetrically. Lines may be different in terms of their physical properties and measures, but if they are equal in terms of their spatial fields, equilibrium will be reached on the picture plane. Such line balance is termed asymmetrical.

In a picture frame, balance a group of lines symmetrically and asymmetrically. Vary the physical properties of the lines.

Problem 4

Lines may be decorative or they may be spatial in character. When lines are of the same thickness and do not cross each other, they tend to decorate a surface without giving any significant sense of space. If lines cross, vary in thickness, and are of different colors, they may express a plastic quality; that is, they may seem to exist in a three-dimensional or space relationship.

On a single sheet of paper make two design patterns of lines, each contained within a frame shape. One should be a design in which the lines have a decorative effect and all seem to lie on the plane of the paper; the other should be made so that the lines seem to exist in space. (fig. 42).

Problem 5

The artist may combine expressive calligraphy and the representational characteristics of line in the same image (fig. 43).

Select a few moderately complex subjects. Draw these experimentally in a continuous contour line, defining the subject but at the same time allowing the drawing instrument to roam freely, making sudden changes in direction and allowing the line to overlap itself. The line should dwell in some areas, moving steadily improvising as it moves, and moving directly from one area to another. Try drawing quickly as well as slowly. The intention is to produce works which are at the same time definitive and spontaneous, expressive and disciplined; the line should have calligraphic qualities (*see Calligraphy* under "Definitions"; *also see* plate 17 and fig. 30).

Problem 6

Different line types can produce different expressive effects. Straight lines are rigid, diagonal lines are exciting, vertical lines are dignified, horizontal lines are quiet and restful. Combinations of these lines can express complex feelings.

Fig. 42A.

Fig. 42B.

Fig. 43.

Create several abstract line patterns expressing the qualities (*not* things) felt in selected nouns, adjectives, and verbs. The expression should lie not in the description of objects but within the nature of the line itself (*see* figs. 31, 33, and 34).

Problem 7

When the form of an object is expressed in one continuous line, the form takes on qualities of expression, depending on the medium used.

Draw several objective forms in a continuous line using the potentialities of the medium. With crayons vary the lightness and darkness of the line; with brush and ink vary the thickness and thinness of the line. Try ink lines on damp paper. Try pencil using a broad stroke with the side of the pencil. Use lines with paint applied thickly as well as thinned with water (fig. 44).

Problem 8

Lines may describe the boundaries of object shapes.

Concentrating the eye on the outer edge of an object, follow the contour with a drawing instrument. When the drawing is completed, vary the lines for spatial and emotional effects (fig. 45).

Fig. 44A.

Fig. 44B.

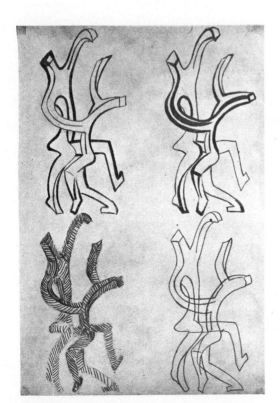

Fig. 45.

Problem 9

Single lines when grouped create areas of dark and light.

Draw parallel lines across the breadth of represented objects, varying the spaces between the lines to produce changes of value (fig. 46).

Fig. 46.

Chapter 5/Shape

Definitions:

Biomorphic shapes: Usually more or less irregular shapes which resemble the freely developed curves found in live organisms.

Cubism: A term given to the artistic style which uses mostly geometric shapes usually two-dimensional in nature.

Decorative shapes: Those shapes which are two-dimensional in nature and seem to lie flat on the surface of the picture plane.

Geometric shapes: Those shapes created by the exact mathematical laws of geometry. They are usually simple in character such as the triangle, the rectangle, and the circle.

Intuitive space: A pictorial spatial illusion which is not the product of any mechanical system but which relies, instead, on the physical properties of the elements and the instincts or feel of the artist.

Linear perspective: A mechanical system for creating the illusion of a three-dimensional space on a two-dimensional surface.

Plane: A shape which is essentially two-dimensional in nature but whose relationships with other shapes may give an illusion of a third dimension.

Plastic shapes: Shapes which are indicated by the artist as being "in the round" and surrounded by space. Shapes displaying the third dimension of depth.

Rectilinear shapes: Shapes whose boundaries usually consist entirely of straight lines.

Shape: An area which stands out from the space next to or around it because of a defined boundary or because of difference of value, color, or texture.

Surrealism: A style of artistic expression which emphasizes fantasy and whose subjects are usually the experiences revealed by the subconscious mind.

Volume: A shape which is three-dimensional in nature and exists in space. On a flat surface the artist can only create the *illusion* of a volume.

Shapes are the building blocks of art structure. Edifices of brick, stone, and mortar are intended by the architect and mason to have beauty of design, skilled craftsmanship, and structural strength. The artist shares these goals in creating a picture. Bricks and stones, however, are tangible objects, whereas pictorial shapes exist largely in terms of the illusions they create. The challenge facing the artist is that of using the infinitely varied illusions of this element to make believable the fantasy which is an inherent characteristic of all art. In other words, an art work is *never* the *real* thing, and the shapes producing the image are never real animals, buildings, people—the subjects from which the artist may work if, indeed, he uses subjects at all. The artist may be *stimulated* by such objects, and in many cases the resultant style may reproduce their basic appearance fairly closely. The alterations of surface appearance necessary for the communication of an idea and to achieve compositional unity if *minor* might be called *semi-fantasy* (fig. 47). On the other hand, the artist may deal with shapes which are not intended to represent at all, or if they are representational at the outset, they may eventually lead the artist into a situation in which copied appearances in the final work are almost totally eliminated. This could be called *pure* fantasy because the final image is entirely the product of the artist's imagination. It is characteristic of the capable artist that, whatever the degree of his fantasy, it finally convinces us that it is a *possible reality.* Any successful work of art, whatever its medium, leads a sensitive observer into a persuasive

Fig. 47. ANIMALS (1941) by Rufino Tamayo. Tamayo has created a semifantasy by using semiabstract shapes to picture beasts, animal-like in general appearance, but of no recognizable species. The stark shapes emphasize the savage environment.
Collection, the Museum of Modern Art, New York. Inter-American Fund

world of the imagination. In the visual arts shapes play an important part in achieving this goal.

DEFINITION OF SHAPE

A shape may be called a visually perceived area of value, color, or line—or any combination of these elements. It may have exact limits by means of which it can be measured or it may be of such delicacy and so gradually blended that one could not determine with any accuracy its true dimensions. It may be defined by the outer reaches of a color or value, or its edges may be specifically stated by a sharp line. There is no end to the variety of shapes, ranging from basic squares, rectangles, circles, and triangles through limitless combinations of angular and curvilinear configurations. Each of these shapes has its own personality derived from the differences in our response to it. In some cases these responses are quite common; in others, much more com-

plex. We share our personality traits with shapes: shyness, aggressiveness, awkwardness, poise—all are indicative of the characteristics we can easily read into shapes. The artist, of course, makes use of these very qualities in developing his work.

USE OF SHAPES

It has been pointed out that the artist is not always interested in using shapes to represent known objects. This is often a matter of degree; in looking at an art work the observer rarely knows the exact nature of the physical objects which may have been involved (plate 20). Thus, the degree of devotion to actual appearance cannot always be accurately assessed; very often a work thought to be realistic does not correspond too closely to the original subject (figs. 48 and 49). There are reasons, of course, beyond mere incompetency for any changes which might have been made. The principal reason is that the

Fig. 48.

Fig. 49. MAUSOLEUM. Object shapes often undergo considerable transformation according to the individual manner of the artist. Such transformation is illustrated in comparison between a photograph and the print of a mausoleum. The object, as such, was not so important as the final art form.

artist is trying to say something *through* the subject; that is, he is *using* the subject—an expression or point of view can't be made without some editing. The artist, then, goes beyond literal copying, transforming object shapes into his *style* or *language*. Sometimes in doing this he so alters the shapes that they become totally unlike those seen in nature. Another reason for alteration of shapes is the necessity for conforming to the discipline of certain fundamental principles of composition in creating a fully unified work of art. These principles determine the ordering of shapes, as well as the other elements of form. In his search for *form* the artist modifies the elements until:

1. The desired degree and type of balance is achieved.
2. The observer's attention is controlled, both in direction and duration.
3. The appropriate ratio of harmony and variety results.
4. The space concept achieves consistency throughout.

These principles are important enough to merit additional investigation.

Balance

As the artist seeks compositional balance, he works in the knowledge that shapes symbolize various amounts of weight. This fact can be dramatized by examining a diagram of a seesaw: placement of shapes of different sizes at varying distances from the fulcrum can be controlled to create feelings of balance or imbalance (fig. 50). As there is no *actual* weight involved, we must assume that the sensation is intuitive, or felt as the result of the various properties composing the art elements. For example, a dark value adds weight to a shape, and substitution of a narrow line for a wider line around a shape reduces its apparent weight.

The seesaw is an elementary example of a few basic elements operating along only *one* plane of action. Developed art works, on the other hand, contain many diverse elements working in many directions. The factors which control the amounts of force generated by the various elements are placement, size, accent, and general shape character (including associational equivalents to be discussed in the section on Duration

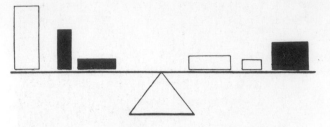

Fig. 50. Diagram showing *amounts of force* or weight symbolized by shapes, using a seesaw as an analogy.

or Relative Dominance in this chapter). The elements are manipulated by the artist until the energy of their dynamic relationships results in arrested tension.

Control of Attention

Direction

As one becomes sensitive to the force represented by the elements, it becomes evident that the artist can use this effect to control the movement of the observer's eyes over his work. Pathways are contrived, providing transition from one pictorial area to another. The artist further attempts to make the travel over the pathways rhythmic, the rhythm at the same time creating pleasurable viewing and serving as an effective unifying device. The character of rhythmic movement depends upon the nature of the artist's expressive intentions; it may be jerky or sinuous, swift or slow.

Duration or Relative Dominance

Paths of eye travel designed by the artist are used to bind together the various optical units, or viewing centers, of the work (figs. 51 and 52 and plate 21). But mere linkage is not enough, for a completely satisfying artistic expression; one would hardly care to travel if all the planned stops on the trip were of equal duration. Similarly, art viewing is more interesting and rewarding if the timing of the itinerary is varied. The artist attempts to organize his pauses so that their lengths are related to the importance of the sights to be seen. The duration of a pause is according to the pictorial dominance of the area, and a number of factors can be used to control it. In a work with the Crucifixion as subject it would be expected that the artist would make the figure of Christ dominant (fig. 53). He could accomplish this through contrast size, value, shape, or location; modification of the physical properties of any of the elements invariably affects spectator attention. The artist develops the importance-scale of his work on the basis of his feelings and reconciles the various demands of the design principles and relative dominance. The degree of dominance is generally in direct proportion to the amount of visual contrast. The principle of relative dominance functions in both representational and nonrepresentational work, and in the same way (*see* fig. 22). The factor (size, for example) making Christ dominant would also work to make a large square dominate

Fig. 51. STILL LIFE: THE TABLE (1928) by Georges Braque.

Courtesy National Gallery of Art, Washington, D.C. Chester Dale Collection others of its kind. There is however another factor, association, which tends to qualify the attention given things. We might be likely to give an oval shape more attention if we were by some chance reminded of a head. Chance interpretation cannot be foreseen by the artist in every case, although he tries to avoid it. If possible, he will use the innate appeal of associational factors to his advantage, weighing them in the balance of relative dominance and forcing them to operate to the benefit of the total organization.

Shape Character

The configuration of a shape gives it the character which distinguishes it from others of its kind. Shape character might be called *natural* when it seems to have been produced by the action of natural forces (stones, leaves, puddles, clouds) or abstract when it seems to have been contrived by the artist. The distinction is not always easily made, for the variations of both are vast indeed. Natural forms generally seem to have been molded into rounded shapes. We see this in the elemental organs and organisms encountered in biological studies (amoebas, viruses, cells, etc.). Biological affinity for the curve has led to the term *biomorphic* to describe the curvilinear shapes in art which suggest the possibility of life.

With the revival of interest in pure abstraction, in which shapes function symbolically, and with increasing awareness of the microcosm through science, the shape type now known as

Fig. 53. CRUCIFIXION by Otto Ocvirk. Examination of this print reveals that the artist has made the figure of Christ paramount primarily through location, size, and value contrast.

Fig. 52. Analysis of the painting by the French Cubist Georges Braque has many elements which contain direction of force.

The diagram with the simplified grouping of dark illustrates the controlled tension resulting from the placement, size, accent, and general character of the shapes used by the artist. The white arrows show the predetermined eye paths by which the artist created visual transition and rhythmic movement.

biomorphic found great use in the hands of artists. The surrealists, whose interests included the mystic origins of being and the explorations of subconscious revelations as in dreams, were particularly attracted to the biomorphic shape (fig. 54). Other artists (Matisse and Braque are examples) abstracted organic forms in a less symbolic and primarily decorative manner (plate 22).

In contrast to the biomorphic shapes are rectilinear (straight line) *geometric* shapes. They generally appear to have the precisionistic, machinelike character of man's invention. They were developed by the cubists in their disection and reformulation of nature (fig. 55). Geometric shapes are rigid, brittle, and generally exciting and when forged together by the artist's instincts form an enduring and frequently austere design (fig. 56).

Biomorphic and geometric shapes may be thought of as shape *families* which are attractive to certain artists because they happen to coincide with the feelings and objectives of those artists. The two families cannot be totally divorced because shapes often happen to share the properties of both. Combined, they are infinitely expressive. It is pictorial expression, often on an abstract or symbolic level, that the artist seeks in his manipulation of shapes.

Plate 20. LE VERTIGE D'EROS (1944) by Matta. Within the limits of the human mind's ability to conceive such things Matta has given us a vision of a completely alien milieu. Though as far as imaginable from everyday reality this environment seems, if not likely, at least possible, thanks to the facility of the artist.

Plate 21. THE MEETING OF SAINT ANTHONY AND SAINT PAUL (c. 1436) by Sassetta and Assistant. In this painting by the Renaissance artist Sassetta "station stops" of varied duration are indicated by contrasts of value. In addition "eye-paths" are provided by the edges of the natural forms which lead from figure to figure.

Courtesy The National Gallery of Art, Washington, D.C. Samuel H. Kress Collection.

Plate 22. THE BLUE WINDOW (1911, Autumn) by Henri Matisse. Matisse has abstracted organic forms for the purpose of decorative organization.

Plate 23. THE ADORATION OF THE SHEPHERDS (c. 1500-05) by Giorgione. Giorgione reflects the period of the early 16th-century when the concept of space was primarily concerned with the illusion of distance.

Plate 25. THE PIAZZA OF ST. MARK'S, VENICE by Antonio Canaletto. The appearance of planes and volumes in space determined by the systematic procedures of linear perspective is well illustrated in this painting by an eighteenth century Venetian artist.

Plate 26. THREE WOMEN (LE GRAND DEJEUNER) (1921) by Fernand Léger. Léger often used sharply defined shape edges which act as barriers or fences to temporarily halt eye travel. However, in order to avoid complete isolation of shapes, the artist uses basic interval, shape direction, and variation in strength of shape edges to encourage unity and visual passage.

Collection, The Museum of Modern Art, New York. Mrs. Simon Guggenheim Fund.

Plate 27. HOMAGE TO THE SQUARE: STAR BLUE by Joseph Albers. The meaning often lies, not in likeness or association, but in the formal relationships developed by the artist.

Contemporary Collection of The Cleveland Museum of Art.

Fig. 55. GUITAR AND FLOWERS (1912) by Juan Gris. In direct contrast to biomorphic shapes are rectilinear or straight line shapes preferred by the Cubists. Shape families such as biomorphic and rectilinear are used by artists to unify, through repetition, their picture surface.

Collection, the Museum of Modern Art, New York. Bequest of Anne Erikson Levene in memory of her husband, Dr. Phoebus Aaron Theodor Levene

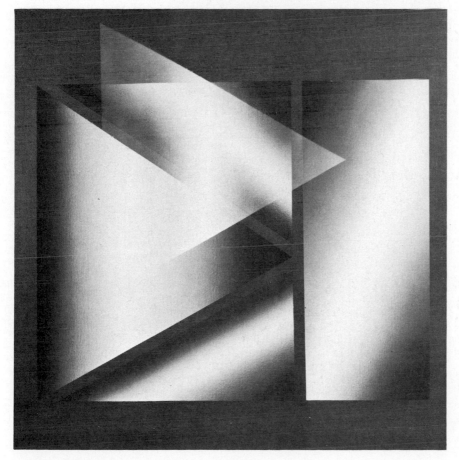

Fig. 56. UNTITLED (1969) by Jack Brusca. The precise, hard edge geometric shapes are a heritage from the Cubists.

Courtesy the Owens-Corning Collection. Owens-Corning Fiberglas Corporation, Toledo, Ohio

SHAPES AND SPACE

Pictorial Depth

Every work of art contains actual or implied shapes and along with them some degree of space. Artists throughout history have reflected the controlling concepts of their time in their use of pictorial space. According to these concepts, spatial phenomena became decoratively flat, shallow, or illusionistically infinite (plate 23; *see* also plate 21). The last hundred years have witnessed the transition from *deep* space to the *shallow* space favored by many contemporary artists. This preference is exhibited today because of the feeling that shallow space permits greater organizational control of the art elements and is more in keeping with the essential flatness of the working surface (plate 24). However, *all* spatial concepts are amply in evidence today, giving an indication of the diversity of our contemporary art scene. Space concepts are used arbitrarily and even in combination when necessary to achieve the desired results.

Volumes and Planes

When shapes are given the thickness which converts them into volumes, or masses, there is automatic implication of the space within which they must exist. The planes which comprise the sides of these volumes may be detached from the parent mass and tilted back into space at any angle and to any depth (fig. 57). They may also be

turned so that they are presented frontally (parallel to the picture plane): When combined with others in this position, they create the illusion of finely graded differences of *depth within a shallow space*. The difference between a plane and a volume lies in the absence of thickness in the plane; it is therefore less substantial and more flexible in exploration of space. However, regardless of spatial suggestion, both volumes and planes are *shapes* whose roles in the two-dimensional arrangement of a work of art must be considered.

Linear Perspective

Linear perspective is a mechanical means of demonstrating the visual appearance of planes and volumes in space. This appearance is based on the location of the artist in reference to the objects drawn; it is accomplished by directing parallel lines toward a common point related to that location (fig. 58 and plate 25). This method of space development was most popular during periods of scientific inquiry and reached its culmination in the mid-nineteenth century. Despite the seeming virtue of agreement with natural appearances, the method has certain disadvantages that in the opinion of some artists outweigh its usefulness. Briefly the liabilities are as follows:

1. It is never an honest statement of actual shape or volume as it is *known* to be.

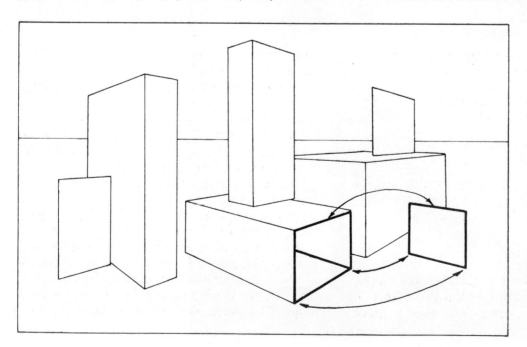

Fig. 57. A drawing showing the essential difference between planes and volumes. Planes are shapes having only two dimensions (height and width), whereas volumes which are made up of planes have the effect of solidity or three dimensions (height, width, and depth). The component planes (sides) of volumes may be detached and inclined back in space at any angle as indicated by the arrows in the drawing.

Fig. 58. INTERIOR OF AN AMSTERDAM CHURCH by Emanuel De Witte. The artist's position is the reference point from which all edges are defined in this work utilizing linear perspective.

Courtesy the Toledo Museum of Art. Gift of Edward Drummond Libbey, 1958

2. The only appearances which can be legitimately portrayed are those which can be seen by the artist-observer from his one position in space.
3. The necessary recession of parallel lines toward common points often leads to monotonous visual effects.
4. The shape distortion created by perspective decreases the design areas available to the artist.

These disadvantages are given only to suggest that familiar modes of vision are not necessarily those which function best in a work of art.

Intuitive Space

Planes and volumes are probably best recognized when seen in terms of linear perspective, the system which creates illusionistic space.

They may also be used to produce *intuitive* space, which is independent of strict rules and formulas. Intuitive space is thus not a "system," but a product resulting from the exercise of the artist's instinct in manipulating certain space-producing devices. The devices which aid him in controlling space include overlap, transparency, interpenetration, inclined planes, disproportionate scale, and fractional representation. In addition, he may exploit the *inherent* spatial properties of the art elements. The physical properties of the art elements tend to thrust forward or back the things they help to define. By marshaling these spatial forces in any combination, as needed, the artist can sense or feel the space into the pictorial image as he adjusts relationships. The space derived from this method is readily sensed by everyone, although judged by the standards of the more familiar linear perspective it may seem strange, even distorted. Nevertheless, it has been the dominant view of space during most of the history of art; it rarely implies great depth but makes for tightly knit imagery within a relatively shallow spatial field (fig. 59).

SHAPE EDGES

The importance of the nature of the extremities of shapes is demonstrated by the terms *soft edge* and *hard edge* used to differentiate between certain styles of contemporary painting. In the description of shape it was mentioned that a harsh border is not always necessary as the limits of value, color, or texture are capable of defining shape. The most obvious conception of shape, however, consists of an outlined area. If the outline is heavy, it can isolate shapes from each other, and repeated outlining of this kind can produce a chaotic situation, with the strong lines creating roadblocks for the eye (plate 26). In order to avert this danger, the artist can utilize the basic interval and direction of the shapes to retain unity, or he can control contour strength at strategic points in such a way as to encourage visual passage through the work. Some artists, on the other hand, prefer working with hazy, indistinct, soft edge shapes; they in turn must realize that, despite their softened, fluid quality, the shapes must still be considered significantly related elements in the composition (fig. 60).

Fig. 59. VIADUCT (1920) by Lyonel Feininger. In this painting the artist has used *intuitive* (or suggested) methods of space control including overlapping planes, transparencies, and planes that interpenetrate one another and incline into space. There are also some indications of disproportionate scale and fractional representation.
Collection, the Museum of Modern Art, New York. Acquired through the Lillie B. Bliss Bequest

Fig. 60. LISTEN TO LIVING (Ecoutez Vivre) (1941) by Matta. This surrealistic painting by Matta demonstrates the gradual blending of shapes which become indistinct and no longer measurable. Such shapes by their softened, flowing character provide a self-acting integration of parts.
Collection, the Museum of Modern Art, New York. Inter-American Fund

Formal Meaning of Shape

All of the principles involved in ordering shapes are of little avail if those shapes are barren of suggesting or *meaning*. Of course, the fullness of *shape meaning* can only be revealed through the relationships developed by the language of art. Nevertheless, shapes contain certain meanings within themselves, some readily recognizable, others more complex and less clear. Some common meanings ascribable to *square*, for example, might be perfection, stability, stolidity, symmetry, self-reliance, and monotony. *Squares* may have different meanings for different people, but the number of meanings which could find general agreement are ample evidence of the common sensations shared when viewing a shape (plate 27). Similarly, circles, ovals, rectangles, and a vast array of other shapes possess distinctive meanings; their meaningfulness depends on their *complexity*, their application, and the *sensitivity of those observing them.* (fig. 61). The artist usually selects his shapes according to the *expression* he wishes to project, but he may be *initially* motivated by the psychological suggestions of shape (fig. 62). Such suggestions are exploited by psychologists in the familiar ink blot tests which are designed to aid in the evaluation of emotional stability. The mere existence of the test points up the fact that shapes can provoke *emotional responses* on different levels. Thus, the artist may use *abstract* shapes to create

desired responses. By using his knowledge that some shapes are inevitably associated with certain objects and situations, he can set the stage for his pictorial drama.

Fig. 61. THREE MEN IN A CIRCLE (1968) by Ernest Trova. The circular elements generate subconscious and generally indefinable reactions which are in contrast to a rectilinear style.

Courtesy the Owens-Corning Collection. Owens-Corning Fiberglas Corporation, Toledo, Ohio

Fig. 62. THE EAST WIND (1918) by Charles Burchfield. The shapes used by Burchfield in this painting are partly psychological and partly symbolic. These shapes suggest the qualities of an approaching spirit-ridden storm.

Courtesy Albright-Knox Gallery, Buffalo. Gift of Seymour Knox

Picture Frame as a Shape

Finally, the very surface on which the artist works is a shape, the *frame* or perimeter around it creating the border. In accordance with principles already mentioned, this *frame shape* presents the germ of a mood, depending upon its *degree of rectangularity*. Horizontal shapes should predominate in a horizontal frame and vertical shapes in a vertical frame. This creates basic harmony *between the frame and its contents* and emphasizes the mood of the original shape.

SHAPE PROBLEMS

Problem 1

Every artist starts with one large shape (the frame shape); his problem is how to divide or break up this area into smaller shapes which are interesting in themselves as well as in their relationships to each other.

With a crayon divide a rectangular shape into five or six areas of unequal size and varied in shape character. Strive for variety but keep some areas simple enough to avoid overcomplexity. Make several experiments of this kind; then select the one most satisfying and fill the areas in with solid color of contrasting tones. Try to make the most interesting shapes stand out through contrast of value and/or color (fig. 63).

Fig. 63.

Problem 2

Shapes which lies on the surface of the picture plane are called decorative shapes and merely divide the plane into pattern. Shapes which overlap divide the space but also create a feeling of depth. Such shapes are called planes and may create movements back and forth in space.

Divide your rectangular shape with overlapping planes. Try to create a movement backward into space but not so deep that the unity of the pattern with the picture plane is destroyed. Create variations by changing the size of the planes and placing them into different spatial relationships to the original picture surface. Have enough similarity in the plane shapes so that they can be considered to belong to the same shape families. Variations could be made by overlapping transparent planes so that new shapes are created (fig. 64).

Fig. 64.

Problem 3

In seeking compositional balance, we must recognize that shapes represent moments of force. The moments or attractions between shapes must counterbalance one another.

Balance and counterbalance several geometric shapes within the boundaries of a picture frame. Consider these shapes as forces which should support one another in controlled tension. Add value and color to the shapes to create interest. Remember that changes of color, value, and texture can affect weight as well as size and variety of shapes.

Problem 4

Shape families represent relationships of areas through the sharing of common qualities (fig. 65).

Create three decorative organizations using:

a. Rectangular shapes which are vertical and horizontal to frame the border.
b. Triangular shapes.
c. Biomorphic shapes.

Fig. 65.

Problem 5

The space concept used with shapes may be shallow, deep, or infinite. Circles, squares, and triangles are basic two-dimensional shapes; spheres, cubes, pyramids, cones, and cylinders are basic three-dimensional shapes.

a. Arrange several circles, squares, and triangles in a shallow space.
b. Transform this into deep space by substituting solid forms such as cubes, pyramids, etc., in a second arrangement.

Problem 6

All shapes do not have a definite border, but may subtly blend one into the other; likewise, some shapes may be defined by a border line only, without a change of value and color.

Using chalk, divide or break up a rectangular space with patches of color. Rub or blend some of these color shapes together so that they lose their distinct edges. Introduce into this design some linear shapes; use some lines to redefine or reaccent areas and superimpose some new linear pattern shapes.

Problem 7

Shapes with contrasting value are much more dominant in a pattern than those which are defined with a linear border only. Such value shapes if large tend to unify several smaller linear shapes.

Make an outline drawing from a section of complex subject matter such as a piece of machinery. Using any shading medium, create several large tone shapes by combining a number of the smaller outlined forms. The lines of the smaller shapes should be left light against the dark background. Against the light background the smaller shapes should be drawn in with dark lines. Positive shapes may be dark against a light background, or this value relationship may be reversed in some parts of the composition. The general purpose is to simplify the basic light-and-dark pattern without losing any of the natural detail (fig. 66).

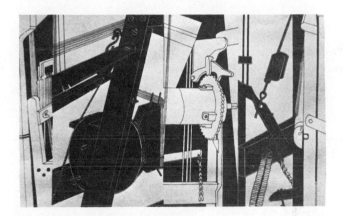

Fig. 66.

Problem 8

The principles of linear perspective may be used to create spatial effects with shape volumes.

Starting with simple geometric solids whose sides are parallel (cubes, rectangular solids), organize the spatial characteristics of a picture field through the perspective of these volumes. Place some solids above and below the horizon, some in which the base is on the ground plane and the top is above the horizon.

This problem may be followed by one which uses more complex volumes based on cylinders, cones, and spheres (fig. 67).

Fig. 67.

Problem 9

Shapes may be used to portray natural objects in many different ways. Shapes frequently undergo transformation or simplification (abstraction) in order to strengthen the pictorial design.

Make a pencil drawing from a photograph, simplifying the subject matter by leaving out some of the little details. In a second picture flatten the object shapes and simplify their contours so that they are almost abstract in nature. You may sacrifice objective identity in order to unify the pictorial organization (figs. 68 and 69).

Fig. 68.

Fig. 69.

Problem 10

Like line, shapes of various kinds can suggest emotional or expressive qualities.

a. Working with either free, geometric, or combinations of shape families, create abstract expressions for such titles as *Tempest, Rowers, Strikers, Ballet Dancers, Circus Clowns*, etc.

b. Try the same thing using invented words such as *Balooma, Irskt, Sleema, Rz-z-z-z, Sloovonious*, etc.

c. Try to express your own reactions to certain situations such as *loneliness, mystery, excitement, triumph, despair, conflict*, etc.

Problem 11

For pictorial unity, it is recommended that we use shapes which will echo or repeat the basic character of the picture frame (frame shape).

Select a real object with fairly complex and interesting outline forms. Use one which might be assumed to have normal or average proportions. Draw and distort the object to fill and repeat the lines of:

a. An exaggerated or stretched-out horizontal frame shape (fig. 70).

b. An elongated vertical frame shape (fig. 71).

Fig. 71.

 Fig. 70.

Chapter 6/Value

Definitions:

Cast Shadow: The dark area created on a surface when another form is placed so as to prevent the light from falling on that surface.

Chiaroscuro: A technique of representation which concentrates on the effects of blending the light and shade on objects to create the illusion of space or atmosphere.

Decorative Value: A term given to a two-dimensional value pattern. It usually refers to areas of dark or light definitely confined within boundaries rather than the gradual blending of tones.

Highlight: The area of a represented shape which receives the greatest amount of direct light.

Local Value: The natural or characteristic value of a shape which is determined by its normal color independent of any effect created by the degree of light falling on it.

Shadow, Shade, Shading: The darker value on the surface of a form which gives the illusion that it is turned away from the imagined source of light.

Tenebrism: A style of painting which exaggerates or emphasizes the effects of chiaroscuro. Larger amounts of dark value are placed close to smaller areas of highly contrasting lights in order to concentrate attention on certain important features.

Value: The relative degree of lightness or darkness given to an area by the amount of light reflected from it.

Value Pattern: The total effect of the relationships of light and dark given to areas within the pictorial field.

1. *Two-dimensional:* Value relationships in which the changes of light and dark seem to occur only on the surface of the picture plane.
2. *Three-dimensional:* The value relationships which are planned to create an illusion of objects existing in depth back of the picture plane.

The visual experiences encountered in the plastic and graphic arts may be divided into two classes: *chromatic* (reds, greens, yellows, and other hues) and *achromatic* (white, black, and the limitless series of greys between white and black). There is nothing divisive about *value* itself, however, as it is an integral part of both chromatic and achromatic appearances. Value is variously termed *tone, brightness, shade,* or even *color.* Some of these terms, as we shall see, have only limited convenience and accuracy when considered in an *art* context. Perhaps the best definition for our purpose is that found in the dictionary, which states that value may be defined as the relation of one part or detail in a picture to another with respect to lightness and darkness.

RELATIONSHIP TO THE OTHER ART ELEMENTS

The student who is investigating art in its constituent parts must consider the relationship of *value* to the other elements of art form: *line, color, texture,* and *shape.* All of these elements must exhibit some value contrast with the material on which they are placed in order to remain visible.

The particular value manifested by a line could be the result of the medium or the pressure exerted on the medium by the artist. For example, depending on the degree of hardness of a

Fig. 72. WOMEN WINDING WOOL (1949) by Henry Moore. In this drawing we have an example of the use of lines in general value areas to create the illusion of volume and texture.
Collection, the Museum of Modern Art, New York. Gift of Mr. and Mrs. John A. Pope in honor of Paul J. Sachs

pencil, you would create a dark or lighter tone or line. Value may be created by a merger of elements as when a number of lines of the same or different qualities are placed alongside or across each other to produce generalized *areas of value* (fig. 72). Shapes are therefore created and distinguished from each other by the use of value. Reproduction of textures relies on the values in the shadows and highlights peculiar to a particular type of surface, while abstract textures contain more or less flat lines and shapes of different values (plate 28). The intoxicating effects of a color often blind people to the fact that the very existence of color is entirely dependent upon the presence of value. A standard yellow, for example, is of far greater lightness than a standard violet, although they may be modified to the point at which they become virtually equal. A common weakness in painting is the unfortunate disregard for the pattern created by *the value relationships* of the color; black-and-white photographs of paintings often reveal this deficiency very clearly. On the other hand, black-and-white pictures without benefit of color or are traditional and commonplace and may be perfectly satisfying as works of art (fig. 73). The application of value to the other art elements

creates *two-dimensional pattern, accent,* and *spatial variation.* A good example of a two-dimensional pattern is a checkerboard. Generally, black and white areas feature examples of accent and spatial variation.

Fig. 73. THE CLOSER HE GETS by Philip R. Wigg. Printmakers, who often work in black and white, have special awareness of the function of value.
Courtesy of the Artist

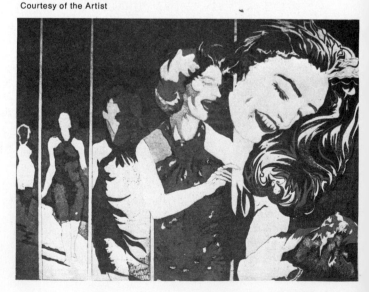

DESCRIPTIVE USES OF VALUE

One of the most generally useful applications of value is in its description of objects, shapes, and space. Descriptive qualities may be broadened to include psychological, emotional, and dramatic expression. Artists from time immemorial have been concerned with value as a problem in translating light as it plays about the earth and its inhabitants. Objects are usually perceived in terms of the characteristic patterns which occur when the mass is exposed to light rays. Objects, at least according to customary occurrence, cannot receive light from all directions simultaneously. A solid object receives more light from one side than from another because that side is closer to the light source and thus intercepts the light and casts shadows on the other side (fig. 74).

Light patterns vary according to the *surface* of the object receiving the light. A *spherical surface* demonstrates this in an even flow from light to dark. An *angular surface* shows sudden contrasts of light and dark values. Each basic form has a basic highlight and shadow pattern. Evenly flowing tone gradation invokes a sense of a gently curved surface. An abrupt change of tone we translate as meaning a sharp or angular surface (fig. 75).

Cast shadows are the dark areas which occur on an object or a surface when a shape is interposed between it and the light source. The nature of the shadow created depends, scientifically speaking, upon the size and location of the light source, the size and shape of the interposed body, and the character of the forms on which the shadows fall. Although cast shadows give very definite clues to the circumstances of a given situation, they only occasionally give an ideal indication of the true nature of the forms. The artist normally uses, reuses, or *creates* those shadows which aid in descriptive character, enhance the effectiveness of the design pattern, and/or contribute substantially to the mood or expression (fig. 76).

Although contemporary artists have generally rejected the use of value to describe form in a traditional chiaroscuro or descriptive sense, a

Fig. 76. Light from an uncontrolled source may cast overlapping shadows which tend to break up and hide the true character of object forms. The unplanned shapes of shadows such as these often disorganize compositional unity.

Fig. 74. A solid object receives more light from one side than another because that side is closer to the light source and thus intercepts the light and casts shadows on the other side.

Fig. 75. A photograph illustrating the even gradation of light to dark on a spherical surface and the sudden contrast of light and dark on an angular surface.

Fig. 77. FEMALE NUDE IN ROBE, SEATED ON PLATFORM ROCKER (1973) by Philip Pearlstein. This painting shows an artist of the contemporary New Realist trend. New Realists are using a kind of chiaroscuro derived from photography to describe volume and space or plastic form.

Courtesy The Allan Frumkin Gallery, Inc., New York

few artists, particularly the New Realists (who stem from Pop influence), do tend to use value in this manner. When value is used in this way to describe volume and space, it could be called *plastic* value. Artists such as Wayne Thiebaud, Philip Pearlstein, and Alex Katz, for example, are obviously influenced by the photograph and cinema. Neither of these disciplines, it should be noted, remain in the disrepute in which artists at the beginning of the twentieth century held them as a part of their rejection of all descriptive reality (fig. 77).

EXPRESSIVE USES OF VALUE

The type of expression sought by the artist ordinarily determines the balance between light and shadow in a work of art. It should be obvious that a preponderance of dark areas will create an atmosphere of gloom, mystery, drama, or menace, whereas a composition which is basi-

cally light will produce quite the opposite effect. Artists will tend to avoid *exact duplication* of cause and effect in light and shadow because such a procedure would create a series of forms which are monotonously light or dark on the same side. The shapes of highlights and shadows are often revised to create desired degrees of unity and contrast with adjacent compositional areas. In summary, lights and shadows exist *in nature* as the by-products of strictly physical laws; the artist must adjust and take liberties with them in order to create his own visual language (plate 29 and fig. 78).

Fig. 78. THE NOSTALGIA OF THE INFINITE (1913–14?) by Giorgio de Chirico. Giorgio de Chirico often used shadow effects, strong contrasts of value, and stark shapes to enhance the lonely, timeless nostalgia that is so much a part of his poetic expression.

Collection, the Museum of Modern Art, New York. Purchase

Chiaroscuro

Chiaroscuro is a word closely related to value and is used frequently in art terminology. The term refers to the technique of representation which displays an obvious use of contrasting lights and darks. The term refers to the way the painter handles those atmospheric effects which permit him to create the illusion that his subjects are on all sides surrounded by space. The development of *chiaroscuro* in painting can be traced to Giotto (1276–1335) who used darks and lights for modeling but expressed shape and space in terms of line. Masaccio, Fra Angelico, and Pollaiuolo, the early Florentine masters, carried *chiaroscuro* a step further by expressing the structure and volume in space with an even, graded tonality. Leonardo da Vinci employed a much bolder series of contrasts in light and dark but always with soft value transitions (fig. 79). The great Venetian painters such as Giorgione, Titian, and Tintoretto completely subordinated line and suggested compositional unity through an enveloping atmosphere of dominant tonality (plates 30 and 31).

Tenebrism

Painters who used violent chiaroscuro are called *tenebrists*. The first tenebrists were an international group of painters who early in the seventeenth century were inspired by the work of Michelangelo di Caravaggio. Caravaggio based his chiaroscuro on Corregio's work and instituted the so-called dark-manner of painting in Western Europe (fig. 80). Rembrandt became the technical adapter and perfector of this dark-manner which he got from migratory artists of Germany and Southern Holland. The dark-manner made value an instrument in the characteristic exaggeration of baroque painting. The strong contrasts lent themselves well to highly dramatic, even theatrical, work of this type. Later the dark-manner evolved into the pallid,

Fig. 79. MADONNA OF THE ROCKS (1483) by Leonardo da Vinci. Leonardo da Vinci used chiaroscuro with strong atmospheric effects and a much bolder contrast of light and dark than his early Renaissance predecessors.
Courtesy Alinari-Art Reference Bureau. Louvre, Paris

Fig. 80. ST. JOHN THE BAPTIST (ca. 1597) by Michelangelo da Caravaggio. Michelangelo was essentially the leader in establishing the dark-manner of painting in the sixteenth and seventeenth centuries. Several of the North Italian painters before his time, however, such as Correggio, Titian, and Tintoretto show evidence of the tendency toward darker value composition.
Courtesy The Nelson Gallery-Atkin's Museum, Kansas City, Missouri. Nelson Fund

muddy monotone which pervaded much of nineteenth-century Western painting. The tenebrists and their followers were very much interested in peculiarities of lighting, particularly as it lent itself to *mood* or *emotional expression*. They deviated from *standard light conditions* by placing the implied light sources in *unexpected locations,* creating unusual visual and spatial effects. In the hands of superior artists such as Rembrandt these effects were creative tools; in lesser hands, they became captivating tricks or visual sleight of hand (plate 32).

DECORATIVE VALUE PATTERNS

Art styles which stress *decorative effects* usually ignore conventional light sources or neglect representation of light altogether. If light effects appear, they are often in composite, *a selection of appearances* based on their contribution to the *total form* of the work. This admixture is characteristic of the art works of primitive and prehistoric tribes, children, traditional East Asians, and certain periods of Western art, notably the Middle Ages. Many contemporary art works are *completely free* of illusionistic lighting. Art work which thus divorces itself from *natural law* is obviously based on *pictorial invention, imagination,* and *formal considerations*. It is not by any means an art necessarily divorced from emotional impact (as witness, Medieval art), but the *emotion* speaks primarily through the *forms* and is consequently less extroverted.

The trend away from illumination values gained strength in the nineteenth century partly as a result of the interest in art forms of the Near East and Far East (fig. 81). It was given a Western *scientific interpretation* when Edouard Manet, a realist, observed that a multiplicity of light sources tended to *flatten object surfaces* (figs. 82 and 83 and plate 33). He found that this light condition would neutralize the *plastic qualities* of objects, thus minimizing *gradations of value*. As a result, he laid his colors on canvas in *flat areas,* beginning with bright, light colors and generally neglecting *shadow*. Some critics have claimed this to be the basic technical advance of the nineteenth century because it paved the way for *nonrepresentational* uses of value and aided in the revival of interest in the shallow space concept (fig. 84.)

COMPOSITIONAL FUNCTIONS OF VALUE

The idea of carefully controlled *shallow space* finds excellent illustration in the works of the early *cubists* Picasso and Braque (fig. 85). In those paintings, space is given its order by the arrangement of *flat planes* abstracted from subject material. At first, the planes were shaded individually and semi-illusionistically, although there is no indication of any one light source. Later *each plane* took on a *characteristic value* and in combination with others produced a care-

Fig. 81. PRINCE RIDING AN ELEPHANT, Mughal: Period of Akbar (1556–1605). Signed: work of Khemkaran. Oriental artists often disregard the use of light (illumination) in favor of decorative value compositions.

Courtesy the Metropolitan Museum of Art, New York. Rogers Fund, 1925

Plate 28. DOG AND COCK (1921) by Pablo Picasso. The contemporary artist (such as Picasso) often uses abstract textures which may depend on the use of value but not for the purpose of description. Values indicating abstract textures, such as the linear or geometric symbols of ''Dog and Cock'' are used for compositional purposes such as variety, accent, or emphasis.

Plate 29. CHRIST AT THE SEA OF GALILEE (1560) by Tintoretto
Tintoretto commonly employs a preponderance of dark values interspersed with flickering lights to create an atmosphere of religious drama.

Plate 30. THE CALLING OF THE APOSTLES PETER AND ANDREW by Duccio. Although line and shape predominate in Duccio's works, some of the early attempts at modeling with chiaroscuro value can be seen.

Plate 31. THE ENTOMBMENT OF CHRIST by Titian (copy of). The great Venetian, Titian, subordinated line, contrasting edges with value and enveloped his figures in a tonal atmosphere that approaches tenebrism.

Plate 32. THE DESCENT FROM THE CROSS (c. 1650-60) by Rembrandt van Rijn. Rembrandt often used inventive, implied, light sources that deviated from standard light conditions in order to enhance the mood or emotional expression.

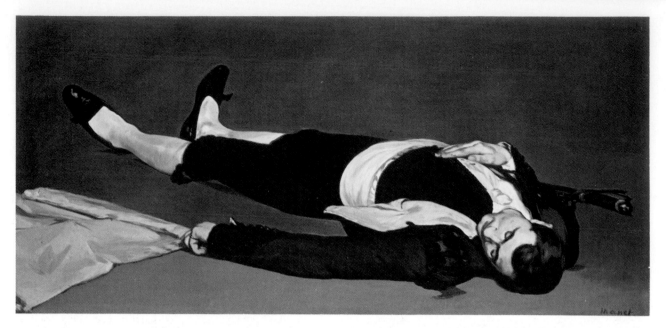

Plate 33. THE DEAD TOREADOR (c. 1864) by Edouard Manet. Manet, a 19th-century naturalist, was one of the first artists to break with traditional chiaroscuro employing instead flat areas of value. These flat areas meet abruptly in comparison to the blended edges used by artists previous to Manet. This was one of the basic technical advances of 19th-century art.

Courtesy The National Gallery of Art, Washington, D.C.
Widener Collection.

Plate 34. BREAKFAST (1914) by Juan Gris. Gris, an example of a later Cubist, not only simplified shape into larger, more dominant areas, but gave each shape a characteristic value producing a carefully conceived light-dark pattern.

Collection, The Museum of Modern Art, New York. Acquired through the Lillie P. Bliss Bequest.

Fig. 84. NUIT DE NOEL (1952) by Henri Matisse. Here, Matisse used value instead of traditional chiaroscuro to produce a two-dimensional pattern.

Collection, the Museum of Modern Art, New York. Gift of Time, Inc., New York, New York

Fig. 82. The photograph above demonstrates how light from one source emphasizes the three-dimensional qualities of the object and gives an indication of depth. This can be particularly observed in a sculptured torso. The photograph below (fig. 83) shows the same group of objects under illumination of several light sources. This form of lighting tends to flatten object surfaces and produces a more decorative effect.

Fig. 85. MA JOLIE (WOMAN WITH A ZITHER OR GUITAR) (1911–12) by Pablo Picasso. The Cubist Picasso in his exploration of the shallow-space concept broke up natural forms into flat planes that are individually shaded and semi-illusionistically rendered.

Collection, the Museum of Modern Art, New York. Acquired through the Lillie P. Bliss Bequest

Fig. 83.

fully conceived *two-dimensional light-dark pattern* (plate 34). Eventually the shallow spatial effect was developed in terms of *three-dimensional* pattern (or balance) through attention to the *advancing* and *receding* characteristics of value. The explorations of these artists in the early twentieth century helped to focus attention on the intrinsic significance of each and every element. Value was no longer forced to serve a *primary role* as a tool of *superficial transcription*, although it continued to be of descriptive usefulness. Most creative artists today think of value as a vital and organic participant in *pictorial organization*, affecting *dominance*, creating *two-dimensional pattern*, establishing *mood*, and producing *spatial unity*.

Open and Closed Compositions

It is easy to see the emotive possibilities of value schemes, particularly as they relate to closed or open composition. Closed designs are those in which values are limited by *the edges of shapes* and *forms*. In open-value composition the value areas may originate and end *as the artist sees fit*, sometimes conforming to the subject shapes, at times working independently of them and on occasion doing both. The artist may employ closely related values for hazy, foglike effects, or he may use dramatically contrasting values, creating sharply crystallized shapes. Thus value may run the gamut from decoration to violent expression (fig. 86; *see also* fig. 53). It is a multipurpose tool, and the success of the total work of art is in large measure based on the

effectiveness with which the artist has made value serve these many functions.

Fig. 86. READING (LA LECTURE) (1926) by Pablo Picasso. The values in this work are used in an open manner; the white value moves in and out of the figure in an arbitrary way, producing a shape not suggested by the original contours.

Collection, the Museum of Modern Art, New York. Gift of Abby Aldrich Rockefeller

VALUE PROBLEMS

Problem 1

Different mediums have varying flexibilities in terms of ability to create tones or values. The average person can easily discern about nine steps of value from white to black, but every medium varies in ability to create these nine steps.

In areas about one inch square, create value scales from the lightest tone to the darkest tone possible. Try to create an individual scale for each of the following mediums: pencil, black crayon, pen and ink, drybrush and ink, tempera paint varied with white and black, and watercolor modified by thinning or thickening the color.

Problem 2

The descriptive qualities of object surfaces are best defined by the value patterns created by light normally coming from above and originating from one source. These descriptive qualities may be enhanced and made more expressive by emphasizing the contrasts of light and dark where the edges of forms come together.

Select a group of simple still-life forms. Place a strong light above this group directed either from right or left. Using any medium, create a picture using the natural group as a model. Copy the light and shadow patterns, feel free to exaggerate the tonal contrasts where forms overlap and where they meet the background (fig. 87).

Fig. 87.

Fig. 88.

Problem 3

A good range of value differences is important in representing the three-dimensional quality of natural objects. In order to achieve the greatest degree of plasticity, solid objects should have very dark shadows, strongly contrasting lights, as well as a range of medium values.

Plan an interesting arrangement of simple tools within a frame shape. Make a shaded drawing of this arrangement on a medium-tone gray paper using white chalk for the light areas and black chalk, soft-charcoal, or ebony pencil for the dark areas. The background may be broken up into arbitrary shapes harmoniously related to the main objects. Emphasize the lights by using dark tones next to them. Edges may be highlighted with white chalk where they adjoin dark areas. Large areas of gray paper may be left untouched for medium tones (fig. 88).

Problem 4

A decorative value pattern is created when each shape in a design has its own value; that is, when there are no gradations within the outlined form. In a composition of this kind the value differences of adjoining shapes have great importance.

Create a decorative composition using abstract or semiabstract curvilinear shapes. Create large shapes at first, but then break them up into smaller areas related to the main forms. Fill in all of the shapes with varied values created with black and white tempera paint. Plan the tones so that there are definite differences in value between adjoining shapes. Strive for good balance between the darks and lights of the composition. In general, negative areas can be dark when next to lighter areas or light when next to dark areas. Decorative lines either in dark or light can also be used to define forms (fig. 89).

Fig. 89.

Problem 5

When values are considered only in terms of the shapes which they create, it is possible for more than one light-and-dark scheme to be effective. Individual artists often favor predominant dark values or predominant light values in their pictures. In fact, the expressive quality of a composition may vary, depending upon whether the values are closely related or highly contrasting in character.

Invent a simple still-life arrangement using familiar forms such as fruit or vegetables. Keep the picture small so that not too much time is required to paint the surface. Using black and white tempera or shading with pencil, create three different light-and-dark schemes for this composition. Do one which is composed of closely related light values; make the second of closely related dark values; and finish the third by emphasizing highly contrasting values (fig. 90).

Fig. 90.

Problem 6

Most well-organized pictorial compositions have a definite dark-light pattern, although they may exhibit a considerable range of values.

Using a color reproduction of a good painting as a model, try to represent its basic value pattern in terms of two tones, black and white. You will notice that there is usually a main large dark shape and a main large light shape.

Using the same picture for a model, develop its pattern in terms of three value tones, black, white, and a medium gray. You will notice that the medium tones serve as a transition between the contrasts of black and white. See if the greatest contrast of light and dark comes on the major shapes. (In doing this problem, forms do not have to be drawn in great detail but may be considerably simplified in character.)

Problem 7

Massing of lines created with pen and ink,

pencil, or any linear medium can be used to create variations of value.

Arrange a group of chairs, tables, tools, or similar objects as subject matter. Different views of the same object could be put together in a planned composition. Add value to the composition by using a massing of lines in the background or negative areas. There can be a variation of values within these areas to create pictorial interest. By making the tones darker next to the white positive shapes, control of attention or dominance can be achieved in the composition (fig. 91).

Fig. 91.

Problem 8

Areas of value do not necessarily have to be rigidly restricted within the outlines of shapes. A given area of tone may belong to two different shapes, creating a greater unity of organization. An area of value does not have to be confined to an object border but may be opened and combined with other shapes.

Draw a simple still-life subject in light lines on a gray paper. Using white tempera, apply areas of light which disregard the object contours. Combine two or more objects or combine objects with the background in order to create an open-value pattern. This will help to unify the shapes in the pictorial composition. The tempera may be thinned to create more than one light tone if desired. Use a brush with dark tempera paint or a felt-tipped pen to accent and define shapes which might otherwise be lost. Lines may also be used in certain areas to accent shapes and provide textural interest (fig. 92).

Problem 9

Repetition of similar values in different parts of a pattern may create eye movements which unify the arrangement. Certainly distribution of the proper sizes of value tones creates controlled tension, stabilizing pictorial organization.

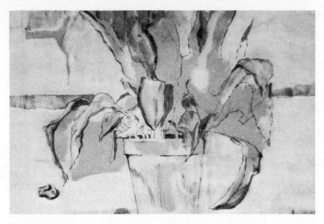

Fig. 92.

Fill a pictorial space with an arrangement of rectangles of varying size. These shapes may be separate, touching, or even overlapping, but a certain amount of empty or background space should be left around the forms. Create a medium value in the background space by using a series of parallel lines placed close together and in either horizontal or vertical relationship. Now fill in some of the rectangular shapes with solid black color and leave others white. See if you cannot create some paths of movement through repetition of the dark values; at the same time distribute them so that a balanced effect will result. Variations in the size of similar value shapes will keep the effect from becoming monotonous. (Where two shapes of dark tone touch each other, a white line may be left to separate the forms.)

This problem may be followed with one which uses rectangular volumes in space such as cubes or pyramids. When these solid forms are used, the values may be used on one or two sides; however, the tones should be planned for the rhythm and balance they create, rather than for mere descriptive effect of light and shade.

Problem 10

Just as with the other elements, a value pattern may have intrinsic meaning or support the emotional character of a mood. Psychologically, we often feel depressed when we note large areas of black, and man has tended to associate it with death, tragedy, and despair. White usually makes us feel buoyant and open or perhaps radiant.

To explore some of the moods or meanings that may be expressed with values, create a pictorial composition incorporating some of the ideas brought to mind by the list of titles which follows: Tempest, Tragedy, Hunger, Riot, Lost, Peace, Strikers, Ballet, Jazz Concert, Carnival. This may be done in a representational style, or more abstract shapes may be employed (fig. 93).

Fig. 93.

Chapter 7/Texture

Definitions:

Actual texture: A surface which may be experienced through the sense of touch (as opposed to surfaces often "imitated" by the artist).

Artificial Texture: Any texture created by man-made invention.

Collage: An art form in which the artist creates the image, or a portion of it, by adhering real materials, possessing actual textures, to the picture plane surface.

Genre: Painting expressing subject matter which concerns everyday life, domestic scenes, sentimental family relationships, etc.

Illusionism: The imitation of visual reality created on the flat surface of the picture plane by the use of perspective, light-and-dark shading, etc.

Invented Texture: Two-dimensional patterns created by the repetition of lines or shapes on a small scale over the surface of an area. The repeated motif may be adaptation or borrowing of nature patterns used in a more regular or planned fashion.

Natural Texture: Textures in actual objects which are created as the result of natural processes.

Paint Quality: The use of the medium on a surface to give it enrichment through textural interest. Interest is created by the ingenuity in handling paint for its intrinsic character.

Papier Collé: A technique of visual expression in which scraps of paper having various textures are actually pasted to the picture surface to enrich or embellish areas.

Tactile: A quality which refers to the sense of touch.

Texture: The surface character of a material which may be experienced through touch, or the illusion of touch. It may be produced by natural forces or through manipulations of the art elements by the artist.

Trompe l'oeil: A painting technique involving the copying of nature with such exactitude that the painted objects may be mistaken for the actual forms depicted.

RELATIONSHIP OF TEXTURE TO THE VISUAL ARTS

Texture is unique among the art elements in that it activates two sensory processes at the same time. In viewing a picture the observer may recognize objects through the artist's depiction of characteristic *shape, color* and *value pattern;* he may also react to the surface character which the artist reminds him is typical of the object. Hence, there may be vivid feelings of touch vicariously experienced and complementing the sensations of vision.

Tactile response is the concern of the artist whether he is working in the *plastic* or the *graphic* field. The sculptor becomes involved with the problem of texture through his choice of media and the type and degree of finish to be given them. It is possible for him to recreate such textures as are characteristic of the subject if he feels so motivated. By cutting into the surface of the materials, he can suggest the tactile qualities of hair, cloth, skin, and other textures which suit his purpose.

The graphic arts do not exist in the round, and any exaggerated attempt to fool the eye into believing they do usually develops into a tour de force or violation of the medium. Although his opportunities to create texture are somewhat more limited than the sculptor's, the graphic artist nevertheless has a formidable array of textural effects available to him. The items in our physical environment on which these effects are based may be *natural* (grass, leaves, stone, treebark, sand, etc.) or *artificial,* that is, those created by man (paper, metal, glass, concrete, stucco, etc.).

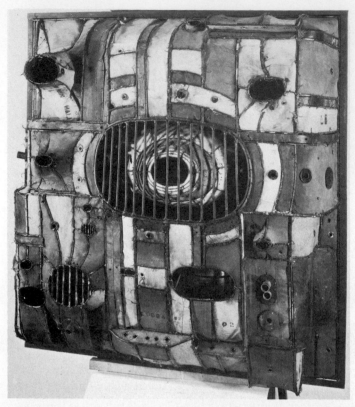

TYPES OF TEXTURE

Actual

If the artist chooses to attach real materials to his work, he is employing *actual texture,* one which can really be sensed through touch. The category of actual texture may even include the medium with which he works as it is applied to the working surface (figs. 94 and 95). Vincent van Gogh's paintings serve as a particularly good example of the surface qualities of medium. In Van Gogh's paintings rough textures have been

Fig. 94. UNTITLED (1961; canvas, metal, and wire) by Lee Bontecou. The actual textures of the materials used by the artist create surface interest and add to the total aesthetic quality of the work. Contemporary sculptors use a wide variety of media, whereas the traditional artist depends for textural interest on manipulation of the one material associated with the medium.

Contemporary Collection of the Cleveland Museum of Art

Fig. 95. PILLOW TALK by Robert Mazur. In this example the surface of the format itself has been altered, creating actual texture.

Courtesy Bowling Green State University, College of Business

produced by building up pigment on the canvas. It is significant that painters such as Van Gogh regard actual textures of any kind as aids to *academic illusionism*, as well as to expression (plate 35). Texture is usually pasted or painted according to the varied needs of the design rather than as a strict description of the properties of particular objects. In many cases the texture of the canvas is left bare as a reminder that the work is part of a flat *painting*, not a *literal* slice of nature.

Papier Collé

The growing appreciation of texture as an integral part of form led to many textural experiments early in the twentieth century. The *cubists* were very much involved in this experimentation. Their exploration of the pictorial functions of texture led to an art form known as *papier collé*, a technique involving the pasting of bits of newspaper, stamps, tickets, and the like, directly on the picture surface. The printed and cut or torn passages of these pieces created patterns which enlivened selected areas (fig. 96).

Collages

Eventually this technique was broadened to include the use of wire, wood, sandpaper, in fact any and all surfaces whose textures were appropriate and usable in the paintings. Compositions made up of scraps of this kind are called *collages*. The picture may be nothing but material arrangements (at times based on subject material, at other times nonrepresentational), or the scraps may be combined with drawn and painted passages.

Some very inventive exploitation of actual texture can be seen in the works of contemporary artists. Aggregates such as sand are sometimes mixed with paint to provide a textured medium (plate 36). Material surfaces of different textural properties are occasionally substituted for conventional canvas. Various textural patterns such as furrows and ridges are produced in the paint by using appropriate, convenient tools of all sources and descriptions. Texture can also be transferred by pressing a material against wet paint. And texture can be further enriched by

Fig. 96. The student work reproduced here is an example of papier collé, meaning that paper shapes have been cut and pasted down to form a picture. The paper used was selected according to the decorative interest provided by its texture. The interest is further enhanced by the fact that the texture does not always correspond to the characteristic surface of objects depicted.

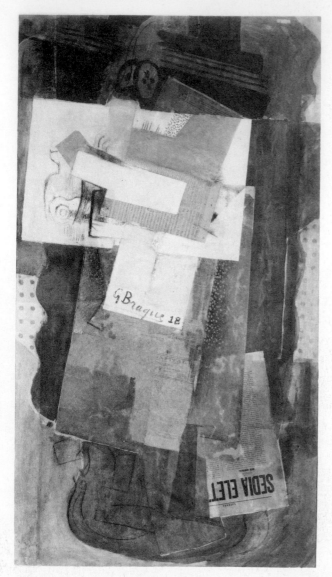

Fig. 97. STILL LIFE (ca. 1917–18) by Georges Braque. This Cubist painter pioneered in invention of the papier collé and collage forms which are works of art created from actual materials having textural interest fastened to a flat working surface. They may be used to stimulate natural textures, but are usually created for decorative purposes.

Courtesy Philadephia Museum of Art. The Louise and Walter Arensberg Collection

Fig. 98. This student collage is a completely nonobjective pattern created by gluing actual materials and objects to a background which in itself is textured. The large areas of simple background are balanced by smaller accents of circular forms. The simplicity of the basic pattern calls for careful adjustment of spaces and proportional relationships.

mixing the medium with various substances that are chalky, oily, coarse, smooth, thin, and so forth. The ethic of such practice is now limited only by the ability of the artist to produce an integrated and harmonious effect (figs. 97 and 98 and plate 37).

Simulated Texture

Simulated textures are very common in the field of art. Such textures call for careful rendering or copying of the light and dark patterns created by surface character. This is essentially an academic procedure, but it may be given creative application. The Dutch and Flemish artists produced amazingly naturalistic effects in still-life and genre paintings. Their work shows the evident relish with which they moved from one texture detail to another. Simulated textures are often associated with *trompe l'oeil* paintings, an obvious attempt to "fool the eye" (fig. 99 and plates 38 and 39).

Invented Texture

A third type of texture is one which may be called *invented*. At times, invented textures may have their source in nature, but they undergo a very positive metamorphosis in the hands of the artist, who changes them according to the needs of his work. In this case, the texture may more properly be described as *decorative pattern*, for it usually becomes two-dimensional in effects. It is nonrepresentational, is ordinarily geometric (although it may also be amorphous and biomor-

Fig. 99. THE HUNTER (1943) by Andrew Wyeth. Skillful manipulation of the medium can effectively simulate actual textures.
Courtesy the Toledo Museum of Art. Elizabeth C. Mau Bequest 1946

phic), and having been created, is potentially of high aesthetic quality. Invented texture may develop out of the artist's programmatic search for a suitable embellishment through accident of technique or a mingling of media. The origin is really of little consequence if the result functions effectively within the framework of the design (fig. 100).

TEXTURE AND PATTERN

The differentiation between *pattern* and *texture* is often ignored or misunderstood and therefore deserves some clarification. *Pattern* can be defined as a decorative design involving some repetition of motif which may or may not have derived from texture. Pattern is ordinarily re-

Fig. 100. GIRL BEFORE A MIRROR (1932) by Pablo Picasso. The stripes and patterns which form such a striking embellishment for this painting can originate in nature or in the artist's mind. They perform an essential function within the design in establishing decorative space, dominant areas, and rhythmic passage through the work. Such textures may be termed *invented*.

Collection, the Museum of Modern Art, New York. Gift of Mrs. Simon Guggenheim

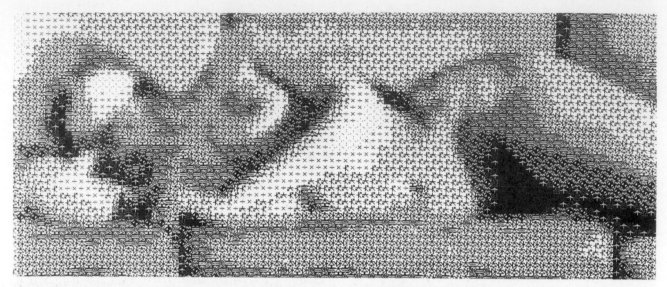

Fig. 101. COMPUTERIZED NUDE (1971) by Kenneth Knowlton and Leon Harmon. This reproduction of a photograph by a specially programmed computer has not only a range of dark and light values, but also a variety of interesting textures. It illustrates the concept that invented textures in themselves can give an ordinary subject a certain amount of aesthetic value.
Courtesy of Bell Telephone Laboratories, Murray Hill, New Jersey

garded as being essentially *two-dimensional* or flat; it has no tactile pretensions. Texture, on the other hand, invariably creates pattern and also invokes a tactile response. A simulated texture is basically a pattern and is textural only to the degree that it reminds one of his sense of touch. An actual texture is of a dual nature: preeminently textural, but also producing pattern. Invented textures may develop to the point at which textural suggestions are of no consequence; at this point, *descriptive* function is exceeded by *decorative* function (fig. 101). No exact line can be drawn between pattern and texture, the distinction would have to be made in terms of the particular area under consideration.

ORIGINS OF CONTEMPORARY TEXTURAL AWARENESS

An interest in texture is an obvious part of contemporary design. The revolutionary art concepts of the last seventy years spawned analyses of naked form and appreciation of simple, even stark, areas. It was necessary to strip objects bare in order to expose and re-evaluate the underlying structure in terms of pictorial form. This re-evaluation is historically complete, and the emphasis on basic form is generally considered desirable. But we now find many evidences of

hunger for adornment of the naked members of pictorial structure. This desire has been aided and abetted by the revelations of the sharp and penetrating focus of the microscope and camera. The urge to decorate is amply revealed by inspection of the professionally designed products and types of home furnishings now being offered. Everywhere use of texture is in evidence: on our walls and floors, in our fabrics, on everything we use and value in our daily living. Most of this is the direct result of the evolution of contemporary art styles, and it continues to exist in those styles through the artist's use of actual, simulated, and invented textures.

FORMAL FUNCTIONS OF TEXTURE

In terms of pictorial function the use of texture has certain perils as well as advantages. Texture contributes greatly to the richness and visual pleasure afforded by a work of art, but only if it is kept within the bounds of judicious restraint. Overuse of texture may place false emphasis on that element, destroying the unity of the work as a whole. Carelessly employed, it may disrupt the coherence of pattern by isolating areas; it can also produce spatial discontinuity. That is, the texture may detach itself from the surface on which it is presumed to exist. Properly used, however, texture becomes an integral part of the value and color plan of the art work.

Emotional Properties of Texture

Texture has the property of enhancing *emotional expression*. By magnifying texture or placing it in unlikely locations, the artist can make the desired effect much more vivid or even shocking. Certain types of textures are generally associated with certain environments, experiences, or objects which in themselves may be symbolic. When we say that a man is as "slippery as a snake," we are equating tactile sensations with attributes of character. Texture in a context such as this may be utilized as a supplementary psychological device (plate 40).

Spatial Properties of Texture

Spatially, finely detailed texture denotes nearness, and conversely blurred or indistinct detail suggests distance. The degree or type of texture of a unit depends on the observer's physical reference. For example, a leaf surface will differ in appearance, depending on whether it is seen through a microscope, at arm's length, or from a considerable distance where its association with other leaves may produce a new and bushy texture. In *academic painting*, the use of texture is always typical of a given spatial situation, but an artist with more creative intentions may take his texture effects from near and far, using them together to achieve *controlled* space variations or to create arresting contradictions (*see* fig. 99).

The use of texture for a *spatial purpose* immediately sets up the requirement that the same texture function effectively in a *two-dimensional* sense as well. The great power of attraction exerted by texture makes it a useful tool in controlling the *relative dominance of the subject material;* the spotting of textures throughout the pictorial area will always affect the existing pattern for good or ill. Texture contrast must be magnified or minimized according to this consideration (fig. 102). An existing shape may tend to dominate the entire picture if it is given an exciting texture. On the other hand, a negligible area, if highly textured, might successfully contend with the larger shape for the observer's attention. Every successful work of art makes each element serve as many roles as possible.

In summary, texture is seen as being useful in describing object, stimulating tactile responses, enriching pictorial areas, clarifying spatial suggestions, and controlling pattern in terms of relative dominance.

Fig. 102. FISHES (1943) by Amelia Pelaez del Casal. The small details of texture on the fish were derived from actual surface quality. This makes them dominant over the large abstract decorative texture in other parts of the painting.
Collection, the Museum of Modern Art, New York. Inter-American Fund

TEXTURE PROBLEMS

Problem 1

Textures can be actual, simulated, invented, or abstracted.

Select five contrasting flat actual textures. Using these actual textures as models, create five simulated textures. Using the actual textures over again as guides, create five abstract textures. In addition, create four invented textures. Mount all of the textures on a cardboard background placing the five actual textures at the left. Group the remaining textures to the right of the actual texture models (fig. 103).

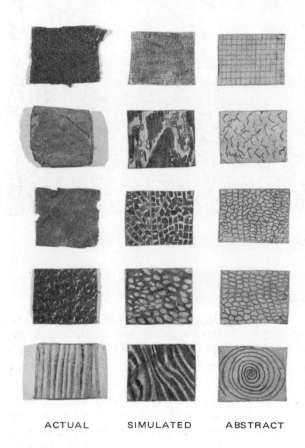

ACTUAL   SIMULATED   ABSTRACT

Fig. 103.

Problem 2

Each medium used by the artist is capable of creating its own distinctive textures. The artist in order to be expressive must understand the varying flexibilities of the different media which may be used.

Divide a large sheet of drawing paper into a number of rectangular areas. Create a design pattern over the whole area of the paper. Finish by changing mediums and style of handling the medium in each rectangular area; for example, drawing ink may be used with fine pen lines in one area and with brush lines in another area. (The example illustrated shows areas of pencil, crayon, ink, watercolor, and tempera paint [fig. 104].)

Fig. 104.

Problem 3

Texture rubbings can quickly guide a student to the infinite varieties of actual and simulated textures.

Place a piece of white paper over a coarse textured surface. Rub over the paper with a soft pencil or crayon. The rubbing technique will bring out a negative impression of the textured surface. Repeat the procedure on a variety of surfaces. Assemble these textures in a chart or a pictorial organization (fig. 105).

Problem 4

The different mediums employed by the artist automatically result in varying surface effects which enhance the character of the shapes used. These changes of textural character may take the place of the interest created by varying shape styles. Frequently, texture variation has become a form of decoration.

These shapes may touch, overlap, or be completely separate, but the organization should be simple in character. In other words, we should depend on texture variation for interest, not on the complexity of the design relationships. Remember to leave a number of areas of plain background around many of the shapes because too much texture variation can become chaotic (fig. 106).

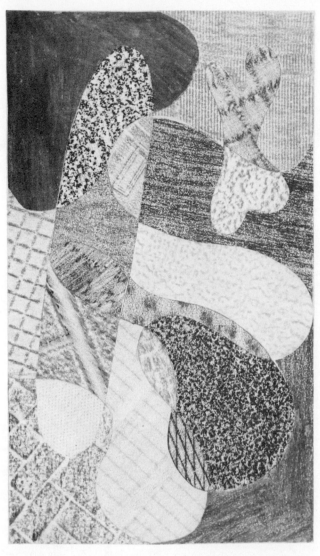

Fig. 105.

Fig. 106.

Using a wide variety of mediums, experiment with their manipulation to see how many different types of surface can be created. Use both point and side of the pencil, varying pressure strokes together for diverse effects. Try mixing mediums such as ink over crayon strokes, watercolor wash over crayon tones, shading with pencil strokes over color washes, pen lines drawn in wet watercolor washes, brush strokes of tempera paint in wet washes of transparent watercolor, and so forth.

These effects should be applied to areas from 1 inch to 4 inches in size. Cut simple shapes such as circles, squares, rectangles, and triangles from these areas and assemble in a simple, decorative shape organization; try using one kind of shape only, but varying the size.

Problem 5

The graphic artist is often deeply interested in making his visual surfaces more varied and exciting. When he is primarily concerned with presenting his picture as a tangible object and not as an illusion of nature, he may use *actual* textures. In creating such an artistic form the artist may add unusual materials to the surface such as papers of varying patterns, colors, and textures. When bits of paper are pasted together on a picture surface, the composition is termed a *papier collé.*

Gather several varieties of paper (i.e., newspaper, construction paper, cellophane, tinfoil, printed color sheets, etc.). Cut, tear, paste, and assemble this paper on a flat surface so that it will have expressive, as well as sound, structural form (fig. 107).

Problem 6

Textures can be used to enrich and lend interest to areas that might otherwise be monotonously bare.

Fig. 107.

Create a design for a record jacket, postage stamp, or some other common item which requires the designer's imagination. Experiment with several invented textures on a separate sheet. Select one of these textures and use it to fill in portions of all of the positive or negative shapes. The texture need not be related to any of the surface characteristics of the subject but should be chosen on the basis of its ability to decorate the chosen areas (fig. 108).

Fig. 108.

Problem 7

In addition to using paper for actual textures, as in papier collé, the artist may add other foreign materials to the picture surface. Among these are such items as string, wire, cotton, cork, rubber, plastic, sponge, sticks, pipe cleaners, sand, gravel, soap, buttons, pebbles, candy, etc. When many such materials are glued to the picture surface, the composition is called a *collage*.

Gather several varieties of textured materials such as those listed in the preceding paragraph. Cut, paste, and assemble these materials together on a picture surface into an expressive arrangement. Also use passages of normal media such as paint, chalk, crayon, pencil, or ink (fig. 109).

Fig. 109.

Problem 8

The interest in pictures or designs made of mosaic tile is largely due to the effects created by putting small colored pieces together. The effect of mosaic may be simulated by using small pieces of colored paper.

Create an abstract design or picture by using small pieces of colored paper cut from magazine illustrations and fitted together to form shapes. An interesting effect

Plate 35. SELF-PORTRAIT (1890, August) by Vincent van Gogh. The massing of paint on van Gogh's canvases creates actual textures. The application of paint is often directly from the tube or "built-up" and scraped clean with the palette knife. The ribbons of paint in his work follow or create the rhythm sensed in nature and frequently simulate natural forms.

Courtesy The National Gallery of Art. Washington. D.C. Chester Dale Collection.

Plate 36. DANCING GALAXY by Gyorgy Kepes. Sand, mixed with the paint, is supported by a careful selection of color to create a total effect similar to surfaces one might see in nature.

Courtesy The Owens-Corning Collection. Owens-Corning Fiberglas Corporation. Toledo. Ohio.

Plate 37. COLOUR-FULL (1968) by Mary Bauermeister. Collages feature the actual textures or real objects se-cured to the picture plane. These are often augmented by painted and drawn passages, sometimes produc-ing simulated textures.

Plate 38. STILL LIFE WITH VIEW OF ANTWERP by Jan Davidsz De Heem. The amazingly "natural" appearances in Dutch and Flemish still-life paintings is largely due to their careful simulation of surfaces.

Plate 39. THE ANNUNCIATION (c. 1428) by Jan van Eyck. Jan van Eyck's work is typically Flemish in that it shows the pleasure with which he selected and simulated textures in his paintings. He delighted in detailed explorations of contrasting materials.

Plate 40. HIDE-AND-SEEK (Cache-cache, 1940-42) by Pavel Tchelitchew. The use of personal, textural style is greatly responsible for much of the emotional quality present in this painting. Here, instead of the obvious invented patterns, we find the subtle textural treatment of organic matter which evokes a feeling of biological mystery.

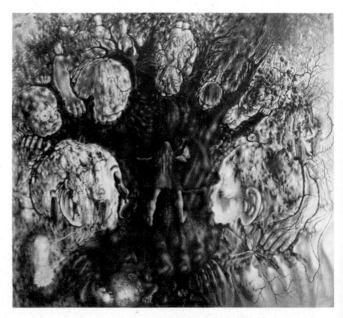

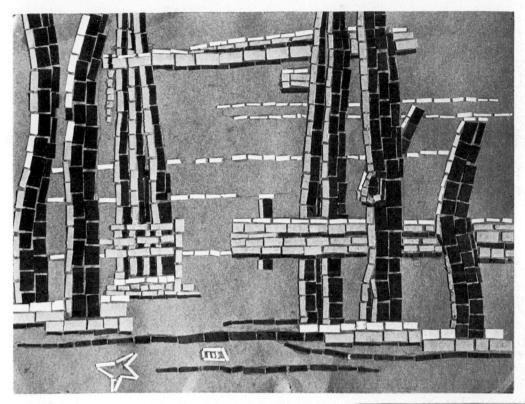

Fig. 110.

can be obtained if some of the colors used already have slight texture variations. To keep the design from becoming *too* confusing take certain necessary precautions: do not use too small or too complex shapes and make sure that the colors chosen for different shapes are definitely contrasting in value (fig. 110).

Problem 9

The effects of texture in a flexible medium such as watercolor are frequently accidental and are especially entrancing because of this unexpected quality.

Experiment with watercolor minglings by placing areas of color together while wet and allow one to flow into the other. This flow can be effected by tipping the paper or by blowing the wet color in various directions. If the paper is dampened before color is applied, a still different type of texture results. Sometimes resemblance to natural shapes is seen in a watercolor mingling; this shape could be further defined by a pen and ink or brush line made while the surface is damp or after it has dried. The result then might be a pictorial representation of natural forms, but with unusual and unexpected textural quality (fig. 111).

Fig. 111.

Chapter 8/Color

Definitions:

Analogous Colors: Those colors which are closely related in hue. They are usually adjacent to each other on the color wheel.

Color: The character of a surface which is the result of the response of vision to the wavelength of light reflected from that surface.

Color Tonality: An orderly planning in terms of selection and arrangement of color schemes or color combinations. It would concern itself not only with hue, but also with value and intensity relationships.

Color Triad: A group of three colors spaced an equal distance apart on the color wheel. There is a primary triad, a secondary triad, and two intermediate triads on the twelve-color wheel.

Complementary Colors: Two colors which are directly opposite each other on the color wheel. A primary color would be complementary to a secondary color which was a mixture of the two remaining primaries.

Hue: Used to designate the common name of a color and to indicate its position in the spectrum or in the color circle. Hue is determined by the specific wavelength of the color in a ray of light.

Intensity: The saturation or strength of a color determined by the *quality* of light reflected from it. A vivid color is of high intensity; a dull color, of low intensity.

Local (Objective) Color: The naturalistic color of an object as seen by the eye (green grass, blue sky, red fire, etc.).

Neutralized Color: A color which has been grayed or reduced in intensity by mixture with any of the neutrals or with a complementary color.

Neutrals: Surface tones which do not reflect any single wavelength of light but rather all of them at once. No single color is then noticed but only a sense of light or dark such as white, gray, or black.

Pigments: Any material or medium used by the artist to create the effect of color on a surface.

Spectrum: The band of individual colors which results when a beam of light is broken up into its component wavelengths of hues.

Subjective Colors: Colors chosen by the artist without regard to the natural appearance of the object portrayed. They have nothing to do with objective reality but represent the expression of the individual artist.

Value: The characteristic of a color in terms of the amount of light reflected from it. It refers to the lightness or darkness of tone, not to its color *quality*.

NATURE OF COLOR

Color is the element of *form* which arouses the most universal appreciation and the one to which we are the most sensitive. It has an instant appeal to a child as well as to an adult; even an infant will be more attracted by a *brightly colored* object than by one which is *dull* in appearance. The average layman who is frequently puzzled by what he calls "modern" art usually finds its color exciting and attractive. He may question the use of distortions of shape, but seldom objects to the use of *color*, provided that it is harmonious in character. In fact, he frequently likes a work for its color style alone.

Color is one of the most expressive elements because its quality affects our emotions *directly* and *immediately*. The average viewer of a work of art does not have to rationalize what he is *supposed to feel* about color, but has an immediate *emotional* reaction to it. Pleasing rhythms and harmonies of color satisfy our *aesthetic* desires. We like certain combinations of color and reject others. In representational art, color serves to identify objects and to create the effect of illusionistic space. Color differs from the other elements in that it deals with certain scientific facts and principles which are exact and may easily be systematized. The general approach in this chapter will be to examine the basic facts or characteristics of *color relationships* and then to see how they function in giving *form* and *meaning* to the *subject matter* of the artist's work.

Source of Color

Color begins with and is derived from *light,* either natural or artificial. Where there is little *light,* there is little *color;* where the light is strong, the color is likely to be particularly intense in character. We notice at such times of day as dusk or dawn when the light is weak that it is difficult to distinguish one color from another. Under bright, strong sunlight, such as in tropical climates, colors seem to take on an additional intensity. Every ray of light coming from the sun is composed of different *waves* which vibrate at different speeds. The *sensation of color* is aroused in the human mind by the way our sense of vision responds to the different *wavelengths* of light which affect it. This fact can be experimentally proved by allowing a beam of

light to pass through a triangularly shaped piece of glass (prism) and then to reflect from a sheet of white paper. The rays of light are bent or refracted as they pass through the glass at different angles (according to their wavelength) and are reflected from the white paper as different *colors.* Our sense of vision then interprets these colors as individual stripes in a narrow band which we call the *spectrum.* The major colors easily distinguishable in this band are red, orange, yellow, green, blue, indigo, and violet. (The scientist uses the term *indigo* for the color which the artist usually calls *blue violet.*) These colors, however, blend together gradually so that we can see several intermediate colors between them (fig. 112 and plate 41).

The colors of the spectrum are, of course, pure and represent the greatest *intensity* (brightness) possible. If we could collect all of these *spectrum colors* and mix them in a reverse process, we would again have white light. The *pigments* or coloring matter which the artist uses are not as strong in intensity nor as pure as the *spectrum colors.* When we work with pigments, all of the colors mixed will not produce *white,* but rather a gray which in a sense is an *impure* or *darkened* form of white.

Since all of the colors are present in a beam of light, how then are we able to distinguish *one*

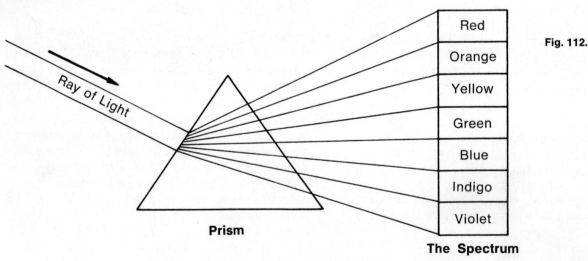

Fig. 112.

Ray of Light

Prism

| Red |
| Orange |
| Yellow |
| Green |
| Blue |
| Indigo |
| Violet |

The Spectrum

color as it is reflected from a natural object? Any colored object has certain physical properties called color quality or *pigmentation* which enable it to *absorb* some of the color waves and *reflect* others. A green leaf will appear green to the eye because it reflects the green waves in the ray of light while absorbing all the other colors. A *pigment* such as the artist uses is a substance which has this property and when it is applied to the surface of an object, gives it the same property. A basic fact to remember is that color in art, depending on *pigments,* can only approximate the intensity of the *spectrum colors* of light. Hereafter when *color* is discussed, the word will be taken to refer to the artist's *pigment* rather than to the sensation of *colored light.*

Neutrals

All objects, of course, do not have the quality of color. Some are black, white, or gray which do not look like any of the colors of the spectrum. No *color quality* is found in these colors; they differ merely in the *quantity of light* which they reflect. Because we do not distinguish any *one* color, these tones are called *neutrals.* From the standpoint of the scientists, these neutrals actually reflect *all* of the color waves in a ray of light. One neutral, absolute black (seldom seen) reflects no light at all and consequently has no color. White may be called the total *addition* of color because it is the result of a surface reflecting all of the color waves in light to an *equal degree.* Black then is usually called the *absence* of color because it results when a surface absorbs all of the color rays *equally* and reflects *none* of them. If white represents one hundred percent reflection of light, then any gray may be considered an impure white because it is created by only *partial* reflection of all the color waves in the spectrum. If the quantity of light reflected is great, the gray is light in value; if the amount reflected is little, the gray is dark in tone. The neutrals are affected by the *quantity of light* reflected, whereas color is concerned with the *quality of light* reflected.

Physical Properties of Color

As previously mentioned, we find in the spectrum such colors as red, orange, yellow, blue, green, and violet. These are only a few colors, and yet we know that hundreds of *color variations* exist. The child or the beginning worker

with color is likely to use only a few simple, pure colors of the spectrum. He does not seem to realize that the simple spectrum colors can be varied in three specific ways. Every color of the spectrum actually exists in *many* forms, although these forms may continue to bear the simple *spectrum name.* There are *many reds,* for example, which differ in character from the *pure red* which we find in the spectrum. Every color which the artist uses must be described in terms of three physical properties: *hue, value,* and *intensity* (fig. 113 and plate 42).

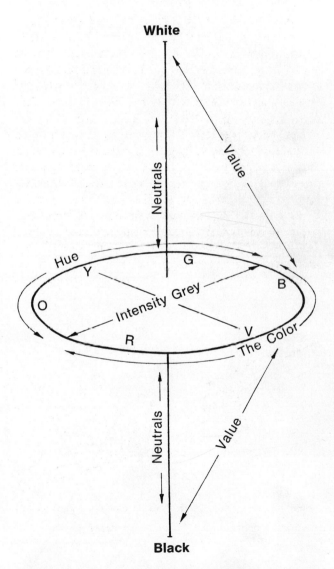

Fig. 113. This diagram demonstrates all three physical properties of color. We can see all of the color variations as existing on a three-dimensional solid (a double cone). As the colors move around this solid, they change in hue. When these hues move upward or downward on the solid, they change in value. As all of the colors on the outside move toward the center, they become closer to the neutral values and there is a change in intensity (*see also* plate 42).

Hue

Hue is the property or characteristic of a color which refers to its *position* in the spectrum. It may also be said to refer to the *color name which* is used to differentiate the colors having different wavelengths of light. For example, yellow is one hue which differs from green, another hue, and has a different wavelength. A color may change its hue only by being mixed with another *color* in the spectrum; this makes an actual change in the wavelength of the ray of light. The same yellow, if added to green, creates a yellowish green or a change in hue. Also, yellow mixed with blue creates green, and the amount of yellow used will determine the kind of green which

Fig. 114. This diagram indicates: first, the primary triad, second, the addition of the three secondary colors, and, third, the placement of the six intermediate colors. In theory, the three primary colors when mixed will neutralize each other and produce gray.

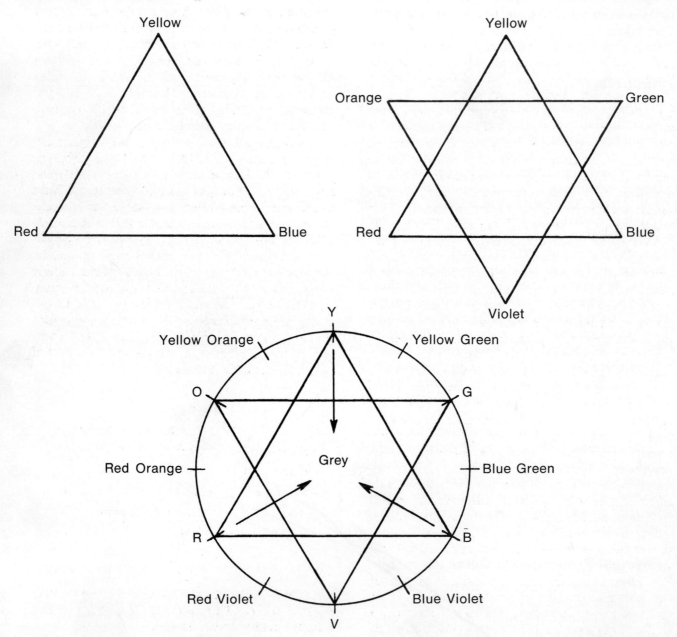

results. Yellow, yellow green, green, and blue green are all different hues because they change their wavelength. However, when these colors are mixed with *pigments,* each contains the *common hue* yellow; such variations are called *analogous hues.*

Many colors of the spectrum may be created by mixing two other colors, such as orange from red and yellow, or violet from red and blue. There are three colors, however, which cannot be created from mixtures; these are the hues red, yellow, and blue. They are called the *primary* colors. When these three primaries are mixed in pairs or all together in equal or unequal amounts, they can produce all of the possible colors. A mixture of the three primaries should theoretically result in white; actually this mixture produces a neutral gray which may be considered a darkened form of white. The important thing to remember is that the three primaries *neutralize* each other so that the resulting tone does not resemble *any one hue.* By mixing any two primaries we arrive at a *secondary* color, such as orange from red and yellow, or green from yellow and blue. In addition, certain *intermediate* colors are created by the mixture of a primary color with a neighboring secondary color. There is actually no limit to the number of intermediate colors because a change of proportion in the amount of primary or secondary colors used will make a change in the resultant hue. In other words, there is no one yellow green possible by mixing green and yellow; if more yellow is used, it is a different yellow green from the one resulting when more green is used (fig. 114).

In order to systematize color relationships, the hues are usually represented as being arranged around a wheel. The three *primary* colors are spaced at equal distances apart on this circle with yellow usually placed at the top. The three *secondary* colors are then placed in between the primaries from which they are mixed. In between each primary and each secondary color an *intermediate* color is placed, the whole resulting in a twelve-color circle. As we move around this color circle, there is a change in the *hue* of the colors because there is an actual change in the wavelength of light rays which produce them. The closer together colors appear on this wheel, the closer their *hue relationships;* the farther apart any two hues are, the more contrasting they are in character. The hues which appear directly opposite each other afford the greatest contrast and are known as *complementary* colors.

Value

In mixing colors, we discover that a wide range of color tones may be produced by using one *hue* and modifying it with the addition of the *neutrals* black or white. This would indicate that colors have characteristics other than hue. The property of color known as *value* distinguishes between the lightness and darkness of colors or the *quantity of light* which a color reflects. It is possible to have many *value* steps between the darkest and lightest appearance of *any one hue.* To change the tone value of a pigment, we must mix another pigment with it which is darker or lighter in character. The only dark or light pigments available which would not also change the hue of a color are black and white.

All of the colors of the spectrum reflect a different *quantity* of light as well as a different *wavelength.* A large amount of light is reflected from yellow, whereas a small amount of light is reflected from violet. Each color at its spectrum intensity has a *normal value* which indicates the *amount of light* it reflects. It can, however, be made lighter or darker than normal by the addition of white or black, as previously noted. It is important to know the normal value of each of the spectrum colors in order to use them most effectively. This *normal value* can be most easily seen when the colors of the wheel are placed in relationship to a scale of *neutral values* from black to white.

	White	
	High light	Yellow
Yellow orange	Light	Yellow green
Orange	Low light	Green
Red orange	Medium	Blue green
Red	High dark	Blue
Red violet	Dark	Blue violet
Violet	Low dark	
	Black	

This chart may be said to indicate the relative *normal values* of the hues at their *spectrum intensity* (purity or brilliance).

Intensity

The third property of color, *intensity* (sometimes called saturation or chroma), refers to the *quality of light* in a color. In this way, it differs from value which refers to the *quantity of light* which a color reflects. We use the term *intensity* in distinguishing a brighter tone of a color from a duller one of the *same hue*, that is to say, a color which has a high degree of saturation or strength from one which is grayed or *neutralized* in character. The saturation point or the purest color is actually found in the spectrum produced by a beam of light passing through a prism. However, the pigment used by the artist which comes closest to resembling this color is said to be at *spectrum intensity*. The purity of the light waves reflected from the pigment produces the variation in the brightness or dullness of the color. For example, a pigment which reflected only the red rays of light would be an intense red, but if any of the complementary green rays were reflected also, the effect would be to dull or *neutralize* the brightness of the red color. If the green and red rays balance each other equally, the resulting tone would be a *neutral gray;* consequently, as a color loses its intensity, it tends to approach or resemble a gray.

There are actually four ways of changing the intensity of colors when mixing pigments. Three of these are accomplished by adding to the hue pigment a neutral that is black, white, or gray. As white is added to any hue, the resulting tone becomes lighter in *value,* but it also loses its brightness or *intensity of color*. In the same way, when black is added to a hue, the *intensity* diminishes as the *value* darkens. In other words, we cannot change value *without* changing intensity, although these two properties are not the *same*. When using the third method of changing *intensity,* a neutral gray of the *same value* is mixed with the *spectrum color*. The mixture then will be a variation in intensity *without* a change in value; the color will become less *bright* as more gray is added but will not get lighter or darker in tone. The fourth way of changing the intensity of any hue is by adding some of the complementary hue. As has been previously mentioned, the mixture of two hues which occur exactly opposite each other on the color wheel such as red and green, blue and orange, or yellow and violet will result in a *neutral gray*. This is because the complementary

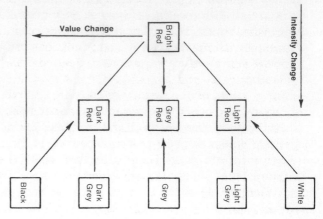

Scale of Neutrals

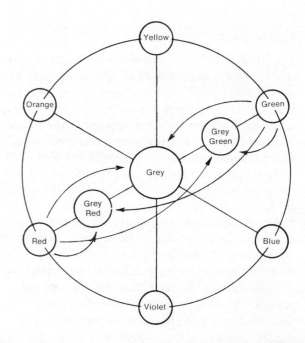

Fig. 115. This diagram illustrates the four means of changing the intensity of color. (1) In the top diagram as white (a neutral) is added to bright red, the value is changed but the resulting color is lowered in intensity. (2) In the same way, the addition of black to bright red creates a dark red closer to the neutral scale because the intensity is changed. (3) When a neutral gray is added to the spectrum color, the intensity is lowered, but the value is neither raised nor lowered. (4) The bottom diagram indicates change of intensity by adding to a color a little of its complement. For instance, by adding a small amount of green to red a gray red is produced. In the same way a small amount of red added to green results in a gray green. When the two colors are balanced (not necessarily equal amounts), the resulting mixture is a neutral gray.

colors represent an *equal balance* of the three *primaries.* The dominating hue in the mixture of two complementary colors will give its specific character to the resulting tone; consequently, this tone, instead of being a pure gray, will be a grayed or neutralized form of the color which is used in the *larger amount.* When hues are neutralized by mixing complements, the resulting colors have a certain liveliness of character not present when they are neutralized with a *gray pigment.* This interesting character is further enhanced when the complementary tones are not actually mixed but are merely placed close together in little dots of broken color. The mixture then actually takes place in the visual sensation of the observer (fig. 115).

Color Relationships

The key to the successful use of color depends upon an understanding of *color relationships.* A single color by itself may have a certain character, but that character may be greatly changed when it is seen with other colors. Colors may be closely related, or they may be contrasting, but the contrast can vary considerably in *degree.* The greatest contrast in hue occurs when two colors are used together which appear directly opposite each other on the color wheel. There is a shorter interval between colors and consequently less contrast when *three* colors are used which are *spaced equally* distant apart on the color wheel. The first group, known as the primary triad, consists of red, yellow, and blue; the second group or secondary triad is composed of orange, green, and violet. The contrast is more striking in the *primary* triad; in the *secondary* triad, although the *interval* between hues is the same, the contrast is softer. This effect probably takes place because in any pair of the triad there is a *common color:* orange and green both contain yellow, orange and violet both contain red, and green and violet both contain blue. Where colors actually appear next to each other on the color wheel, we have the shortest interval and consequently the closest relationship. Three or four *neighboring* hues (analogous colors) always contain *one common color* which dominates the group (fig. 116).

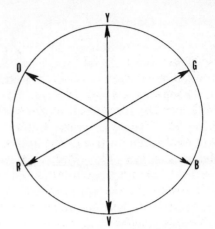

Complementary Colors
(Extreme contrast)

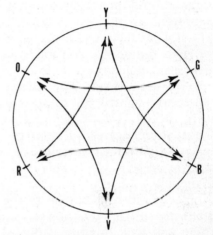

Triad Color Interval
(Medium contrast)

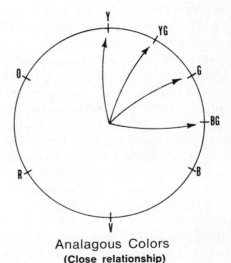

Analagous Colors
(Close relationship)

Fig. 116.

Warm and Cool Colors

All of the colors which we know are usually thought of as belonging to one of two groups, the *warm color* or the *cool colors*. Red, orange, and yellow colors are usually associated with the sun or fire and are considered *warm*. Any colors containing blue, such as green, violet, or blue green, are associated with air, sky, and water and are called *cool colors*. This quality of warmth or coolness in a color may be affected or even changed by the hues *around* or *near* it. The artist may mix a color on his *pallette* and then find it appears entirely different when it appears on the *canvas* in juxtaposition with other colors.

Simultaneous Contrast

The effect of one tone upon another is sometimes expressed as the RULE OF SIMULTANEOUS CONTRAST. According to this rule, whenever two different color tones come into direct contact, the contrast will intensify the *difference* between them. The effect is most noted, of course, when the colors are directly *contrasting* in hue, but it occurs even if the colors have some degree of *relationship*. For example, a yellow green surrounded by green will appear to be yellow, whereas if it were surrounded by yellow, it would be more noticeably green. The contrast used can be in the characteristics of *intensity* or *value* as well as in *hue*. A grayed blue will look *brighter* if placed against a gray background; it will look *grayer* or more neutralized against a bright blue background. The most obvious or strongest effect occurs when directly opposite or *complementary hues* are juxtaposed; blue is brightest when seen next to orange, and green is brightest when seen next to red. When a warm tone is seen in simultaneous contrast to a cool tone, the warm tone is warmer and the cool tone cooler. A color always tends to bring out its complement in a neighboring color. When a neutralized gray is placed next to a strong positive color, it tends to take on a *hue character* complementary to the positive color. When a person wears a certain color in clothing, it tends to emphasize or bring out the *opposite color* in his complexion.

All of these changes in color feeling should make us realize that no one color should be used for its character alone, but should be considered in relation to the other colors present. For this reason, it is better to develop a color composition *all at once* rather than try to finish one area completely before going on to another. Only after gaining a knowledge of the basic facts of color and effects of color relationship can we go on to its function as an *element of form* in composition.

USES OF COLOR

Being familiar with the sources of color and its principal properties will be of little value to us unless we can understand how these facts are used by the artist to accomplish his purpose. Color serves several different purposes in artistic composition. It must be understood, however, that these purposes are not always separate and distinct but frequently overlap and are interrelated. Color may be used in the following ways:

1. To give spatial quality to the pictorial field.
   a. Color may supplement, or even substitute for, value differences in order to give plastic quality.
   b. Color may create interest through the counterbalance of backward and forward movement in pictorial space.
2. To create mood and symbolize ideas.
3. To serve as a vehicle for the expression of personal emotions and feelings.
4. To attract and direct attention as a means of giving organization to a composition.
5. To accomplish aesthetic appeal by a system of well-ordered color relationships.
6. To identify objects by describing the *superficial facts* of their *appearance*.

The last of these functions was considered of greatest importance when painting was looked upon as a purely *illustrational* art. For a long period in the history of Western art, color was looked upon as something which came from the object being represented. Color in painting used to indicate the natural appearance of an object is known as *local color* (plate 43). A more expressive quality is likely to be achieved when the artist is willing to disassociate the color surfaces in the painting from the *object* to which the color supposedly belongs. In place of local color, an entirely *subjective* color treatment may be substituted; the colors used and their relationships become the *invention of the artist* for purposes other than mere representation (plate 44). This style of treatment may even *deny* color as an *objective reality*; that is, we may have purple cows, green faces, or red trees. Most of the functions of color mentioned previously are largely *subjective in character;* they are of particular importance in contemporary art and should be examined separately.

Plastic Quality of Color

As used by the present-day artist, color which does not describe the surface of an object may be used to give the essential reality of its plastic character. This ability of color to *build a form* comes from the advancing and receding characteristics of certain colors. Colors when placed upon a *surface* actually seem to have a *spatial* dimension. For example, a spot of red on a flat surface seems to take a position *in front* of that surface; a spot of blue color, similarly placed, seems to *sink back* into the surface. In general, warm colors seem to advance, and cool colors seem to recede. The character of such effects, however, may be altered by differences in the value and/or intensity of the color. These spatial characteristics of color were first noted by the French artist Paul Cézanne in the latter part of the nineteenth century. He admired the sparkling brilliancy of the *impressionist artists* of the period but thought that their work had lost the *solidity* of earlier painting. Consequently, he began to experiment with expressing the bulk and weight of forms by modeling with *color tones.* Previous to Cézanne's experiments, the traditional academic artist had modeled form by a *change of values* in monotone (one color). The artist then tinted over these tones with a thin, dry *local color* characteristic of the object being painted. Cézanne discovered that a *change of color* on a form could serve the purpose of a *change of value* and not lose the intensity of expression. He felt that the juicy richness of positive colors served to express the actual structure of a solid object. Later contemporary artists realized that Cézanne's advancing and receding colors could also create those backward and forward movements in space which give liveliness and interest to the picture surface (plate 45). Many abstract artists have used the relationships of balance and movement in space to give *content* (meaning) to a painting, although no actual objects are represented. Color has been used as just another means along with line, value, and texture to accomplish this purpose.

Color and Emotion

A second use of color is its ability to create mood, to symbolize ideas, and to express personal emotions. Color itself, as found upon the canvas, may express a mood or feeling, although it is not *descriptive* of the objects represented. Light, bright colors make us feel happy and gay, while cool, dark, or somber colors are generally depressing in character. The different hues of the spectrum may have different emotional impact. Psychologists have found that red is happy and exciting, whereas blue may be dignified, sad, or serene. Also, different *values* and *intensities* of the hues in a color tonality may have an effect on its *feeling tone*. A decided value range (strongly contrasting light or dark hues) gives a color scheme vitality and directness; closely related values and low intensities suggest subtlety, calmness, and repose (plate 46). We cannot escape the emotional effect of color because its appeal is directly to our senses.

The artist may also take advantage of the power of color to *symbolize* ideas; thus he may make his work stronger in content or meaning. Such ideas or abstract qualities as *virtue, loyalty, honesty, evil,* and *cowardice* may be symbolized by the colors which have come to be traditionally associated with them. In many cases, we do not know the origin of these associations, but are nevertheless affected by them. For example, blue is associated with loyalty and honesty (*true blue*), red with danger, yellow with cowardice (*yellow* streak), black with death, green with life or hope, white with purity or innocence, and purple with royalty or wealth. Some colors may have many different associations; for example, red may mean fire, danger, bravery, sin, passion, or violent death. The colors in a painting may enhance the impact of the *subject matter* by suggesting or recalling the *meanings* associated with them (plate 47).

In addition to expressing meanings by association, the artist may use color to express his own *personal emotions*. Most truly creative artists evolve a personal style of color tone which comes primarily not from the subject, but from their own *feelings* about it. Albert Pinkham Ryder expressed what he felt about the sea in a very original style of color. John Marin's color is essentially *suggestive in character* with little expression of form or solidity. It is frequently delicate and light in tone in keeping with the medium (watercolor) with which he works. The color seen in the paintings of Vincent van Gogh is usually vivid and hot, intense in character, and applied in snakelike ribbons of pigment. It is his use of texture and color which accounts for the intensely personal style of his work (plate 48). The French artist Renoir used a luminous, shimmering color in his painting of human flesh so that his nudes have a glow which is not actually present in the human figure. The emotional approach to color appealed particularly to the expressionistic painter who used it to create an entirely *subjective treatment* having nothing to do with *objective reality*.

Aesthetic Appeal of Color Tonality

The final use of color is in its ability to invoke in the observer sensations of pleasure because of its well-ordered system of color tonality (plate 49). This appeal refers to the sense of satisfaction we get from seeing a well-designed rug or drapery material whose color combination is harmonious. The same appeal may be found in a purely nonobjective painting. There are no *exact rules* for arriving at pleasing effects in color relationship, but there are some *guiding principles* which may help us develop a feeling for them. We may develop the ability to create pleasing color by studying and analyzing color schemes which appeal to us; this study should be followed by experiment and practice in *color organization*. The problem will be, *first*, the *selection* of hues which are to be used together in a composition and, *second*, their *arrangement* in the pictorial field in the proper amounts for color balance. No color is important in *itself* but is always seen on the picture surface in a *dynamic interaction* with the other colors present. It must be remembered that combinations and arrangements of color are for the purpose of expressing content or meaning; consequently, any arrangement ought to have a definite *feeling tone*. In talking about pleasing color, we must realize that there can be brutal color combinations as well as refined ones; these are satisfying in the sense that they accomplish the artist's purpose of exciting us rather than of having a quieting effect. Some of the German expressionist painters have proved that these brutal, clashing color schemes can have definite aesthetic value when they are done in a purposeful manner (plate 50).

Color Balance

In all good color combinations, there are some relationships and some contrasts. Where colors are related in *hue*, they may exhibit some contrast in *value* and/or *intensity*. The basic problem is the same one present in all aspects of form organization, *variety in unity*. There must be relationships between the color tones, but these *relationships* must be made alive and interesting through *variety*. A simple device for creating unity and balance is the *repetition* of similar color tones in different parts of the composition. An important aspect of color balance is based upon our psychological perception of complementary hues. If we look fixedly at a spot of intense red for a few moments and then shift our eyes to a white area, we will see an afterimage of the same spot in green blue, the psychological complement. The phenomenon may be noted when *any pair* of complementary colors is used. This psychological fact is the basis for our use in many color schemes of a note of *complementary color* to balance the *dominating hue* used (plate 51).

The pleasing quality of a color pattern depends frequently on the amounts or proportions of color used. In general, it may be said that *equal amounts* of different colors are not as interesting as a color arrangement where *one color* or one kind of color *predominates* (plate 52). We are often confused by color schemes where all of the tones demand equal importance because we cannot find a *dominant area* on which to fix our attention. The dominance of any one color in a pattern may be due to its hue, its value, or its intensity; it may also be affected by the character of the surrounding hues (plate 53). A small, dark spot of color, through its *lower value*, may dominate a large light area. A spot of *intense* color, though small, may balance a larger amount of a *grayer*, more *neutralized* color. Also a small amount of warm color will usually dominate a larger amount of cool color, although both may be of the same intensity. Complementary colors, which of course vie for our attention through simultaneous contrast, may be made more attractive if one of them is softened or neutralized.

Color Combinations

Any attempt to base the aesthetic appeal of color pattern on certain fixed theoretical color harmonies is not satisfactory. For one thing, the effect will depend as much on how we *distribute* our tones as on the *relationships* of the tones themselves. Most combinations, however, may be reduced to *two basic types* of color organization. In the first one, we depend upon the *unity of the hues* being dominant; in the second, we use hue combinations which depend for their interest on *strong contrast* and *variety* of color. Here, of course, the basic problem is to unify these contrasts without destroying the general strength and intensity of expression. In the *unified color scheme*, the opposite is true; we must introduce enough *variety of color* to keep the effect from becoming *too monotonous*. In the first type of color pattern (unity), the hue intervals are closely related as in analogous colors; in the second type (contrast), the hue intervals are further apart, the greatest possible interval being that between two complementary colors.

Unified Color Patterns. Unity is often made dominant in a color scheme by the use of *one hue only*. Naturally, variety can only be achieved in a combination of this kind by using contrasting values or intensities (plate 54). This scheme may be varied by the introduction of a *small amount* of a subordinate contrasting *hue* or even a contrasting *neutral* such as white or black (plate 55). Another way of relating colors where unity is desired is to *key* a number of colors toward *one hue.* This one hue will serve as a harmonizing factor if a little of it is mixed with *every color* used in the combination. The same effect may be created by glazing over a vari-colored pattern with a single tone of color, which becomes the *key color.* A third type of unified pattern is found when we use all warm or all cool colors in combination. Again, however, a small amount of a complementary or a contrasting

neutral may be used for variety in the color pattern (plate 56). As a rule, where warm and cool colors are balanced against each other in a composition, it is better to allow one temperature to dominate.

Contrasting Color Patterns. Color schemes based upon a strong *contrast of hue* or intensity have great possibilities for expressive effect (plate 57). These contrasts may sometimes be controlled by the *amount of contrasting color used.* Where the *basic unity* of a color pattern has been established, we may use strong contrasts of color in *small accents;* their size, then, prevents them from disturbing the basic unity of the color theme. Another commonly used method of controlling *contrasts* is to separate all or a part of the tones by a *neutral* line or area. Absolute black or white lines are the most effective neutrals for this purpose because they are so positive in character themselves. They not only tie together the contrasting hues, but also serve to *enhance their color character* because of value contrast. The use of the neutral black leading between the brilliant colors of stained glass windows is an example of this unifying character. Such modern painters as Georges Rouault and Beckmann found a *black line* effective in separating their *highly contrasting* colors (plate 58). A similar unifying effect can be brought about by using a large area of neutral *gray* or a *neutralized color* as a *background* for clashing contrasts of color.

Finally, we should remember that combinations of color frequently defy the exactness of any rules and are still satisfying to the eye. The artist uses color, as he does the other elements of art structure, to give a highly personalized meaning to the *subject matter* of his work.

COLOR PROBLEMS

Problem 1

Hue Change

Mix with tempera paint the twelve colors and mount them in the spaces indicated on the chart (fig. 117).

Problem 2

Intensity Change

Use any pair of complementary colors to create the horizontal intensity scale. At either end, the

colors should be at spectrum intensity. Gradually mix a little of the complement with each color until you arrive at a neutral gray which is placed in the middle rectangle (fig. 118).

Value Change

In the left-hand vertical column create a value scale from white to black by mixing tempera paint.

In the right hand column of Figure 118 place any hue from the color wheel, matching it to its

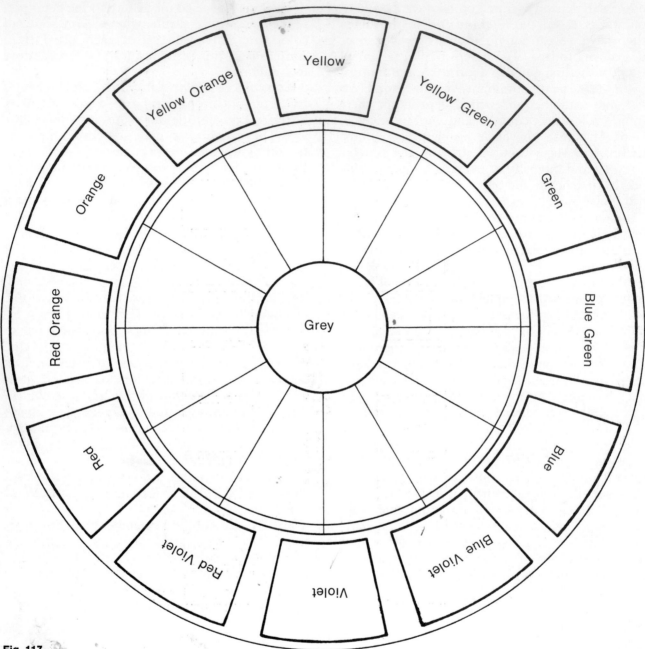

Fig. 117.

corresponding value in the left column. Mix white with this color so as to match it with the lighter values. Repeat by mixing the same hue with black to match the darker values.

Problem 3

Any color may vary in appearance, depending upon the color which is placed next to it. An application of the "rule of simultaneous contrast" will indicate the apparent changes in a color as it is placed against different colored backgrounds.

Make experiments in simultaneous contrast by using areas of background in the form of rectangles about 2½ by 3½ inches in size. Paste squares or circles of color about ¾ inch on these backgrounds.

a. Using a spot of primary or secondary color of high intensity, mount it first on a background of its complement and then on a background of any related color.
b. Use the same color in a lower intensity and mount it on the same backgrounds.

Intensity Change

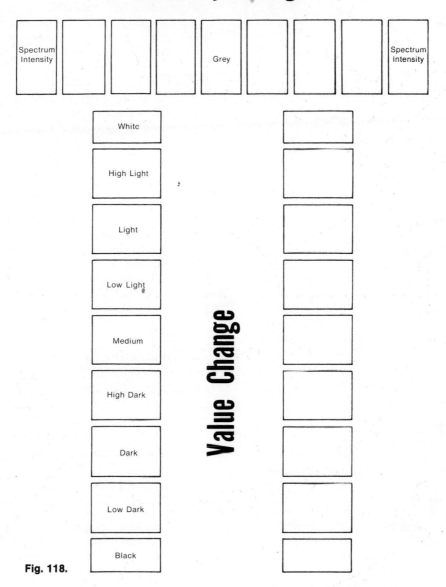

Fig. 118.

c. Use a low intensity of any primary color and mount it first on a background of plain gray or black. Then put it on a background of its own hue at a high intensity.

d. Using a neutral gray, mount it first on a background of any pure primary or secondary. Next place the same gray against a background which is the complement of the first color used.

Mount all these experiments in pairs on a large chart. Check with the text to see if the effects are the same as indicated in the section Simultaneous Contrast (p. 90).

Problem 4

The use of certain "standard" color combinations should be explored by the student. It should be noticed, however, that the use of such schemes without sensitivity to the quality and relative amounts of color used will not accomplish a satisfying result.

Lay out a page of drawing paper with five 4 by 5 inch rectangles. Within these rectangles repeat a simplified geometric design and paint each one with a different type of color combination. Use some neutrals (black, white, or gray) in each color combination. Use the following standard color schemes for this problem:

a. Monochromatic
b. Analogous
c. Complementary
d. Split-complementary (the use of one color next to the direct complement)
e. Triad (secondary or intermediate)

Problem 5

Plastic use of color implies spatial relationships created by certain types of color organization. Colors which are warm in hue character and have high intensity seem to advance, whereas those which are cool and have low intensity seem to recede. Also colors which are complementary to their background seem to occupy a space in front of it.

Plan a pattern of simple planes overlapping in space. Vary the size and position of the planes in order to create interest. Cut these shapes from a variety of colored papers and paste them on a background of neutral or neutralized color. Choose the colors so that they will help to establish the spatial recession of forms.

Problem 6

Every color of the spectrum exists in many forms or modifications, although these forms continue to bear the simple spectrum name. Modification of a color by mixing it with neutrals or even a little of its complement does not change its basic hue.

The intention of this problem is to demonstrate the many modifications which may be created from a basic color scheme. Use a simple abstract pattern created by placing a small shape and a medium-size shape on a larger background area (about 2½ by 3½ inches). Choose any three contrasting colors widely separated on the color wheel and paint the design with these colors in their spectrum intensity. This represents the basic color scheme.

Using each one of these colors, see how many modifications you can make by adding varying amounts of black, white, or gray or a little of the complementary color. Paint swatches of each color modification a little larger than the original pattern. Choose a modification of each of the three original colors and combine them to make a color variation of the original pattern. Make another selection to create a second variation of the pattern. Continue combining forms of the original colors until you have ten or twelve variations. (The

original pattern can be created by cutting the shapes used from the color swatches and pasting them on background shapes also cut from these swatches.) Mount the original color scheme and variations in a pleasing arrangement on a large piece of illustration board. Label the original basic color pattern.

Problem 7

Colors make a direct appeal to the emotions. Generally speaking, such emotional states as anger, melancholy, jealousy, and the like, have come to be associated with specific colors. Sensitive color employment in combination with appropriate use of the other elements of form may express greatly varied emotional feelings.

Select a black-and-white reproduction of a painting (or even a photograph) which seems to contain a specific mood. Reproduce this work in any medium using a color scheme expressive of that mood. Pay no attention to the naturalistic qualities of color but make sure that all other factors (particularly the light-and-dark pattern) are true to the work being reproduced.

Problem 8

The Impressionistic painters of the nineteenth century developed a technical painting method to simulate the illusion of light, color, and atmosphere. Because they knew that light was composed of varying wavelengths of color, they painted surfaces with dabs of different colors placed side by side in an attempt to catch the vibrating quality of light rays. They realized that the eye would mix or fuse these colors into the variations or color mixtures which they desired.

Set up a group of simple still-life objects and draw it in simple outline form. Using tempera paint, express the quality of color in the objects by painting dots or short dabs of color on the picture surface. Instead of mixing colors on a palette, merely place them on the paper so that they will mix when the eye perceives them from a distance. For example, dots of pure green could be used with dots of blue or yellow to create modifications of hue and value. In some areas, dabs of complementary color might be used to modify the local colors seen. Dabs of cool color could be used in shadow areas to create spatial recession. It will probably be necessary to create definite value differences between forms in order that they may stand out one from the other. Do not feel bound by rules in this problem but feel free to experiment with different tonal effects. Also, the dots of color do not have to be completely separate but may mix or overlap with each other.

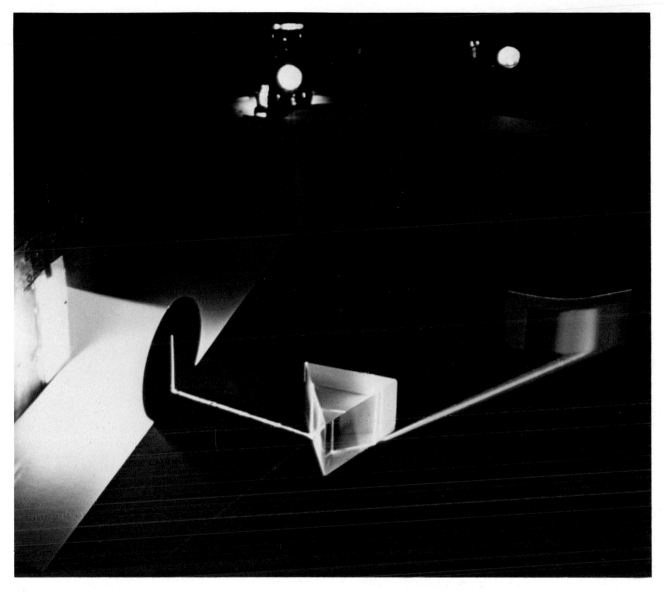

Plate 41. PRISM AND SPECTRUM. A beam of light passes through a triangularly shaped piece of glass (prism). The rays of light are bent or refracted as they pass through the glass at different angles (according to their wavelengths) producing a rainbow array of hues called the spectrum.

Fritz Goro photograph, courtesy Time-Life books.

Plate 44. MOTHER AND CHILD (1928) by Marie Laurencin. This French artist used color to construct a personal (or subjective) interpretation which sets the charming mood of the painting.

Plate 45. STILL LIFE WITH APPLES AND PEACHES by Paul Cézanne. Cézanne uses changes of color as a means of modelling form. Cool colors are used as a means of indicating recession rather than a mere darkening of the characteristic tones.

Plate 46. ROUEN CATHEDRAL, WEST FACADE SUNLIGHT (1894) by Claude Monet. Monet, a French impressionist, features subtlety and delicacy of color. Two main hues are used in related variations.

Plate 47. THE TRAGEDY (1903) by Pablo Picasso. Picasso's personal style of color during the early 1900's seems fraught with imminent sadness due to the dominantly blue hue. His use of such blues came to be regarded so highly that this time in his career is often called his "Blue period."

Courtesy The National Gallery of Art, Washington, D.C. Chester Dale Collection.

Plate 48 SUNFLOWERS (1887) by Vincent van Gogh. Vincent van Gogh, during the late 1880's, developed a mature style featuring dominantly hot and lively hues painted with a verve that indicates his personal discovery and passion for the sunny climate of Mediterranean France.

Courtesy The Metropolitan Museum of Art, Rogers Fund, 1949.

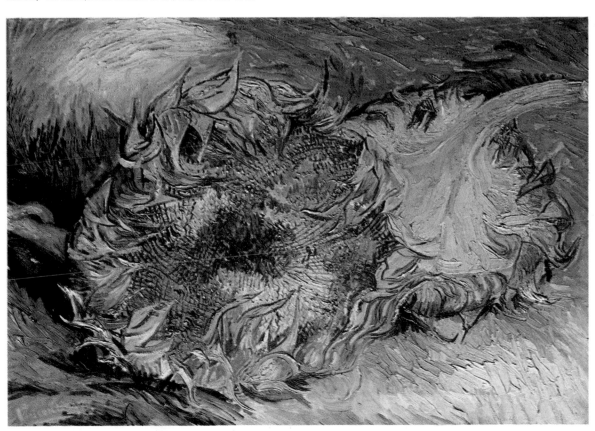

Plate 49. FRUITS AND GUITAR (1938) by Georges Braque. The Cubist painter, Braque, commonly achieves aesthetically pleasing arrangements of color and value areas. His inventive hues are probably the choicest of early 20th-century painting and his selectivity of placement is equally significant.

Courtesy The Art Institute of Chicago.

Plate 50. CHRIST AMONG THE CHILDREN (1910) by Emil Nolde. The Expressionists usually employed bold, clashing hues in order to emphasize their emotional identification with a subject. Intensity of feeling is created by the use of complementary and near-complementary hues.

Collection, The Museum of Modern Art, New York. Gift of Dr. W. R. Valentiner.

Plate 51. THE GOLDEN WALL (1961) by Hans Hoffman. The large areas of red in this painting serve to unify its color tonality. A smaller area of green is used to give balance to the total color pattern. Complementary colors balance and enhance each other.

Courtesy The Art Institute of Chicago. Collection of Mr. and Mrs. Frank G. Logan.

Plate 52. PROPELLERS (1918) by Fernand Léger. Although a variety of strong colors appear in this painting, the careful repetition of a key hue (yellow) creates harmony and color balance.

Collection, The Museum of Modern Art, New York. Katherine S. Dreier Bequest.

Plate 53. RUE A SANNOIS by Maurice Utrillo. Blue is used as a dominant hue in the painting by Utrillo. He achieves a dynamic balance by his use of smaller areas of complements and neutral white.

Plate 54. TWO LITTLE CIRCUS GIRLS (1879) by Auguste Renoir. Here, unity is achieved by the French artist, Renoir, through a dominantly warm color scheme in order to invoke a sense of childhood grace and charm. Although very slight traces of cool color are found in the painting, variety is basically achieved through modulations of value.

Plate 55. STILL LIFE by Paul Cézanne.
Cézanne has arrived at a dominantly
cool tonality in this painting, using
contrasts of red and yellow in small
amounts so the pattern is not disturbed.

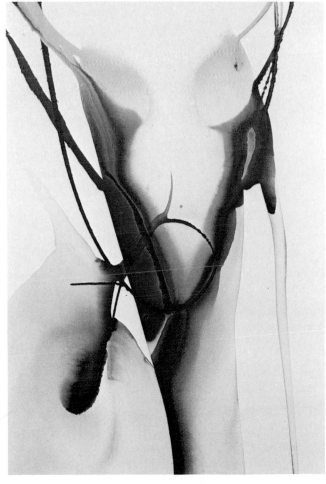

**Plate 56. PHENOMENA SHIELD AND
GREEN (1969) by Paul Jenkins.** Analogous (related) colors can serve to
produce harmony, while touches of a
complementary color contributes variety.

Plate 57. THE OLD PORT OF MARSEILLE by Maurice de Vlaminck. Vlaminck, another expressionist, uses the preferred contrasting hues of these emotionally inclined painters. The hues are neutralized, so that unity is achieved without loss of liveliness.

Plate 58. CHRIST MOCKED BY SOLDIERS (1932) by Georges Rouault. Again we have an expressionist contrast of clashing complements. The pattern and harmony of the painting in this case are stabilized without loss of expression through the heavy neutralizing lines of black suggested to Rouault by medieval stained glass.

Collection, The Museum of Modern Art, New York. Given anonymously.

Problem 9

A natural subject may be interpreted by the artist in many different styles of color tonality, either unified or contrasting in hue character. As the local color character of the objects is ignored, the artist is enabled to express a personal feeling or emotional quality.

Again, set up an arrangement of three or four simple still-life objects. Using any medium or combination of mediums, interpret the subject matter in several different color organizations selected from the following:

a. Strongly contrasting hues and values
b. Closely related hues and values
c. Dominant cool colors with warm accents
d. Dominant warm colors with black or white accents
e. A dark-toned color scheme but with contrasting hues
f. A light-toned color scheme with contrasting hues
g. Contrasting colors used with black or white lines

Lines and textures in neutral tones may be used as decorating embellishments on, in, or around the color shapes. Areas of shadow may be ignored or considered color shapes. Remember that the expressive quality of the color pattern is more important than the naturalistic appearance of the subject matter.

Chapter 9/Space

Definitions:

Atmospheric (aerial) Perspective: The illusion of deep space produced in graphic works by lightening values, softening contours, reducing value contrasts, and neutralizing colors in objects as they approach the horizon, while following the general principles of linear perspective.

Decorative Space: A concept in which the visual elements have interval relationships in terms of a two-dimensional plane.

Four-dimensional Space: A highly imaginative treatment of forms which gives a sense of intervals of time or motion on the picture surface.

Intuitive Space: Relationships of the visual elements on the surface of the picture plane so as to give a feeling of the third dimension without actually giving a true illusion of solidity and depth.

Infinite Space: A pictorial concept in which the illusion of space has the quality of endlessness found in the natural environment. The picture frame has the quality of a window through which one can see the endless recession of forms into space.

Orthographic Drawing: A two-dimensional graphic representation of an object showing a plan, a vertical elevation and/or a section.

Plastic Space: A concept in which the visual elements on the surface of the picture plane are made to give the illusion of having relationships in depth as well as in length and breadth.

Shallow Space: Sometimes called "limited depth" because the artist controls his use of the visual elements so that no point or form is so remote that it does not take its place in the pattern of the picture surface.

Space: The interval or measurable distance between preestablished points.

Three-dimensional Space: A sensation of space which seems to have thickness and depth as well as length and breadth.

Two-dimensional Space. Measurable distances on a surface which show length and breadth but lack any illusion of thickness or depth.

Although *space* is not considered an *element* of two-dimensional art, its presence is nevertheless felt in every work of art, presenting fundamental problems which must be faced by the artist. Space is here conceived as a *product* rather than as a *tool;* it is created by the tools or art elements which were discussed in the preceding chapters. The importance of space lies in its function, and a basic knowledge of its implications and use is essential to every artist. Space, as defined in this chapter, is limited to the graphic fields, that is, two-dimensional surface arts such as drawing, painting, printmaking, and the like. The space which exists as an illusion in the *graphic* fields is actually present in the *plastic* areas of sculpture, ceramics, jewelry, architecture, and so forth. Their three-dimensional space concepts will be discussed in Chapter 10.

SPATIAL PERCEPTION

All spatial implications are mentally conditioned by the environment and experience of the viewer. Vision is experienced *through* the eyes, but *interpreted* with the mind. Perception involves the whole pattern of nerve and brain response as well as the visual stimulus. Man uses two eyes for the perception of objects in nature and continually shifts his focus of attention. In so doing, two different types of vision are used, *stereoscopic* and *kinesthetic*. Having two eyes set slightly apart from each other, man sees two different views of the object world at the same time. The term *stereoscopic* is applied to his ability to overlap the views which are slightly different into one image. This visual process creates an illusion of three-dimensional depth, making it possible to judge distances.

In kinesthetic vision, man experiences space in the movements of the eye from one part of a work of art to another. Space is experienced while viewing a two-dimensional surface because we unconsciously attempt to organize its separate parts so that they can be seen as a whole. In addition, man explores object surfaces with *eye* movements in order to make *mental* recognition of them. Objects close to the eye require more ocular movement than those more distant, and this factor adds spatial illusion to man's kinesthetic vision.

TYPES OF SPACE

There are two basic types of space available to the artist; both are fundamental to spatial conception: decorative space and plastic space.

Decorative Spatial Concept

The graphic artist should realize that the actual surface to which he is physically limited in his art is two-dimensional and that suggestions of space as they occur on this surface are almost entirely a matter of premeditated illusion. The usual *picture plane* (paper, canvas, board, etc.) has height and width (see form) but no depth which could be of any significance to the artist. This depthless surface could be called *decorative space* or a space which exists *across* the plane rather than *in* it. When he adds any element of art to this blank surface plane, the artist begins to cut, divide, and rearrange the decorative space into smaller units. When this happens, the illusion of depth may appear either *accidentally* or as a result of the *intention* of the artist. The depth (or three-dimensional space) and the divisions across the surface (or two-dimensional space) are of vital concern to the artist, for they must both be organized into a coherent whole. Decorative space invariably exists in the sense that distances between images or elements can be measured *across the picture*

plane. It exists in theory only in the sense that the image is completely confined to the picture plane. Thus, in terms of depth, decorative space becomes a matter of degree. Decorative space ceases when it is obvious that the artist intends to divorce the *image* from the *plane* on which it physically rests. It is doubtful that the human mind will accept the idea of a perfectly flat surface in an art work. Because of memory overlays of objective experiences, the slightest manipulation of line, value, or color will generate *an illusion of depth-space* (figs. 119 and 120).

Plastic Spatial Concept

The term *plastic* is applied to all images which assume the qualities of the third dimension. Man bases much of his art on his experiences in the objective world, and it is a natural conclusion that he should explore the resources of pictorial space.

Deep and/or Infinite Space

An art work which emphasizes *deep space* denies the *picture plane* except as a starting point from which the space begins. The observer of such a work seems to be moving continuously in the far distances of the picture field. This spatial feeling will be recognized by those who have looked through an open window over a landscape which seems to roll on and on into infinity. The infinite quality of *illusionistic space* is created by the recognition of spatial indications which are produced by certain relationships of art form. Size, position, overlapping images, sharp and diminishing details, converging parallels, and perspective are the traditional methods of indicating deep spatial penetration.

Infinite spatial concepts, sometimes called atmospheric perspective, dominated Western art from the beginning of the Renaissance (about 1350) to the middle of the nineteenth century. During this period, generations of artists such as Uccello, Botticelli, Ruisdael, Brueghel, Rembrandt, Poussin, and Corot, to name only a few, developed and perfected the *deep space illusion* because of its obvious accord with *visual reality* (plate 59). Present-day art is largely dominated by the *shallow space concept,* but many contemporary artists work with strongly recessed fields. Any space concept is valid if it demonstrates consistent control of the elements in relation to the spatial field chosen.

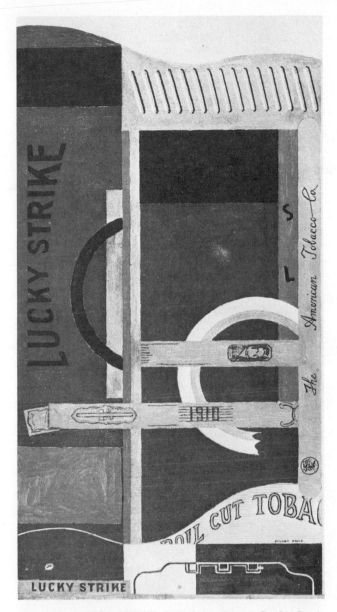

Fig. 119. LUCKY STRIKE (1921) by Stuart Davis. Davis worked with planes generally parallel to the picture surface. Certain devices such as overlapping and transparency are employed but never in such a way as to seriously contradict the concept of flatness.

Collection, the Museum of Modern Art, New York. Gift of the American Tobacco Company, Inc.

Fig. 120. THE KNIFE THROWER, (1947) from *Jazz* by Henri Matisse. No depth was intended in this decorative and ornamental abstraction. The flatness of the shapes is exaggerated by avoiding modeling, but vitality is maintained by variations of contour, value, and color. A silhouetted effect is the dominant feature.

Courtesy Philadelphia Museum of Art. McIlhenny Fund

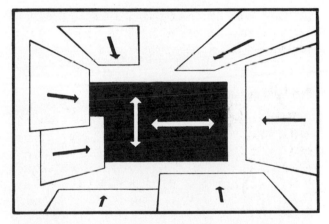

Fig. 121. As a variation on the concept of shallow space, artists occasionally define the planes which make up the outer limits of a hollow boxlike space behind the picture plane. The diagram shows this concept, although in actual pictorial practice a return to the picture plane would be made through objects occupying the space defined. The back plane acts significantly as a curtain which prevents penetration into deep space (*see also* fig. 181 and plate 60).

Shallow Space

Artists often take an intermediate spatial position, keeping some of the qualities of deep space, but relating them to the picture plane. Awareness of the presence of the picture surface usually limits the space of a composition. Varying degrees of *limited space* are possible, ranging from the near-decorative to the near-infinite. Limited or *shallow space* could be compared to the restricted spatial feeling of a box or stage (fig. 121). Egyptian, Oriental, Byzantine, and medieval artists used comparatively shallow space in their works. The works of the early Renaissance were often based on shallow sculpture reliefs (plate 60). In the neoclassic paintings of Jacques Louis David, a nineteenth-century artist, most of the figure action was limited to a single plane in the foreground. David interwove his figures decoratively on a stagelike plane which was limited by a backdrop of flat architecture (*see* fig. 181).

Many modern artists have elected the use of shallow space on the theory that it admits of more positive control and is more in keeping with the flatness of the working surface. Gauguin, Matisse, Modigliani, and Beckmann are typical advocates of the limited spatial concepts (fig. 122).

TRADITIONAL METHODS OF SPATIAL INDICATION

Artistic methods of spatial representation are so interwoven and interdependent that an attempt to isolate and examine all of them would be impractical and inconclusive. The illustration of all spatial means would be an interminable task and leave the reader with the feeling that art is entirely "formula-istic."

Fig. 122. BRIDE AND GROOM (1915–16) by Amedeo Modigliani. Modigliani dealt with simplified monumental forms given plasticity by subtle linear and value treatment and enriched by sensitive paint application. The space behind the figures is usually limited to broad, severe shapes which restrict the vision of the viewer to a narrow corridor of space.

Collection, the Museum of Modern Art, New York. Gift of Frederic Clay Bartlett

Our comprehension of space which comes to us through objective experiences is enlarged, interpreted, and given meaning by the use of our *intuitive faculties*. Spatial order develops when the artist *senses* the right balance and the best placement and then selects vital forces to create completeness and unity. Obviously, then, this process is not a purely intellectual one but a matter of instinct or subconscious response (fig. 123).

Fig. 123. ROOM INTERIOR (1960) by Jack Troutner. Many indications of space appear in this composition, but they are freely varied to fit the demands of artistic unity. The sense of space is felt by the observer, although he realizes that the indications follow no particular formula of mathematical perspective.

Since the *subjective* element plays a part in the control of space, one can readily see that emphasis on formula here, as elsewhere, can quench the creative spirit. Art is a product of man's creativity and is always dependent on individual interpretations and responses. Space, like other qualities in art, may be both spontaneous or premeditated, but always results as the product of the artist's will. If an artist has the impassioned will to make things so, they will usually be so, *despite inconsistency and defiance of established principles.* Therefore, the methods of spatial indication which are discussed in the following pages are those which have been used frequently and which guarantee one effect of space, though not necessarily one which is always exactly the same. These traditional methods are presented here merely as a means of giving the student a basic conception of the more significant spatial forces.

Size

Man usually interprets largeness of scale as meaning nearness. A smaller scale conversely suggests spatial distance. If two men were to stand at distances of five and fifteen feet from us, the nearer figure would appear larger than the other. The difference of scale between the two figures would not ordinarily be understood as showing a large and a small man (although this could conceivably play a part in our perception), but men of approximately the same size placed at varying distances from us. Therefore, if we are to use depth-scale as our guide, a figure, regardless of all other factors, must assume a scale to correspond to its distance from us. This concept of space has not always been so in art. In many broad periods and styles of art and in the works of children large scale is assigned according to importance, power, and strength, regardless of spatial location (fig. 124 and plate 61).

Position

For many artists and observers, there is an automatic inference that the *horizon line,* providing a point of reference, is always at *eye level.* The position of objects is judged in relation to the horizon line, the bottom of the picture plane is seen as the closest visual point, and the degree of rise of the visual units up to the horizon line indicates subsequently receding spatial positions. There is evidence to suggest that this

Fig. 124. THE ADORATION OF THE MAGI by Master of the Blessed Clare. The importance of the Madonna accounts for the unexpectedly large scale of her figure. This disproportionate size produces a strange conflict with the semirealistic space with which the size of the angels is more in harmony. The adjustment of size to equal importance is known as hieratic scaling.

Courtesy Lowe Art Museum, Kress Collection. University of Miami manner of seeing is instinctive (having grown out of continued exposure to the objective world), for its influence persists even in viewing greatly abstracted and nonobjective work (plate 62). The alternative, of course, is to see the picture plane as entirely devoid of spatial illusion and the distances of the visual elements as actually measurable across the flat surface. It is difficult to see this way even when we discipline ourselves to do so, for it calls on us to divorce ourselves entirely from ingrained environmental factors.

Overlapping

Another way of suggesting space is by overlapping planes or volumes. If one object covers part of the visible surface of another, the first object is assumed to be nearer. The device of overlapping is a powerful indication of space, for once the device is used, it takes precedence over other spatial signs. For instance, if one ball were placed in front of another of a larger size, the overlapping ball would appear closer than the overlapped ball, despite the smaller size of the interposed sphere (fig. 125).

Sharp and Diminishing Detail

Because of the construction of the human eye, man is not able to see *with equal clarity* near and distant planes at the same time. A glance out the window will confirm the fact that close objects

Fig. 125.

appear sharp and clear in detail, whereas those at great distances seem blurred and lacking in definition. Artists have long been cognizant of this phenomenon and have used it widely in illusionistic work. In recent times, artists found that they could use this method and other *traditional* methods of space indication in works which are otherwise quite *abstract*. Thus, in abstract and nonobjective conceptions, sharp lines, clearly defined shapes and values, complex textures, and intense colors are associated with foreground or near positions. Hazy lines, indistinct shapes, grayed values, simple textures, and neutralized colors are identified with background locations. These characteristics are often included in the definition of atmospheric perspective.

Converging Parallels

The general principle of spatial indication of converging parallels can be illustrated through the use of a rectangular plane such as a sheet of paper or a table top. By actual measurement, a rectangle possesses one set of short parallel edges and one set of long-parallel edges. If the plane is arranged so that one of the short edges (A) is viewed head-on, its corresponding edge (B) will appear to be much shorter. Since these edges appear to be of different lengths, it is readily apparent that the other two edges (C and D) which connect them must seem to converge as they move back into space. Either set of lines when separated from the other set would continue to indicate space quite forcefully. The principle of converging parallels is found in many works of art which do not abide by the *rules of perspective*. It is closely related to perspective but it is not necessarily restrictive in a creative sense (fig. 126).

Linear Perspective

Linear perspective is a geometric system used for converting sizes and distances of known objects into a unified spatial order. Its use involves the application of some of the other spatial indications such as size, position, and converging parallels. This system has been since the Renaissance the principal device for spatial representation in the art of the Western world.

The general understanding of perspective did not originate with the Renaissance, but the wave of scientific inquiry which swept many coun-

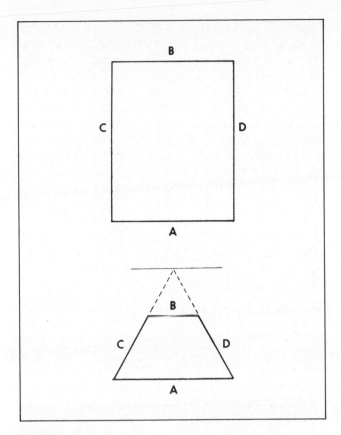

Fig. 126.

tries during that period brought this spatial system to a point of high refinement. The Renaissance artist focused his attention on one view, a selected portion of nature, seen from one position at a particular moment in time. The use of *vanishing points, eye levels* and *horizon lines,* and guide lines gave this view mathematical exactitude. To a certain extent, artists became prisoners of the system which they had helped to produce. Being a system of inflexible rules, perspective places emphasis on *accuracy of representation,* an emphasis which does not favor *creative expression.* If, however, the artist sees perspective as an aid rather than an end in itself, it can be very useful to him. This attitude conceives of perspective as something to be used *when* and *if* the need arises in the creation of a picture. Many fine works of art which ignore perspective or show "faults" in the use of the system have been and are being created. In such cases the type of spatial order created by linear perspective simply is not compatible with the aims of the artist. Perspective then is something which should be learned by the artist simply to make it available to him (plate 63, *also see* plate 25 and fig. 58).

The traditional Oriental artist could be cited as a dramatic countertype to the Renaissance artist of the West. Ancient canons prescribed convergence of parallel lines as they *approach* the spectator, creating a *reverse perspective.* This type of presentation closes the space in depth so that the picture becomes a stage and the spectator an actor-participant in an active spatial panorama rarely losing its identification with the picture plane (fig. 127). Similar space concepts have been employed in the West during various historical periods. It is revealing to notice that ideas on pictorial space usually agree with the prevailing mental climate of the society which produces the art. In this sense space is a form of human expression.

Fig. 127. A COURTESAN DREAMING by Kubo Shunman. The reversal of normal perspective in the table is a deliberate device used by this Japanese artist to limit the depth of space in the painting.
Courtesy the Metropolitan Museum of Art, New York. Bequest of Mrs. H. O. Havemeyer, 1929. The H. O. Havemeyer Collection

SPATIAL PROPERTIES OF THE ELEMENTS OF ART STRUCTURE

As work with the elements of art structure proceeds, it becomes necessary that we recognize and control the spatial effects which arise from their use. Each of the elements possesses some inherent spatial qualities, but it is the interrelationship between elements that yields the greatest spatial feeling. Many types of spatial experiences can be achieved by manipulating the elements, that is, by varying their position, number, direction, value, texture, and color. The resultant spatial variations are endless.

Line and Space

Line, by its physical structure, implies continued direction of movement, an agent for indicating spatial presence. Since, by definition, a line must be greater in length than in breadth (or else there would be difficulty in distinguishing a line from a dot or shape), it tends to emphasize one direction. The extension of this dominant direction in a single line creates continuity, moving the eye of the observer from one unit or general area to another, thus creating transition which unifies the front, middle, and background areas.

The physical properties of line contain other spatial ingredients. Long and short, thick and thin, and straight, angular, and curved lines take on different spatial positions and movements in contrast with each other. The indications of three-dimensional space mentioned earlier in this chapter are actively combined with the physical properties of line. A long and thick line, for instance, appears larger in size (a spatial indication) and hence closer to the viewer than a short and thin line. Overlapping lines establish differing spatial positions, especially when they are set in opposite directions (i.e., vertical against horizontal). A diagonal line seems to move from the picture plane into deep space, whereas a vertical or horizontal line generally seems to remain comparatively static. In addition, the plastic qualities of such overlapping lines can be increased by modulating their values. The plastic illusion invariably suggests change of position in space. A single line may similarly be modulated in value and dimension to add to its plastic qualities (fig. 128).

The spatial indication of line convergence (which occurs, subject to rule, in mechanical perspective) is always in evidence wherever a complex of lines occurs. The types of spatial suggestions arising out of this general principle are of such infinite variety that particular effects are usually the product of the artist's *intuitive* explorations (fig. 129). Wavy, spiral, serpentine, and zigzag line types adapt to all kinds of space

Fig. 128. LEUCORYX (1949) by Robert Shuler. Variation of line width suggests movement in space. When the line serves for mass, the spatial movement modifies its plastic qualities, causing it to take on new dimensions.
Courtesy of the artist

Fig. 129. LA LEÇON D'ANATOMIE by Stanley William Hayter. Active lines can weave their way between the various spatial levels, periodically joining, overlapping, and moving behind each other.
Courtesy Bowling Green State Universtiy. School of Art Print Collection

through their unexpected deviation of direction and accent. They seem to move back and forth from one spatial plane to another. Unattached single lines seem to define their own space and may have plastic qualities within themselves. Lines also serve to clarify the spatial dimensions of solid shapes.

Shape and Space

In terms of space, *shape* may refer to planes, solids, or volumes, all of which occupy space, and are therefore entitled to consideration in this chapter. A plane, which to the artist is physically two-dimensional, may create the illusion of three-dimensional space (fig. 130). The space appears two-dimensional when the plane seems to lie on the picture surface (fig. 131). The space appears three-dimensional when it edges seem to converge at a point toward either the front or back of the picture plane.

Solids, volumes, and masses automatically suggest three dimensions. Such shapes express the space in which they must exist and actually become a part of it. Planes, solids, and volumes can be made to take a distant position by diminishing their size in comparison to others in the frontal picture areas and by neutralizing their value, color, intensity, and detail. This treatment relates back to the indications of space outlined earlier in this chapter (fig. 132).

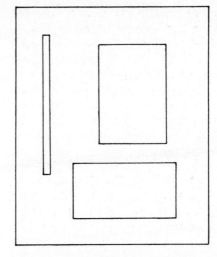

Fig. 131. Since the shape outlines consist of horizontals and verticals repeating the essential two-dimensional nature of the picture plane (as determined by the horizontal and verticals of the border), this diagram is an example of two-dimensional space-shape relationships.

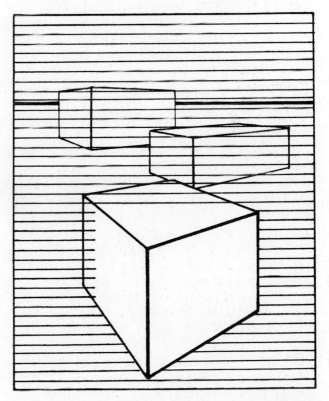

Fig. 132. The relationship of planes in this diagram describes an effect of solids or volumes which in turn seem to occupy space. The size, overlapping, and placement of these volumes further increase the effect of solidity. The horizontal shaded lines are used to indicate an imaginary position for the picture plane in order to cause a projection of the near-volume into the observer's space, or in front of the picture plane.

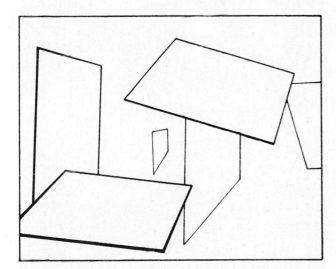

Fig. 130. In this example, the outlines of the two-dimensional shapes (or planes) are varied in thickness and placement, while two edges converge towards the back to give the effect of three-dimensional space. The overlapping of planes in the diagram also enhances the effect of hollowing out behind the picture plane.

Value and Space

The plastic effect of value can be used to control pictorial space. Light and dark spatial positions are based upon a consistent order of light source which operates reciprocally. When a light source is assumed to be in *front* of a work, the objects in the foreground will appear light. The middle and background objects will become progressively darker as they move away from the picture plane (plate 64). When the light source is located at the back of the work, the order of values will be reversed. The order of value change is consistent in gradation from light to dark or dark to light.

In the natural world, foreground objects are seen with clarity and great contrast, while distant objects are ill-defined and gray. Therefore, neutral grays when juxtaposed with blacks or whites will generally take a distant position.

Cast shadows are sometimes helpful in describing plastic space, but may be spatially confusing and even injurious to the design if they are not handled judiciously (*see* figs. 78 and 207).

It is very important to notice that *value-modeling can be abstract* in the sense that it need not follow the *objective natural order* of light and dark. Many artists have totally ignored this natural order, using instead the inherent spatial position resulting from the *contrast of dark and light* (fig. 133).

Fig. 133. MAP: SPIRIT OF '76 by Tony King. The format with its papier collé surface is perfectly flat, but use of light and dark values creates a strongly three-dimensional illusion.
Courtesy The Owens-Corning Collection. Owens-Corning Fiberglas Corporation, Toledo, Ohio

Texture and Space

Because of the surface enrichment which texture produces, it is frequently a temptation to think of this element purely in terms of *decorative* usefulness. Actually, texture functions *plastically* by describing the depth position of surfaces. Generally speaking, sharp, clear, and bold textures seem to advance, while fuzzy, dull, and minuscule textures recede. Textures when modified through varied use of value, color, and line should function as a significant contribution to the total pictorial unity.

Texture is one of the visual signs used to produce the decorative surface so valued by contemporary art. The physical character of texture is related to allover patterned design and, as such, operates effectively on decorative surfaces. When patterned surfaces are repeated and distributed over *the entire pictorial area,* the *flatness* of the picture plane becomes of vital importance. The works of Pablo Picasso frequently illustrate the contemporary use of texture surfaces to preserve the concept of the *flat picture plane* (fig. 134; *see also* fig. 133).

Color and Space

One of the outstanding contributions of the modern artist has been his reevaluation of the plastic potentialities of color. Color is now integrated directly into the form of the picture by being used in a positive and direct manner to model the various spatial planes of surface areas (*see* Chapter 8, Color). Since the time of Cézanne, a new awareness of the advancing characteristics of color is evident in art. Prior to this time, deep space was considered as beginning *with* the picture plane and *receding from it.* Today many artists, chiefly through the use of color, deal with the spaces on or *in front* of the picture plane. Hans Hofmann, the contemporary abstractionist, often used intense colors to advance shapes *beyond the picture plane* (*see* plate 51).

Analogous colors through their relationship create spatial movement, and contrasting colors provide varied accents or focal points of interest. Both are used to exploit the limitless dimensions of space (*see* plate 54).

RECENT CONCEPTS OF SPACE

Every great period in the history of art has espoused a particular type of space conception. These spatial preferences reflected basic conditions within the civilization which produced them. Certain fundamental space attitudes seem to recur in varied forms throughout recorded history. During the period of their influence, these attitudes become a norm of vision for the people, gradually conditioning them to see things in much the same way. As an epic social change ushers in a new space attitude it is resisted at first by the public but finally becomes the standard filter through which people see things. These changes were fairly cyclical and even predictable through the Renaissance. The acceleration of change prompted by the cataclysmic revelations of modern science has today produced new concepts which are without precedent. The artist is today groping for ways of understanding and interpreting these ever-widening horizons, and as he does, his explorations are met by characteristic recalcitrance from the public.

Search for a New Spatial Dimension

The artist of the Renaissance, conditioned by the outlook of the period, set as his goal the optical, scientific mastery of nature. He sought to accomplish this by reducing nature, part by part, to a *static geometric system.* By restricting his attention to one point of view, the artist was able to develop perspective and represent some of the illusionary distortions of actual shapes as seen by the human eye.

The modern artist, equipped with the findings from new scientific and industrial materials and technology, has extended the search into nature initiated by the Renaissance. He has probed into nature's inner and outer structure with the microscope, camera, and telescope; with the automobile and the airplane, he has had the opportunity to see more of the world than any of his predecessors. The radically changed environment of the artist has brought about a new awareness of space. It has become increasingly evident that the essence of space cannot be described from the one point of view characteristic of the Renaissance, and a continuing search has been instituted for a new graphic vocabulary to describe visual discoveries. Since one outstanding feature of the modern world is motion, new artistic representation must move, at least illusionistically. Motion has become *a part of space,* and this space can be grasped only if a certain *period of time* is allotted to cover it. Hence, a new dimension is added to spatial conception— the fourth dimension which combines the elements of space, time, and motion and presents an important graphic challenge. This challenge is the discovery of a practical method for representing things in motion from every viewpoint on a flat surface. In searching for solutions to this problem, the artist has turned to his own experience as well as to the work of others.

Plastic Image

Paul Cézanne, the nineteenth-century Post-Impressionist, was an early pioneer in the attempt to express the new dimension. His aim was to render objects in a manner more true to nature. This nature, it should be pointed out, was not the Renaissance world of optical appearances; instead, it was a world of forms in space, conceived in terms of a plastic image (fig. 135). In painting a picture of a still life, Cézanne would select *the most characteristic viewpoint* of all his objects; he would then change the eye levels, split the individual object planes, and combine all of these views in *the same painting,* creating a composite view of this group. Cézanne would often shift his viewpoint of a single object from the right side to the left side and from the top to the bottom, always creating the illusion of *looking around the object.* If one wished to see these multiple views, one would be forced to move around the object or revolve it in front of him. This act would involve *motion, space, and time.*

The *cubists* adopted many of Cézanne's pictorial devices. They usually showed the object from as many views as suited the discrimination

of the artist. Objects were rendered in a type of *orthographic drawing* in which the basic intention was division into essential views which could be drawn in *two dimensions*. The basic view is called a *plan*, one which might be thought of as the top view. When the plan was used as a basis, the *elevations* (or profiles) were taken from the front and back and the *sections* from the right and left sides. The juxtaposition of these views in a painting illustrated the *movement of the objects in space*. Such a painting was a composite which showed much more of the object than would normally be visible. The technique seems a distortion to the lay spectator conditioned to a static view, although within the limits of artistic selection everything is present which one would ordinarily expect to see (figs. 136 and 137).

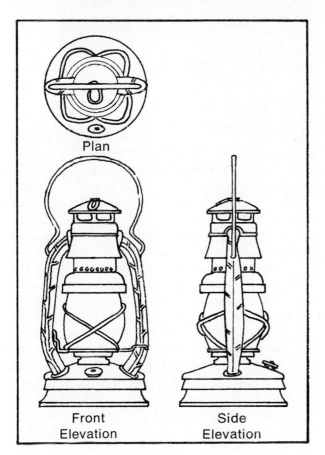

Plan

Front Elevation   Side Elevation

Fig. 136. KEROSENE LAMP by Tom Haverfield. This student work illustrates the following excerpt from the text—"Objects were rendered in a type of orthographic drawing in which the basic intention was division into essential views which could be drawn in two dimensions."

Fig. 137. The juxtaposition of orthographic views in a drawing illustrates the movement of objects in space. Such a drawing is a composite which shows much more of an object than would normally be visible.

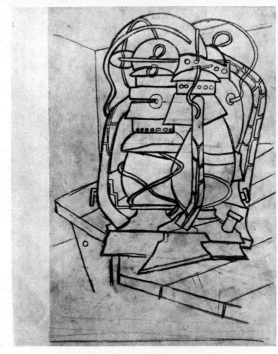

Fig. 138. THE CHESSBOARD (1917) by Juan Gris. Spatial movements formed in abstractly designed paintings give variety and interest to the pattern relationships. Natural spatial indications are ignored in favor of a more subjective interpretation of the objects represented.
Collection, the Museum of Modern Art, New York. Purchase

In the works of the cubists, we find the suggestion that a picture can have a life of its own,
and that the creation of space is not essentially
a matter of portrayal or rendering. Step by step
the cubist works to illustrate that the greater the
departure from *object resemblance*, the clearer
the *spatial order* may become. One of the off-
shoots of this discovery was the synthetically
designed picture, one which divorces itself from
the model (fig. 138).

Pictorial Representations of Movement in Time

From time immemorial, artists have grappled
with the problem of the representation of movement on the stationary picture surface. In the
works of prehistoric and primitive man, the efforts were not organized but were isolated at-

tempts to show a limited phase of observed
movement.

Greek sculptors organized the lines in the
draperies of their figures to accent *a continuous
direction*. By means of this device, the eye of
the observer is directed along a constant edge
or line. This was an early attempt to add movement to otherwise static figures.

The artists of the Medieval and Renaissance
periods illustrated the life and passion of Christ
by repeating a series of still pictures. The representation of the different phases of Christ's life
(either in sequence form or combined in a single
work) created a visual synopsis of His movement, the space He covered, and the time He
took to cover it. These pictures were the ante-
cedents of the modern comic and motion-picture
techniques which actually fill the gaps between
the still views in the final product.

Plate 59. WHEATFIELDS (c. 1670) by Jacob van Ruisdael. Early Dutch landscape painting, which aimed at the maximum illusion of visual reality, emphasized the infinite space concept. Diminishing sizes of objects and hazy effects of atmospheric perspective give the viewer a sense of seeing into far distances.

Plate 60. ST. ANTHONY DISTRIBUTING HIS WEALTH TO THE POOR (c. 1444) by Sassetta and Assistants. A shallow stage-like space is achieved in this early Renaissance painting. The work is composed in terms of two flat planes represented by the figures in front and the architectural structure in back.

Plate 61. SUNDAY AFTERNOON ON THE ISLAND OF LA GRANDE JATTE (1884-86) by Georges Seurat. The obvious progression of sizes in the figures of Seurat's painting are a strong indication of spatial recession. At the same time, these figures are carefully placed to give balance to the pattern of space and shape relationships.

Plate 62. BREEZING UP (1875-76) by Winslow Homer. The horizon line in this painting describes a separation of space into a ground plane below and a sky plane above. The smaller size and higher position of the distant boat helps to achieve the spatial effect.

Plate 63. A DUTCH COURTYARD (c. 1668) by Pieter de Hooch. This Dutch painting of the 17th century is an indication of the impact which the fixed perspective system of the Renaissance, 200 years previously, had upon the way artists "saw" space.

Plate 64. THE WATERMILL WITH THE GREAT RED ROOF (c. 1663-65) by Meindert Hobbema. Concerned with the lyric qualities of landscape painting, Hobbema commonly used backlighting. This created a unified gradation of dark moving towards a light though consistently atmospheric background.

Courtesy The Art Institute of Chicago.

Plate 65. DYNAMIC HIEROGLYPHIC OF THE BAL TABARIN (1912) by Gino Severini. The works of the Futurists were devoted to motion for its own sake. They included not only the shapes of figures and objects, and their pathways of movement, but also their backgrounds. These features were combined in a pattern of kinetic energy.

Collection, The Museum of Modern Art, New York. Acquired through the Lillie P. Bliss Bequest.

Another representational device used for the suggestion of movement is the superimposition of many stationary views of the figure or its parts in a single picture. This device catalogs the sequence of position of a moving body, indicating the visible changes of movement.

Twentieth-century artists have attempted to fuse the different positions of the figure by filling out the pathway of its movement. Figures are not seen in fixed positions, but as *moving paths of action*. The subject in Marcel Duchamp's *Nude Descending a Staircase* is not the human body but the type and degree of energy it emits as it passes through space. This painting signified important progress in the pictorialization of motion because the plastic forces are *functionally integrated with the composition* (fig. 139).

The works of the Futurists (see Futurism, Chapter 11) were devoted to motion for its own sake. They included not only the shapes of fig-

ures and objects and their pathways of movement, but also their backgrounds. These features were combined in a pattern of kinetic energy. Although this was not entirely new as a form of expression, it provided a new type of artistic adventure—simultaneity of figure, object, and environment (fig. 140 and plate 65).

The exploration of space in terms of the four-dimensional space-time continuum is in its infancy. As research reveals more of the mysteries of the natural world, art will continue to absorb and apply them according to their effect on human relationships. It is not unreasonable to assume that even more revolutionary concepts will emerge in time, producing great changes in art style. The important thing to remember is that distortions and unfamiliar forms of art expression do not occur in a vacuum—they usually represent earnest efforts to apprehend and interpret our world in terms of the latest frontiers of understanding.

Fig. 140. LEASH IN MOTION (1912) by Giacomo Balla. In an effort to conceive a solution to the problem of suggesting motion as it is involved in time and space, Balla invented the idea of repeated contours. This soon became a device commonly imitated in newspaper comic strips, thus losing aesthetic uniqueness.

Courtesy George F. Goodyear and the Buffalo Fine Arts Academy

Fig. 139. NUDE DESCENDING A STAIRCASE, No. 2 (1912) by Marcel Duchamp. "The subject in Marcel Duchamp's painting is not the human body but the type and degree of energy it emits as it passes through space."

Courtesy Philadelphia Museum of Art. The Louise and Walter Arensberg Collection

SPACE PROBLEMS

Problem 1

In conjunction with linear perspective, artists of the past frequently used diminishing contrasts of hue, value, and intensity of color and texture to achieve deep penetration of space on a two-dimensional surface. This is known as the infinite concept of space or atmospheric perspective.

Create a pictorial composition based on the theme "Objects in Space." Conceive of the picture plane as the near side of a volume of deep space. Use the indications of space suggested in the opening paragraph, plus softening edges of objects as they are set back in depth. The human figure may be used to help suggest the scale of objects in space. Foreground, middle ground, and deep space may be indicated by the size of similar objects.

Problem 2

Certain artists of the past, particularly the Egyptians, conceived of space in art as a two-dimensional arrangement. In effect, objects to be shown were placed vertically above one another or side by side. This is essentially a decorative space concept.

Attempt to keep the sense of the picture plane by eliminating all signs of three-dimensional space such as diminishing hue, value, and intensity of color or texture. Utilize objects such as those in Problem 1, but attempt to give the appearance that they lie upon and are a part of the surface of the picture. This is essentially a two-dimensional problem in semiabstract patterns (fig. 141).

Fig. 141.

Problem 3

Many artists today prefer some of the qualities of design provided by a decorative space concept but wish to retain some suggestion of three-dimensional depth.

a. Without radically altering the two-dimensional surface of the picture plane, create a semiabstract form using some of the spatial tools in Problem 1: i.e., gradation in size, placement in picture plane, overlapping, transparency, open or closed composition, closely related hues, values, and brightness. The effect created should be of a measurable depth, i.e., as if the furthest penetration into the space back of the picture plane were a few inches rather than infinite depth (fig. 142).

Fig. 142.

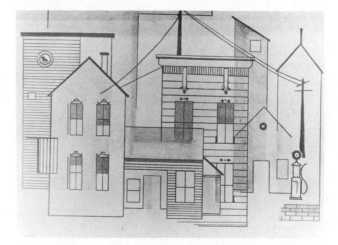

b. In this problem, conceive of the space back of the picture plane as somewhat similar to the effect in Problem 3a, but with the side planes, top plane, and ground plane as well as the back plane clearly defined by color, value, texture, or other means. Movement in depth should be resolved by returning it to the foreground through various devices. Use planes and solids to give form and pattern to the enclosed space. The concern is primarily with space itself in this problem, as contrasted to the relationship of objects in space in Problem 1.

Problem 4

Interior space problems have frequently been solved in varied ways by artists.

In this problem, conceive of an interior of enormous proportions defined by objects lighted from a fixed position in the space; a great railway or air terminal lighted by windows in the roof. The effect should be similar to Problem 1 and Problem 3b combined.

Problem 5

There are various ways of organizing objects in space. The following problems represent two variations of space organization.

Utilizing either abstract solids or realistic objects, organize the resultant volumes into a diagonal or circular series of movements penetrating into semideep space (fig. 143).

Fig. 143.

Problem 6

Many artists consider the unfilled portions of space as important as the solids occupying the space.

Beginning with objects such as those in a still-life setup or a landscape, define either a fairly deep space or a shallow space by emphasizing the hollows (negative areas) around and between the objects through the use of devices such as value, texture, and color. The result should be an abstraction which is concerned with the importance of negative areas in any kind of spatial organization as opposed to the attention to volumes in Problem 5.

Problem 7

Many contemporary artists consider transparency an important way of defining space.

Using linear perspective or parallel convergence of lines, create the effect of looking through transparent planes set at different angles to one another within a volume of space. Define several different distances in depth by having some planes opaque or semitransparent with color, texture, and value mix as the transparent planes meet.

Problem 8

Obviously decorative textures are visual signs often used by the contemporary artist to limit spatial indication. These decorative relationships permit more free interpretation of object shapes and permit variations which can contribute to organic unity of the pictorial elements.

The result is a shallow or decorative space concept.

Create a composition of forms derived from still-life, sculptural, or architectural forms. Omit indication of naturalistic light-and-shade, substituting decorative textures of lines, spots, stripes, and the like. Break up background areas into arbitrary shapes which seem related to objects and use treatment of decorative texture in some of these spaces as well. Solid tones of varying values and/or color may be used to keep the overall design from becoming too busy and overelaborate (fig. 144).

Fig. 144.

Problem 9

Cézanne and the Cubists often combined several viewpoints of a plastic image in one painting. The juxtaposition of multiple views in a single painting implies movement of the observer around the objects.

Select a single object to be used as a model for this problem. On three pieces of tracing paper draw the top or plan view, the elevation of profile view, and a section view of the same object to the same scale. Place these drawings one over another and combine in a single work the most characteristic parts of each view. Add value differences for contrast, variety, and enhancement of spatial position (fig. 145; *see also* figs. 136 and 137.)

Fig. 145.

Problem 10

An early representational device for suggesting movement as used by twentieth-century artists was superimposition of stationary views of a figure or its parts in a single picture.

a. Select a moving figure or object as a model. Draw a series of pictures representing this figure or object as it rotates, tilts, or falls in space. Each of the drawings should indicate a slight change of movement in space or position. Superimpose and place the drawings together in such a way as to suggest a continuous movement in space. This problem is not intended to create a complete pictorial organization but is an experiment in representing movement on a flat surface (fig. 146).

b. Select parts of the sequence of motion referred to in the above experiment. Combine these within the limits of a frame-shape so as to create an organized pattern. Add value differences for contrast, variety, and enhancement of spatial position.

Problem 11

Varying sizes of forms and their positions in relationship to each other and to the planes in picture space are traditional methods of space indication.

Make a contour drawing of a human figure which

is reasonably accurate as to proportion but greatly simplified in detail. Repeat this drawing about twelve times on a sheet (or sheets) of light gray construction paper, varying the size of the figures dramatically.

Cut the figures out and place them on a 9-by-12-inch sheet of white paper which has had a horizontal line drawn across it at an elevation of approximately 6 inches.

Using this line as an indication of the horizon, place the figures in location appropriate to their size in terms of distance. Some figures should be isolated and others gathered together to form groups. Make the figures overlap occasionally to accent spatial differences. Mix up the sizes in figure groups and note the variations in figures which are in proximity. Give the illusion of difference in stature as well as depth-distance (i.e., the figures would seem to indicate various age levels).

Note—Linear Perspective is a mechanical technique of optical illusionism which produces a standardized spatial effect based on the single viewpoint of the observer-artist. Many art teachers believe, and with some justification, that the inherent dangers in perspective outweigh its value. Others feel that it is an established form of vision and, as such, deserves some consideration, even though there may be violent disagreement on the desirable depth of instruction. We believe that there is some legitimacy to both of these views. The intricacies of perspective are too great to be covered successfully in this textbook. Consequently such problems are omitted, and the extent of study in this phase of art is left to the judgment of the individual instructor. If this book is not being used in connection with classroom work, the reader is advised to seek further information on perspective in works which deal specifically with the subject.

Fig. 146.

Chapter 10/The Art of the Third Dimension

Definitions:

Atectonic: The opposite of tectonic; a quality of three-dimensional complexity, involving fairly frequent and often considerable extension into space, producing a feeling of openness.

Bauhaus: Originally a school of architecture in Germany which flourished between World War I and World War II. The Bahaus attracted many of the leading experimental artists of both the two- and three-dimensional fields.

Form: 1. The total organization of a work of art (see Chapter 3, Form). 2. Three-dimensional sense: a portion of a three-dimensional work which has a certain degree of concavity or convexity.

Mass: The physical bulk of a solid body of material.

Patina: 1. A film, usually greenish in color, which results from oxidation of bronze or other metallic material. 2. Colored pigments, usually earthy, applied to a sculptural surface.

Shape (three-dimensional): The silhouette of an object or a portion of that object with awareness of the forms within.

Silhouette: The area existing between or bounded by the contours, or edges, of an object. The total shape.

Tectonic: Pertaining to the quality of simple massiveness, lacking any significant extension.

Three-Dimensional: Possessing the measurements of length, width, and thickness; a solid, surrounded by space.

Void: The penetration of an object to its other side, thus allowing for the passage of space through it. An enclosed negative shape.

Volume: 1. The space occupied by an object (preferred meaning). 2. The object itself.

In the preceding chapters, examination of art fundamentals was limited to discussion of the graphic arts. These art forms (painting, drawing, and printmaking) exist on a flat surface, and any sensation of space that they generate is the product of *illusion* created by the artist. This chapter deals with the unique properties of three-dimensional work and the creative concepts evolving from these properties.

Artists and critics use a number of terms to designate the three-dimensional quality of objects in space: among them are *form, volume,* and *mass.* The term *form* here can be misleading because it is likely to be confused with the larger meaning of *form* as defined in earlier chapters of this book. *Volume* can also be confusing, as it is often used to define the space occupied by an object, as well as the object itself. The term *mass* is somewhat less confusing because it almost invariably refers to an object in space, frequently with reference to its weight. *Shape* is another term that can also create difficulty as it most frequently pertains to flat images. Sculpturally, the term *shape* applies to the silhouette or outline of a work.

BASIC THREE-DIMENSIONAL CONCEPTS

In the widest sense all things in our environment have three-dimensional qualities, although in many cases these qualities are so microscopic that we tend to disregard them. In being three-dimensional, objects displace space, as indicated by the rectangular and ovoidal shapes in figure 147. The weight of these solids is felt and is established by planes which, whether flat or rounded, seem to push into space. The dimensions demonstrated by such objects are height, width, and depth.

Fig. 147.

Although the two solids illustrated are three-dimensional, their spatial indications are minimal. Any designed three-dimensional object whose dimensional features are restricted is not taking full advantage of its major asset. Viewers who are accustomed to the basic flatness of *graphic* works tend to see masses as a series of two-dimensional views rather than as total space-displacing units.

Fig. 148.

In figure 148, the four bricks as far as spatial dimension is concerned have been arranged in a

very restrictive manner. Collectively, they form a large, minimal rectangular solid. The individual bricks are distinguished only by the cracklike linear edges seen in the frontal and side planes. These linear edges are reminiscent of graphic techniques in which object surfaces are embellished without regard to the third dimension.

Fig. 149.

The four bricks illustrated in figure 149 are separated by indentations similar to the mortar joints used by masons. These gaps although relatively shallow nevertheless produce distinctively clearer and darker edges than those shown in figure 148. Line engravers use a similar technique in handling metal plates (*see* fig. 153). Although the darker edges indicate greater three-dimensional complexity than previous illustrations, the plastic quality still has decided limitations. The channeled edges in an engraved plate can actually be felt. Many shallow relief sculptures function within the kinds of limits imposed by the act of engraving (*see* fig. 154). Since depth is an integral ingredient of the plastic arts, the artist should make maximum use of this dimension within the limits of his concept.

Fig. 150.

The bricks in this arrangement show the increasing utilization of space (fig. 150). They are positioned so that the planes moving in depth are contrasted with the frontal and side planes, moving toward and away from the viewer. The light which strikes the grouping now produces stronger shadows and more interesting value patterns.

Fig. 151.

Although still in a compact and closed arrangement, the rotation of the bricks now brings new directions and spatial relationships into play (fig. 151). The work is becoming more truly sculptural as contrasts of movement, light, and shadow increase.

Fig. 152.

The greater variety of brick positions, particularly with the introduction of the diagonal in the tipped brick, creates far greater exploitation of space than other groupings (fig. 152). The *void* or open space adds a new and very significant factor which gives even greater emphasis to the three-dimensional quality of the arrangement by producing a direct link between the space on each side.

The visual appearance of three-dimensional objects such as chairs, motor cars, and buildings is to a considerable degree determined by the considerations of *plastic* form, or the creative arrangement of masses. These considerations are tempered by utilitarian and mechanistic functional requirements. Thus, the sculptor has a far greater degree of creative freedom since he is not restricted by problems of *use*. There is a generally accepted notion that the sculptural form of functional objects should expose, not hide, their function. Frank Lloyd Wright, the celebrated American architect, needed to understand both the fundamentals of engineering and art in order to shape many new materials to fit the function of his buildings. In this way he showed himself to be an artist in his handling of three-dimensional form (fig. 155).

Although the fundamentals of three-dimensional form are the principal concern of this chapter, this emphasis does not imply that the *plastic* arts are better than the *graphic* arts. Such an evaluation is not determined by dimensions or media. Any artist selects the means and form by which he will reach his creative goal, and his work is judged within the terms of these choices.

Fig. 154. **DEATH BY VIOLENCE, 1963, bronze by Giacomo Manzu.** Study for one of a series of panels for the doors of St. Peter's, The confining spatial limitations of relief sculpture are evident in this work by Manzu. In order to create a greater feeling of mass he has used sharply incised modeling which, in technique as well as effect, is similar to the engraved lines of the printmaker's plate. The crisp incising creates sharp value contrasts which accent movement as well as depth.

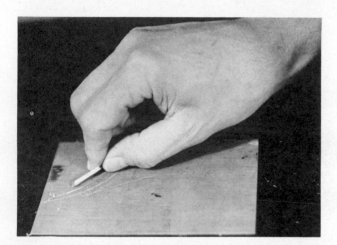

Fig. 153. The engraver uses his instrument, the burin, to cut furrows in the metal which will hold ink to produce a line. The engraved plate is a very shallow sculptural relief which is used to produce linear illusion in the print.

COMPONENTS OF THREE-DIMENSIONAL ART

Subject matter, form, and *content,* the components of graphic art, function in much the same manner with regard to the plastic arts. The emphasis on each of the components may vary within the three-dimensional arts of architecture, ceramics, metal work, and sculpture. Subject matter, for example, is taken from those objects and concepts having affinity for the third dimension and/or their functional needs. The human figure may be suitable as a subject for the sculptor, the ceramist, or the jeweler, but not for the architect. The human figure is *served* by the architect, but not depicted by him. One might say that the *subject matter* suitable for an architect are those consciously constructed forms that serve the *functional* aspects of human activity.

Formal organization is more complex in three-dimensional art than it is in the graphic arts.

Actual materials developed in actual space through physical manipulation exist in a tactile, as well as in a visual, sense. The resultant complexities expand the *content* or meaning of the form and add greater aesthetic dimension.

Materials and Techniques

In working with the three-dimensional arts, one will find that materials and techniques play more important roles than they do in the graphic arts. It is impossible to conceive of a three-dimensional structure without some consideration of its physical materials. Having become involved with these materials, the artist soon finds that he must conform to the physical laws governing their use. The clay modeler must understand the characteristics of clay and adapt

Fig. 155. ARMCHAIR (American, Ray Evans House, Beverly Hills, Illinois), Furniture, woodwork-oak by Frank Lloyd Wright. To Wright form and function were inseparable. The chair, which functions for sitting, should be considered along with the whole architectural environment. This armchair, an integral part of an enclosure of interior space to be lived in, was designed by Mr. Wright in the original scheme of the Ray Evans House.

Courtesy the Art Institute of Chicago. Gift of Mr. and Mrs. F. M. Fahrenwald

them to his concept. The structural characteristics of materials generally determine the techniques which can be used. For example, one would not use a saw to cut clay but would manipulate the material with his hands, a block, or a knife. The nature of the material sets limits to the structure to be created and the technique to be used. An understanding of materials and their techniques is necessary for their three-dimensional control. They are not ends in themselves, but are necessary ingredients in the development of the artist.

The Elements of Three-Dimensional Form

Three-dimensional form is composed of the visual elements *shape, value, space, texture, line, color,* and *time.* The order of listing is different from that for two-dimensional art and is based on significance and usage.

Shape

The artist working in three dimensions instinctively begins with shape. Shape, a familiar element in the graphic arts, takes on expanded meaning in the plastic arts. It implies the totality of the mass lying between its *contours,* including the *planes* creating the projections and depressions. We may speak of the overall space-displacing shape of a piece of sculpture or architecture, of the flat or curved shape that moves in space, or of a negative shape that is partially or totally enclosed. These shapes are generally measurable areas which are limited by and/or contrasted with other shapes, values, textures, and colors. It is important for the three-dimensional artist to clearly define the actual edges of shape borders. Ill-defined edges often lead to viewer disinterest

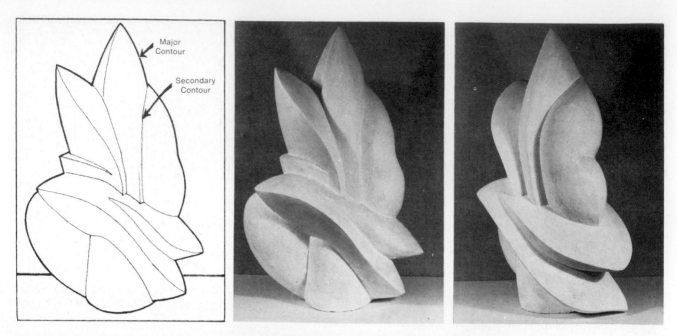

Fig. 156. *Left,* The major contour surrounds the silhouette, or the total visible area of the work. Secondary contours enclose internal masses. *Middle* and *Right* (Student work, plaster). Each change in position reveals new aspects of a three-dimensional work.

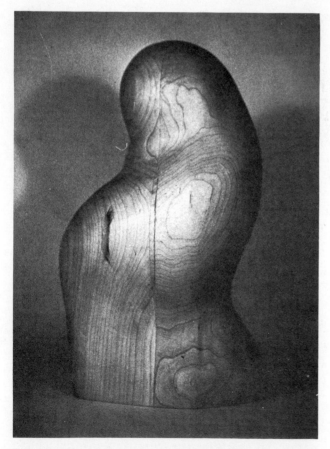

Fig. 157. (Student work, wood). In this example, tectonic because of its massive simplicity, secondary forms have less significance than they might in a more complex structure.

or confusion because they lack the authority to direct attention. The shape edges guide the eyes through, around, and over the three-dimensional surface in controlled movement.

In three-dimensional art, the visible shape depends on the viewer's position. A slight change of position will result in a change in shape. The outer limits are seen as *contours.* These contours are not essentially linear, however, as they are in graphic art. A major contour is viewed as the outer limit of the total three-dimensional work as seen from one position (fig. 156). Secondary contours are perceived as shapes moving across, back and forth, and between the major contours. Some three-dimensional works are constructed so that the secondary contours are negligible (fig. 157).

A shape can be a negative *space,* a three-dimensional open area surrounded by solid material. The open shape of this penetrated material is called a *void.* Alexander Archipenko, Henry Moore, and Barbara Hepworth are prominent twenty-century sculptural innovators who have pioneered in the use of the *void* (fig. 158). The void has provided varied opportunities for these artists: It has exposed interior surfaces, opened a direct route to the other side of the sculpture, reduced excessive weight, and created new spatial relationships for otherwise unexciting sur-

Fig. 159. (Student work, alabaster). Values are more abrupt and have greater contrast on angular forms than on curved forms.

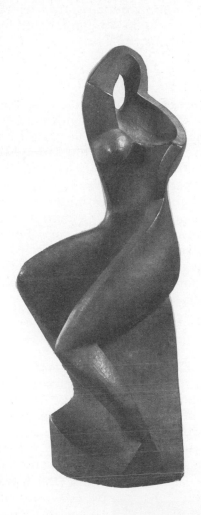

Fig. 158. WOMAN DOING HER HAIR (seated Black Concave) (ca. 1958 Bronze casting from plaster based on original terra cotta of 1916), by Alexander Archipenko. A significant example of scuptural form where the shapes create negative space, or a *void*. Archipenko was one of the pioneers of this concept which helped establish, a short time later, the fourth dimensional use of time, or motion in space. Courtesy the Kunst Museum, Dusseldorf, Germany and the Art Reference Bureau, Inc.

faces. Void shapes should be considered integral parts of the total form. In linear sculpture, enclosed void shapes become so important that they often dominate the width, thickness, and weight of the materials which define them.

Value

As the artist physically manipulates three-dimensional shapes, contrasting values appear through the lights and shadows produced by the forms. Value is the quantity of light actually reflected by the object surfaces. As in the other visual arts, three-dimensional values range from white to black. Surfaces which are high and facing a source of illumination will be light, while surfaces which are low, penetrated to any degree, or facing away from the light source will appear dark. Any angular change of two juxtaposed surfaces, however slight, will result in a change of value contrasts. The sharper the angular change, the greater will be the contrast (fig. 159).

When any part of a three-dimensional work blocks the passage of light, shadows result. Three-dimensional objects are solid, and any variation in arrangement creates partially or totally shadowed areas (fig. 160). The shadows change when the position of the work or of its source of illumination changes. If a work has a substantial shape variation and/or penetration, the shadow patterns will be more likely to define the work, regardless of the position of the light source. Sculptors who create mobiles demonstrate interest in the changing of light and shadow. The intensity of light will markedly change the shadow effect.

Value changes can also be affected by the addition of a pigmented medium to the surface of a three-dimensional work. Light pigments generally strengthen the shadows, while dark pigments weaken them. The more lightly pigmented media work best on those pieces which depend on secondary contours; darker pigmentations are most successful in emphasizing the

Fig. 160. (Student work, clay). The modeling by the artist, the source of illumination, and the opacity of the medium combine to create cast shadows, as seen from this view.

major contour. Thin linear structures which depend more on background contrast for visibility most often appear in strong dark or light silhouetted value (fig. 161).

Space

Space is created by adding the new dimension of depth to the height and width present in the work of the graphic artist. The plastic artist can change spatial effect by manipulating his three-dimensional materials. As he cuts the material away, the space moves inward, and as he adds material, the space moves outward. The artist can control space just as he controls the other elements. Space in the *graphic arts,* however, is an illusion and cannot be measured; it is a product resulting from use of the other elements. Thus, it is not itself considered an *element* as it is in the *plastic arts.*

Texture

Texture serves to enrich a surface, to complement the medium, and to enhance expression or content. Textured surfaces range from the hard glossiness of glass or polished marble to the roughness of fingerprinted clay (and bronze when cast) or weathered wood (fig. 162). Certain surfaces are indigenous to media, and tradition-

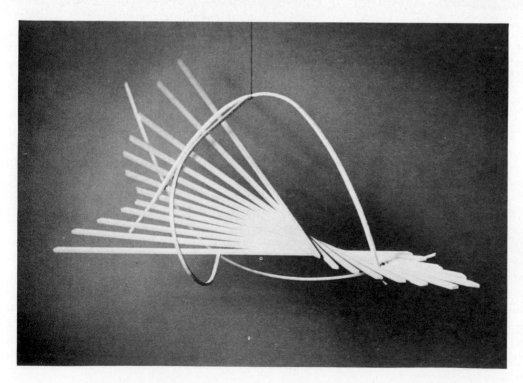

Fig. 161. (Student work, balsa wood mobile). The value of the background is an important factor in the visibility of some types of work.

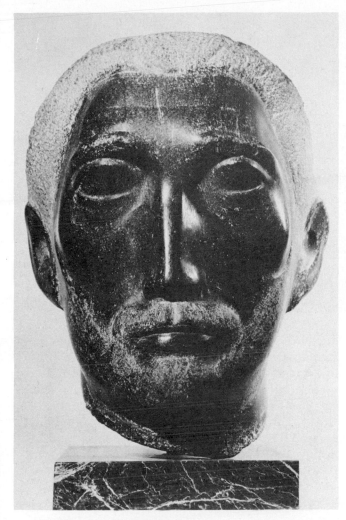

Fig. 162. HEAD OF CHRIST (1940) by William Zorach.
Zorach has polished portions of the surface of this head of
Christ in order to bring out the natural textural quality of
granite. He has roughened selected surfaces, which seems
suitable for stimulation of subject characteristics.
Collection, the Museum of Modern Art, New York. Abby Aldrich Rockefeller Fund

**Fig. 163. PORTRAIT OF RON RUSSEL (1974, painted
plaster) by Paul Johnson.** The surface character of a work
is selected by the artist to express his conception of the
subject's character and/or physical characteristics.
Courtesy of the Artist

ally, these intrinsic textures have been respected. However, artists sometimes surprise us
with a different kind of treatment. Patterns also
occur in the grain of wood; they are not truly
texture, although they function as such in orna-
menting the surface. The artist usually employs
texture as a distillate of the distinctive qualities
of the subject. The sleek suppleness of a seal, for
example, seems to call for a polished surface, but
the character of a rugged, forceful person suggests
a rough-hewn treatment (fig. 163). The actual,
simulated, and invented textures of the graphic
artist are also available to the plastic artist and
are developed from the textures inherent in his
materials.

Line

Line is a phenomenon not actually existing in
nature nor in the third dimension. It is primarily
a graphic device used to indicate the meeting of
planes or the outer edges of shapes. Its definition
might be broadened, however, to mean also the
axis of a three-dimensional shape whose length
is greater than its width. Within this context,
line would relate to the thin shapes of contemporary linear sculpture using wires and rods.
Development of welding and soldering techniques made possible the shaping and joining of
thin linear metals in sculpture. Such artists as

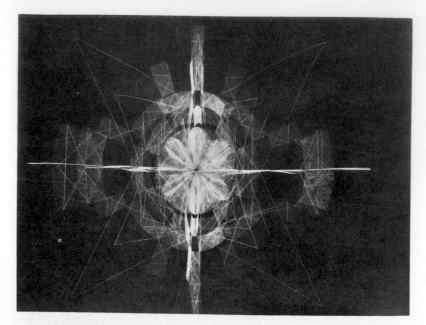

Fig. 164. VARIATION WITHIN A SPHERE, No. 10, The Sun (gold-filled wire) by Richard Lippold. Development of welding and soldering techniques for use in sculpture made possible shaping and joining of thin linear metals, as in this work by Lippold. Courtesy the Metropolitan Museum of Art. Fletcher Fund, 1956

Richard Lippold and José de Rivera have expanded the techniques of linear sculpture (figs. 164 and 166).

The incising of line in clay or in any other soft medium is similar to the graphic technique of drawing. In the history of three-dimensional art, incised lines were common, being used to accent surfaces for interest and movement. Giacomo Manzu, an Italian artist, employs such lines to add sparkle to his relief sculpture (*see* fig. 154).

Color

Color is also indigenous to sculptural materials. Sometimes it is pleasant, as in the variegated veining of wood or stone (fig. 165), but it can also be bland and lacking in character, as it is in the flat chalkiness of plaster. Pigment is often added when the material needs enrichment or when the surface requires color to bring out the form more effectively. The elements of value and color are so interwoven in sculpture that artists often use the terms interchangeably. Thus, an artist may refer to value contrasts as "color," actually thinking of both simultaneously. Many applications of color are an attempt to capture something of the richness and form-flattering

Fig. 165. HOLE (1973, alabaster) by William Provident. The artist must use the beauty of the graining or veining of the material to complement the form of his work. Excessive patternization can be a danger, for it can obscure structure. Courtesy of the Artist

Fig. 166. BRUSSELS CON-STRUCTION (1958, stainless steel) by Jose de Rivera. The concept of attracting the observer to a continuous series of rewarding visual experiences as he moves about a static three-dimensional work of art, led in the present century to the principle of having the work of art become kinetic or mobile, as with this sculpture set on a slowly turning motorized plinth.

Courtesy the Art Institute of Chicago. Gift from Mr. and Mrs. R. Howard Goldsmith.

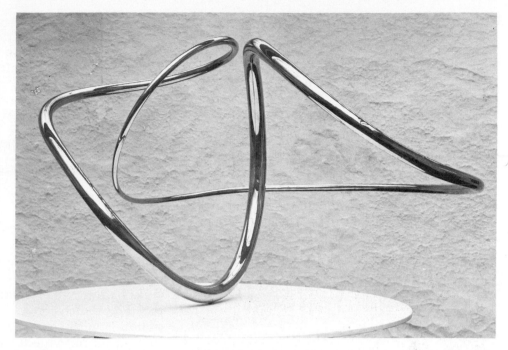

qualities of the patina often found on bronzes oxidized by exposure to the atmosphere. This approach stresses subdued color subordinated to structure of the piece. There have been, however, periods (for example, early Greek art) during which application of bright color was commonplace. Some revival of this technique is evident in contemporary works. In every case the basic criterion for its use is compatibility with the form of the work (plate 66).

Time

Time is an element unique to the three-dimensional arts. It is envolved in graphic arts only insofar as contemplation and reflection on meaning are concerned; the physical act of view-ing the work as a totality requires only a second. However, in a plastic work there is an added dimension which means that it must turn or that one must move around it if it is to be seen completely. It is important to the artist that the time required for the work's inspection be a continuum of rewarding visual variation. Each sequence of the viewing experience must display interesting relationships and lure the observer ever further around the work, extending the *time* spent on it.

In the case of sculpture called *kinetic,* the sculpture itself, not the observer, is in movement. Such works require time for their movements. Mobiles, examples of this kind of sculpture, present a constantly changing, almost infinite series of views (figs. 166 and 167).

Fig. 167. MOBILE: HORIZONTAL BLACK WITH RED SIEVE (1957, steel) by Alexander Calder. This noted artist introduced physically moving sculptures, called mobiles. Kinetics require time for observation of the movement, thus introducing a new dimension to art in addition to height, width, and space. The result is a constantly changing, almost infinite series of views of the parts of the mobile.

Courtesy the Toledo Museum of Art

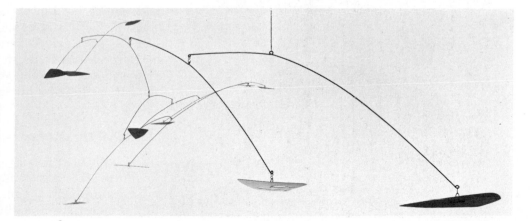

Principles of Three-Dimensional Order

The basic components of graphic art—*subject matter, form,* and *content*—also relate to the three-dimensional fields. Subject matter, the starting point, may be realistic or naturalistic, abstract to lesser degrees of likeness, or exist only as theme or concept. The underlying *content* or meaning derives from the artist's handling of form, as it does in graphic work. *Form* and its principles of order, which are the controlling factors in each work, have the same central importance. Although the principles are the same as those observed in two-dimensional work, the three-dimensional object with its unique spatial properties calls for a somewhat different application of those principles.

The plastic artist has the added responsibility of making his work function successfully from a variety of views. This makes the observance of the principles of order a much more complicated matter; the artist's satisfaction with one aspect of his work is not enough to make it a wholly effective piece. As a result, the three-dimensional work represents a continuous series of adjustments designed to give it a spatial wholeness or

Fig. 168. (Student work, welded steel). A work which features open space, usually as the result of thin, outreaching form, is called *atectonic*.

unity. The problems faced in arriving at this solution are related to the basic nature of the work as conceived by the artist. It may be tectonic, massive and simple with few and limited projections, or it may be atectonic, to a large degree open space with frequent and extensive, often quite thin projections (fig. 168; *see also* fig. 157). All works of architecture, jewelry, sculpture, ceramics, and fibers fall into or somewhere between these two classifications.

Obviously, when one considers the matter of artistic equilibrium (involving degrees of symmetry and asymmetry), the difficulties increase if the subject is of *atectonic* complexity, particularly when the balance must be felt from any viewpoint. *Balance* is partly the result of *proportion,* a significant three-dimensional factor. Proportion creates the silhouette, the basic shape, of the three-dimensional work; it determines the posture or major thrust of the work (*see* fig. 164). *Rhythm* is introduced with the adjustment of secondary masses to the major core masses which have established the basic proportion (*see* fig. 161). The secondary masses are varied in attitude and placement to develop movement around the core, relating the internal and external space to it. Semi-enclosed negative shapes resulting from incorporation of external space are significant factors in the *balance* and total silhouette (*see* fig. 168). The three-dimensional artist seeks *economy* because he, like his fellow workers in other areas, is interested in coming directly to the point by eliminating irrelevancies (*see* fig. 157). *Relative dominance,* the principle of assigning each area its proper degree of emphasis, is of course a vital concern of every artist (*see* fig. 160).

The dual concepts of *variety* and *harmony* are those which in proper combination produce unity in all forms of art, but there are differences of application in each field. In three-dimensional field, the issue is in the similarities and differences of the *plastic* forms involved. This means that the physical properties of size, character, location, and attitude, familiar to the graphic artist, should be considered, but in terms of translation into the third dimension.

Functional Three-Dimensional Art

The bulk of this book has addressed itself to the pure or fine arts, those works of art designed to have no practical function. However, in the three-dimensional arts, the situation changes, for

Courtesy Collection of the Whitney Museum of American Art. Gift of the Friends of the Whitney Museum of American Art.

Plate 66. WOMEN AND DOG (1964) wood plaster, synthetic polymer, and miscellaneous items by Marisol. 72 x 82 x 16 inches. An example of Pop Art which reveals the willingness of some contemporary artists to use bright color to heighten three dimensional characteristics of form at the same time that it enriches surfaces. The form further suggests sources in previous twentieth century styles; while the use of combine-assemblage tends to fuse the medias of sculpture and painting into one.

Plate 67. PENDANT NECKLACE, cast silvergilt with transparent enamel, cultured pearls, and a 55 carat rutilated kunyite, by Harold Hasselschwert. Articles of jewelry, although decorative in intent, often become sculptural in concept.

Plate 68. CONFLAGRATION, free hand-blown glass with hot design on opaque white glass, cased in colorless glass (1972) by Dominic Labino. The forming of glass requires an understanding of three-dimensional principles, as well as knowledge of the chemistry and techniques of the medium.

67.   68.

Plate 69. TWO PORCELAIN JARS by Charles Lakofsky. The aesthetic form of his ceramic ware is an important consideration of the potter.

Plate 70. SISAL HANGING by Kathleen Hagan. Contemporary textile design frequently goes beyond its largely two-dimensional traditions.

Plate 71. TOUCH TONE TRIM LINE TELEPHONE. This example of product design incorporates a streamlined aspect that enhances the three-dimensional beauty of the curved and planular shape relationships.

Courtesy of Bell Laboratories, Murray Hill, N. J.

69

70.

71.

Fig. 169. BELL TOWER, ST. JOHN'S ABBEY AND COLLEGE, Collegeville, Minnesota (Ca. 1967). Marcel Breuer, Architect. This structure, based on the traditional campanile of Romanesque cathedrals, is typical of the contemporary approach to three-dimensional design in architecture.

most of these works are intended to be used. Clearly, this fact has strong influence on the design of a three-dimensional work and more often than not puts some restriction on the creative latitude of the artist. Perhaps it would be well to list some of the general areas of three-dimensional design whose works usually serve some useful purpose:

1. Architecture (fig. 169)

2. Metal work (jewelry, and the like) (plate 67)

3. Glass design (plate 68)

4. Pottery (plate 69)

5. Weaving (fiber work) (plate 70)

6. Product design (plate 71)

7. Furniture design *(see* fig. 155)

There is a great deal of variety among the areas of design just listed, incomplete as it is. The items range in size from buildings to rings and in function from something to hold up one's garments to something that serves as personal adornment. Although they are all three-dimensional, their specific use modifies the degree to which three-dimensional design is the concern of the artist. A building is generally observable from all sides, and it has interior spaces as well as external surfaces. A piece of handmade fabric, on the other hand, may be little more three-dimensional visually speaking than a painting or drawing.

One thing these objects have in common, however, is *function* and its effect on their design. A famous architect, Louis Sullivan, made the oft-repeated remark that "form follows function." This concept has influenced several decades of design, changing the appearance of tools, telephones, silverware, chairs, and a vast array of other familiar and less familiar items. Sometimes this concept was misapplied. The idea of streamlining was practical when it was applied to moving objects such as trains and cars, but it had no logical application when used on spoons and lamps. Streamlining was helpful in a larger sense, however, in eliminating irrelevancies from design. Even the idea of simplification can be overdone. The *Bauhaus* notion of the house as a "machine for living" helped architects rethink architectural principles, but it also produced many cold and austere structures against which there was inevitable reaction.

The contemporary designer is very much aware of the function of the objects he designs and tries to design them so that they express and aid this function. On the other hand, he is probably more conscious than his fellow artists of a few years ago of the need for these objects to be aesthetically pleasing. All of this points up the necessity for the designer to be a "practical artist," applying the principles of formal order within the strictures of utilitarian need.

THREE-DIMENSIONAL PROBLEMS

Problem 1

Three-dimensional linear sculpture is usually made of metal wires and rods welded or soldered together. This type of work may be simulated by using balsa wood.

Select strips of balsa wood of varying lengths and thickness and glue them together to create a structure to be suspended in space. Begin with larger forms and then introduce smaller forms which may be accented by filling in the open spaces with colored paper, tissue paper, or cellophane (figs. 170 and 171).

Problem 2

Open structures and/or mobiles can be produced using strips of wood.

Construct open cubes or pyramids from balsa strips. Accent some of the interior planes by stretching a series of threads or strings which go from one side to the other. They may then be suspended from each other in various ways to create a mobile. Adjust the balance by moving the threads. Fishing tackle swivels can be used for suspension (fig. 172).

Fig. 171.

Fig. 170.

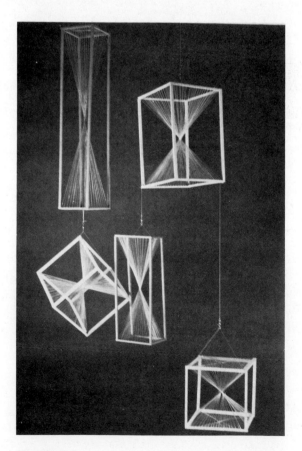

Fig. 172.

Problem 3

Voids add interest to a three-dimensional structure and should be varied in character and structure.

Cut strips of ¾-inch soft pine. Fasten the strips together with small nails and/or glue to create open box-like forms of different sizes. They can be next to, on top of, or within each other to create unified structures. Consideration of size and space will result in greater interest (fig. 173).

Fig. 173.

Problem 4

The sculptor may organize the space around and within a main mass by cutting into it or by building it outward.

Cut five or six blocks of varying size and proportion from soft white pine. Cut smaller blocks from within the larger blocks. The second step will leave blocks which now contain negative shapes. Assemble any number of the blocks by gluing them together. Work for variety in inward-outward movement (fig. 174).

Problem 5

A work is considered harmonious when its different parts contain similarities.

Start with one block about 7 to 10 inches in size. This may be a simple rectangular form or one which is partly curved. Divide this block into three shapes

Fig. 174.

by cutting it with a band saw. Experiment with arranging these three shapes together into one main mass. Slight alteration of shape may be made if necessary. When satisfied with the total effect, glue the shapes together (fig. 175).

Problem 6

Economy is achieved by using abstraction, as it is in the graphic arts. When resistant materials are used, simplified concepts are encouraged.

Plan a simple human or animal form by making several preliminary sketches. Transfer various views of a selected sketch to the four sides of a block of plaster, wood, salt, or water clay. The proportions of the images on each side must match. Carve away the figure by using the appropriate tools (if wood is chosen, a saw may be used). When the excess material has been removed, the forms may be smoothed and the edges rounded (fig. 176).

Problem 7

Cardboard (mat board or illustration board) is a material easily manipulated when experimenting with three-dimensional form. It may be cut easily with scissors, razor, or sharp knife and the pieces glued together.

a. Make three simple forms which have flat planes such as cubical or pyramidal shapes. Experiment

Fig. 175.

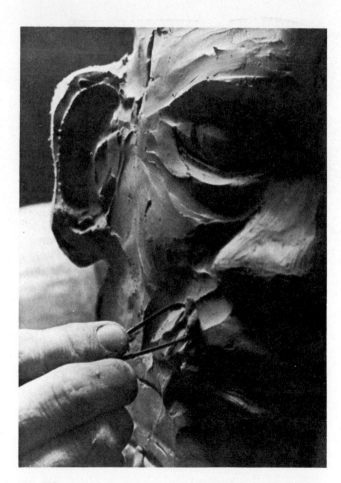

Fig. 176.

Fig. 177.

with various arrangements of these three shapes so that they create one sculptural mass. Holes may be cut into the planes to create interesting voids. Interpenetration of forms can be used if there is careful advanced planning (fig. 177).

b. A simulated relief sculpture can also be created by gluing flat pieces to a background (fig. 178).

c. Strips of cardboard or heavy paper can also be used within a boxlike frame to create a spatial effect (fig. 179).

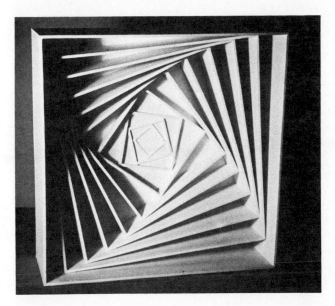

Fig. 178.

Fig. 180.

Fig. 179.

Problem 8

The advent of welded metal and the use of wire have expanded linear three-dimensional form in sculpture.

Select a subject to be used as a model for this problem or work directly and let the linear material suggest the subject and/or the form for a single sculpture. Form and bend manually malleable wire of about 12 feet in length and ⅛ inch in diameter. Work the wire as a graphic artist would a continuous line in a drawing, stopping only to change direction or to join an intersection of wire. Generally, it is best to begin with larger shapes and progress to smaller shapes and details. Remember that the directional qualities of line and wire can suggest movement. Work for interest from a variety of views (fig. 180).

Chapter 11 / Forms of Expression

DEFINITION OF EXPRESSION

The fixing of an image, whether it be oil pigment on canvas or pencil upon drawing paper, is only one aspect of the act of artistic creation. The character or personality of this formal image is determined as much by the artist's mental and emotional response to subject matter as by his choice of media and manipulation of tools. Kepes says:

The image grows in the sense that man sees what he wants to see. As each tool has its own unique way of living on the picture surface, so each individual has his own way of binding optical signs into shapes and images that he would like to see.[1]

Expression in art is primarily concerned with the intangible quotient of creativity previously mentioned in Chapter 2, The Nature of Art. It is this unique creative urge and its formal crystallization which art critics consider when making the distinction between ordinary artists and those who are truly marked with genius.

The artist may be said to express his feelings about life growing out of his continuing experiences with people, places, events, objects, and ideas. These experiences, interwoven with the associations and sentiments of memory, are molded or reworked in the mind through the artist's understanding of artistic values. Finally, this feeling image is given *form* and *meaning* through the artist's mastery of his chosen medium. Expression becomes the stylistic *form* in which the artist couches his sensual-visual *meaning*; it is an attempt to say something about his *subject* in terms of his own time. Expression is thus directly related to the basic components of a work of art.

CLASSIFICATION OF EXPRESSION AS STYLISTIC FORM

There are two broad classifications of *expression* as stylistic form: *individual* and *group*. Group expressions are those of a society as a whole which come into being and achieve sophistication with the birth and growth of its culture. An example of group expression is the development in ancient Greek civilization of idealism wherein the artist saw humanity transfigured by its destiny. Within such group expression, social changes affect *style* so that quite discernible variations of attitude toward *subject, form,* and *meaning* take place. These variations can be traced from the lively *conceptualism* of early Greece (seventh century B.C. to early fifth century) through the refined *perceptualism* of the Classic Age (late fifth century to fourth century B.C.) to the Hellenistic Age (fourth through the third centuries B.C.) when there was a gradual loss of artistic values in favor of purely associational, imitative, and academic qualities.

The individual expressiveness in the handling of subject matter, form, and content seems more appropriate to our own time than to the group expression of the past. This is probably due to present-day extollation of self-assertion and individualism. Although general groupings or categories of artists with similar intentions may be made in the art of the nineteenth and twentieth centuries, hosts of variations within these basic directions are discernible. The contemporary accent on individuality has resulted in a greater

1. Gyorgy Kepes, *Language of Vision* (Chicago: Paul Theobald & Co., 1951), p. 194.

diversity of artistic expression since mid-nineteenth century than in art previous to that time.

A summarization of the movements in the art of today will make us realize that the traditions of the past did not suffer wholesale rejection. Actually, these traditions have merely been reevaluated in the light of modern tastes. The changing concepts of physical beauty down through the ages illustrate the fact that each period has its own standards of taste—women in paintings by Rubens look rather bulky in comparison with our modern concept of fashion-figure slimness. In a like manner, certain artists of the past who were once rejected are now preferred to many others; occasionally, even a whole artistic tradition, once considered of great significance, may be relegated to a lower level of consideration. No tradition of the past, whatever its direction, should be completely rejected because it is possible to find something of beauty or quality in each of them. It is essentially a matter of orienting ourselves to see those qualities in the same way that their creator saw them. It is this manner of seeing which explains why once-rejected traditions are now wholly acceptable and even preferred to those which were at one time considered to be of greater significance.

The varied forms of expression in contemporary art may be accounted for by the psychological and sociological changes that occurred in the late nineteenth- and early twentieth-century art. The scope of this book does not permit us to completely explore these backgrounds, so this chapter is limited to a simplified account of the successive movements and an attempt to explain their primary artistic aim. Many fine books and articles giving more complete treatment are available to challenge students who wish to explore these backgrounds more deeply.

Nineteenth-Century Forerunners of Twentieth-Century Art

All of the forms of expression in nineteenth-century art have contributed in some degree to the character of art movements in the present century. Surprisingly, twentieth-century art in general may be considered a reaction to all art since the latter half of the eighteenth century. Without a background of understanding, it becomes impossible to see that present-day art developed out of the art produced in the past.

Until the middle of the last century, artists were still directly inspired by the visual appearance of the world around them. With the invention of the camera, however, science disposed of difficulties remaining in the imitation of natural appearance. By that time, artists as well had so completely solved the problem of representing reality that they were compelled to search for new directions of expression. Some turned toward introspection in their search for new forms; others looked toward the reevaluation of concepts of artistic form which prevailed prior to the Renaissance. These included the ideals of ancient Greek art, forms of expression used by primitive man, and styles characteristic of the medieval period. The opportunity to examine photographs of hitherto unknown art manners (Oriental art and that of the American Indian) provided a background for evolution in new directions.

Economic influences, many of which still affect the art of today, also played a part in this search for new principles of expression. For the past two hundred fifty years, the artist had depended for his economic welfare on the patronage of a wealthy clientele. Rather than assert their own inventiveness and individuality, artists gradually adopted the less aesthetic viewpoint of their patrons, the wealthy aristocrats and burghers. Many artists were content to supply works of art which were designed to satisfy and flatter the vanity of their patrons. A few great artists naturally evaded such bonds of artistic degradation and drew their inspiration from the society around them as well as from universal meanings.

Neoclassicism

The earliest new principle—actually the rediscovery of older intentions in art—was an attempt to seek freedom from this economic bondage. Reaction to the earlier "patronized" form of art resulted in the formation of formal institutions such as the French Academy. The art of the Academy was characterized by rules for achieving correct works of art which contained messages of a high moral order. Artists involved in the Neoclassic movement at the beginning of the nineteenth century did not reject patronage so much as they rejected the class of people who had patronized the artist of the eighteenth century. Such prominent artists as Jacques Louis David and Jean Auguste Ingres largely replaced the patronage from the effete French aristocracy with that from the Napoleonic State and the upper middle class (fig. 181).

Romanticism

The first group of artists to reject any kind of servitude to a patron, or even to a class of patrons, were the Romantics. They may be considered the first revolutionaries of modern times because of their concern with the work of art itself rather than with its significance for a patron or even for an observer. The true revolutionary realizes that he does not have to seek an audience; if he has something worthwhile to say, people will eventually be convinced of his viewpoint. This has become one of the fundamental principles underlying the creative art of our time. As a result of this revolt, the artist has based his expression upon his own inspiration and his study of past traditions; he is again tuned to the world of all human experience. However, in this world the artist has found many contradictions; as a result, we find many contradictions in present-day art.

The most important artists of the Romantic

Fig. 181. OATH OF THE HORATII (1786) by Jacques Louis David. A cold, formal ordering of shapes with emphasis on the sharpness of drawing characterized the Neoclassic form of expression. Both style and subject matter seemed to be derived from ancient Greek and Roman sculpture.
Courtesy the Toledo Museum of Art. Gift of Edward Drummond Libby

Fig. 182. EL FAMOSO AMERICANO MARIANO CEBALLOS (ca. 1815) by Francisco Goya. The Romanticism of Goya is here displayed in both his choice of subject matter and characteristic dramatic use of light-and-dark values.

Courtesy Philadelphia Museum of Art. Purchased: the McIlhenny Fund

group were: Eugene Delacroix in France, Francisco Goya in Spain, Joseph M. W. Turner in England, and Albert Pinkham Ryder in the United States. Illustrations of the paintings of some of these men show the characteristics of the movement (fig. 182 and plates 72 and 73).

Realism and Naturalism

Where the art of the Romantics had been a reaction to the pseudoclassic, academic formulas of Neoclassicism, the Realist movement was a reaction against the exotic escapism and literary tendencies of Romantic art. Wishing to avoid the pretentious attitudes of the previous group and stimulated by the prestige of science, the Realists wanted to show the world as they thought it

appeared to the average layman. Although attempting to avoid mere surface appearances, they wanted to give a sense of immediacy which they found missing in the idealistic expression of Romantic and Neoclassic artists (fig. 183; *see also* plate 62). A related group, now known as Naturalists, wanted to go beyond the results achieved by the Realists. Their attempts to make a visual copy of nature, exact in all its minute details, were probably influenced by the results obtained with the newly invented camera (plate 74; *see also* fig. 2 and plates 33 and 43).

Impressionism

In the nineteenth-century movement of Impressionism, we find a strong shift toward the contemporary view in art; the *form* of the work of art (materials and methods) was emphasized rather than significant *subject matter* from nature. Where previous movements had developed the trend toward freedom of choice in subject matter, the Impressionists contributed a new technical approach to painting which stressed the artist's interest in the appearance of his work in terms of *form* as much as in the appearance of nature. Impressionism represented the transition between tradition and revolution. The Impressionists still wished to show nature in its most characteristic way, but were mildly revolutionary in using technical aids to represent special conditions of light and atmosphere.

The Impressionists' interest in the illusion of light and atmosphere required intensive study of the scientific light theory of color and the effect of light on the color of objects. They discovered the principle of juxtaposing complementary colors in large areas for greater brilliance; they interpreted shadows as composed of colors complementary to the hue of the object casting those shadows. To achieve the vibratory character of light, they revived the old principle of *tache* painting, a technique in which the pigment is put on the canvas in thick spots which catch actual light and reflect it from the surface. The tachist method of painting seems to have been invented by the Venetians of the sixteenth cen-

Fig. 183. ADVICE TO A YOUNG ARTIST by Honoré Daumier. Influenced by a climate of scientific positivism, the artists of the Realist movement strived toward a recording of the world as it appeared to the eye, but interpreted with overtones of timeless quality. This painting by Daumier suggests not so much the particular appearance of costume and setting but rather the universal quality in the subject—the "idea" that the working people of all ages have similar qualities.

Courtesy National Gallery of Art, Washington, D.C. Gift of Duncan Phillips

tury and may be seen in the work of Titian (*see* plate 31). Later application of the technique may be found in the painting of Hals, Goya, and Constable. The Impressionists employed the style in a new way by using complementary hues in the dabs of pigment; when seen at a distance, they tend to form fused tones from the separate hues.

Local color was all important to the Impressionists because their whole intent was to capture the transitory effects of sunlight and shadow or of any kind of weather condition. Landscape became the favorite subject matter of the Impressionist painter because of the variability of local color under changing weather conditions.

Traditional ways of artistic interpretation underwent a second alteration when the Impressionists discovered the fascinating possibilities of unexpected angles of composition. The new photographic views of the natural scene were often different from the conventional arrangements used by artists for many years. This attitude was also partially encouraged by the character of oriental block prints being imported into France for the first time. These prints were often cropped down for shipment to Europe; as a result, many had curious, truncated composition which seemed unique to western artists.

Artists representative of Impressionism in France about 1870 were Claude Monet, Camille Pissarro, Auguste Renoir, and sometimes Edgar Degas (plates 75 and 76; *see also* plates 8, 46, and 54). There were deficiencies in Impressionist theory which caused some artists in the group to separate and pursue their own direction. One of the principal deficiencies was the loss of structural form resulting from the acceptance of surface illusion alone. A second was related to the effect which outdoor lighting has on the way an artist sees color. In strong sunlight, it was difficult to avoid making greens too raw, and there was a tendency to overload the canvas with yellows.

Nineteenth-Century Sculpture

At this point it seems appropriate to turn to nineteenth-century sculpture in order to trace the factors leading to the changing values in the twentieth century. However, we must retain the original principle that this text is an elucidation of fundamentals and, therefore, restrict the discussion primarily to sculptors who manifested an outstanding influence on the course of sculpture.

First, we should point out variances between the points of view and procedures of painters and sculptors. This we have done in Chapter 10, The Art of the Third Dimension. In beginning this analysis of sculptural expression let us reiterate some features of that chapter. Of importance in this frame of reference is the fact that the major difference between painting and sculpture lies in the elements of material and regard for space.

Painters work with flexible materials in an additive manner, and in their concern for space must not only invent their own illusion, but also invent the kinds of volumes or nonvolumetric shapes that seem to occupy that space.

Sculptors, on the other hand, work with tangible materials, creating actual volumes in actual space. Obviously, the thinking of sculptors is dominated most by the weight and mass of the materials they employ. Yet, paradoxically, the thinking of nineteenth-century sculptors was primarily painterly, or additive. Clay modeling dominated the procedures and thinking. Modeling is primarily an additive, rather than a subtractive, process. Thus, when it is said that nineteenth-century sculptors lost sight of traditional sculptural values, it was due to the strong dominance modeling had during that time.

Another factor leading to revolutionary changes in sculpture during the early twentieth century was caused by inhibitions imposed by the vested authority of various European academies. More so than in painting, commissions to sculptors were awarded on the basis of fidelity to nature and to observance of the classical principle of using the human figure to personify abstract ideals or symbolic meanings. Is it any wonder that the best sculptural talent was submerged by such strictures on originality of expression, or that sculptors more than painters in the nineteenth century lost sight of the older fundamentals of their craft?

It can be stated with some confidence that there really was a void in innovative sculpture during the nineteenth century until Auguste Rodin. True, there were men who could handle the tools of sculpture with virtuoso dexterity, and there is a great deal that is admirable in their handling of resistant materials like marble or malleable materials such as the clay from which bronze castings are made. Unfortunately the thinking behind their work was not definably different from ideas that had been in existence for about three hundred years, or since the early

Fig. 184. TIGER DEVOURING AN ANTELOPE (1851, bronze) by Antoine Louis Barye. Barye's use of emotionalized romantic form is similar in dynamism to the intense coloristic qualities of Romantic painters such as Delacroix and Turner.
Courtesy the Philadelphia Museum of Art. The W. P. Wilstach Collection

Renaissance. Antonio Canova, the outstanding early nineteenth-century classical sculptor, and Jacques Louis David, his counterpart as a painter, merely reestablished the classical ideal of the allegorical figure representation. If we compare Canova with any of the great originators of the past such as Donatello or Michelangelo, however, he pales into insignificance. His figures seem artistically lifeless. Their expression depended on attention to surface detail and on mannered gestures demonstrating a somewhat borrowed attitude in representing beauty of the human form, rather than a new way of using sculptural materials to express human life. The Romantic sculptor, Antoine Louis Barye, seems more original in his grasp of the essentially dynamic, monumental, and ferocious character of animal life, his favorite subject (fig. 184). But the idea behind Barye's use of animals in combat or feeding on their prey followed the essentially Romantic principle of evoking human emotional parallels which had been in existence at least since the seventeenth century. Then they had been expounded by the great Dutch philosopher Baruch Spinoza. Old values and thinking were merely being reiterated rather than new forms being invented expressive of man in nineteenth-century life.

The examples just given may help the student to grasp why of all nineteenth-century sculptors only Auguste Rodin was the dominant figure working in the three-dimensional form during the century. Rodin was an artist who looked to the past as well as to the future. He provided in the historical sense the break between traditional representation and nineteenth-century emphasis on modeling and the beginning of the new attitudes stressing materials, form, and expression exploited by twentieth-century sculptors.

Although he was never a direct follower of the Impressionist movement, Rodin worked in a manner which was often like that of the painters of the movement. But Rodin went far beyond Impressionism. His search into the realm of new ways to express emotional states directly through form was to be one of the crucial directions that evolved in the early part of the twentieth century. Rodin's attitude parallels the endeavors of expressionistic Post-Impressionist painters such as Vincent van Gogh and Toulouse-Lautrec.

Rodin's impressionistic effects come from dependence on the way light falls upon his forms to suggest the musculature and bony structure of his figures. Soon, he expanded this impression of form to express the inner condition of man as it was understood toward the end of the century (an often-used theme of Symbolist painters, followers of Paul Gauguin).

In his late work, Rodin also tended to see sculptural form in terms of fragmentary objects, probably the result of criticism of his early work as being too literal. Rodin's *Age of Bronze* of 1870 (fig. 185) was so implicitly naturalistic that salon critics insinuated that he had cast it from a living model. Tremendously upset by this criticism, Rodin moved away from ostensibly literal effects toward the expression of psychological or emotional states. During this change he rediscovered the principle of suspended or fleeting movement, due partly to its exploration by some contemporary painters (Degas, Toulouse-Lautrec) and partly to his own study of the great seventeenth-century sculptor Giovanni Lorenzo Bernini. Rodin greatly admired Michelangelo also and tried to restore sculptural values such as the feeling for the ponderousness and texture of stone and the contrast between highly polished surfaces and unfinished roughness which he discovered in Michelangelo's work, and which he felt had been lost since that sculptors' time.

In his renewal of such old aims, Rodin was led to an interest in the play between volume and mass and the interplay between hollows and protuberances. Clay and wax remained his favorite materials in which to sketch or create new forms, and he carried the great malleability of these materials into finished bronze castings so well that the observer can feel the tactile sensations of thrust and pressure used in the process of forming. Thus, Rodin no longer used a primarily modeling approach to produce naturalistic figures as his nineteenth-century predecessors had aimed to do.

Certainly, Rodin was a paradox during his lifetime since he was first denounced for being too natural and, then, in his late work criticized again for creating unnatural distortions. He ran the gamut between sweetly bland sculptures in marble and plaster to others that suggested mauled, distorted, amputated bodies—fragments of human form in plaster and bronze. From Michelangelo he learned the trick of letting a figure or head emerge from a roughly finished

Fig. 185. AGE OF BRONZE (1876, bronze) by Auguste Rodin. Rodin was excited by the possibility of expressing human psychological states. In early works, such as the example illustrated, he used a quasi-Impressionistic effect of natural light to suggest the quality of human anatomy as the outward form of mental processes.

Courtesy the Detroit Institute of Arts. Life Interest Gift of Robert H. Tannahill

Fig. 186. DANAÏDE (1885, marble) by Auguste Rodin. An example of the sculptor's later work in marble which reflects Michelangelo's influence in its partially revealed form emerging from the roughly finished stone. The psychological effect of such a work helped to bring about twentieth century expressionist art.

Courtesy the Musée Rodin, Paris, France and the Art Reference Bureau, Inc.

block of stone (fig. 186). These figures and parts of figures tend to suggest man's striving against fateful forces. Expressionistic sculpture was initiated by the strange psychological effect of such works since some early twentieth-century sculptors used it mainly for emotional effect.

Like Michelangelo, Rodin also enlarged limbs or gave them a painful twist as did Bernini, and he gave figures unnatural torsion and dimension in order to emphasize the effect of inner torment and potential power. Thus, the tense, turbulent, distorted side of Rodin's work predicted the future and paved the way for the sculptors of the twentieth century to escape the academic inhibitions that had ruled so much art in the nineteenth century. Rodin's career also reconfirms the fact that it is always the individual genius who leads the way to new ideas and forms. Most artists, substantive though they may be, tend to profit from only one or two of the directions foreseen by the genius.

Post-Impressionism

Late in the nineteenth-century, painters who had once been inspired by Impressionist theories began to abandon many of the principles of the movement. The most important artists in this reaction were Paul Cézanne, Paul Gauguin, and Vincent van Gogh. From these three pioneers stem the major expressions or directions of twentieth-century art.

This group of artists was later classified under the term Post-Impressionism, an ambiguous title

Fig. 187. PINES AND ROCKS (ca. 1904) by Paul Cézanne. Cézanne looked for the essential "essence" of natural forms rather than for mere surface description. In this painting, the artist has simplified the tree and rock shapes to produce a solid compositional unity.

Collection, the Museum of Modern Art, New York. Lillie P. Bliss Bequest

meaning "following Impressionism." This vague title does not satisfactorily indicate the far-reaching objectives of the artists in the movement. These artists sought (1) a return to the structural organization of pictorial form, (2) an emphasis on decorative organization for the sake of unity as well as for the enchanting patterns which might result, and (3) a more or less conscious use of exaggeration of natural appearance for emotionally suggestive effects (commonly called *distortion*) (*see* fig. 135). Cézanne may be said to represent primarily the first of these aims, Gauguin, the second, and Van Gogh, the third; each, however, incorporated some aspect of the other's objectives in his form of expression. It was these similarities which cause them to be grouped in the same movement, although, unlike the Impressionists, they worked independently toward their goals.

Cézanne was the dominant artist in the Post-Impressionist movement. In a manner contrary to the haphazard organization and ephemeral forms of the Impressionists, he saw a work of art in terms of the interrelationships of all of its parts. He retained the individual color spots of the former group, but in his painting these became building blocks in the total physical structure of the work (*see* plates 45 and 55). Although he may be called an *analyst* of reality rather than a *recorder* of reality (like the Impressionists and Naturalists), he went beyond mere analysis. Reality, for him, was not the object in nature from which he drew his inspiration, but rather represented all of the artistic conclusions arrived at in the completed work. He conceived of reality as the totality of expression derived from the appearance of nature as it became transformed in the mind and under the artist's hand. Therefore, although Cézanne found his beginning point in nature (as was traditional), he became the first artist of modern times to consider the appearance of his *pictorial form* more important than the *forms of nature*, themselves (*see* plate 15).

In this search for his own kind of reality, he looked beneath the surface matter of the world for the universal or changeless form. He once wrote to a friend that he found all nature reducible to simple geometric shapes such as cones, spheres, and cubes. The essentialness of these forms seemed more permanent to Cézanne than the transient face of nature (fig. 187). Due to the intellectual processes involved in his realizations of form, he is considered a classicist in spirit; nevertheless he became the forerunner of mod-

ern Cubism as well as of other intellectualized abstract forms of the twentieth century.

In contrast to the architectural character of Cézanne's forms, the works of Paul Gauguin show the invention of a vivid, symbolic world of decorative patterns (plate 77). They owe their particular character to the type of form expression found in medieval frescoes, mosaics, and enamels. Although his themes were inspired by the barbaric peoples of the South Seas, the works always demonstrate a sense of the sophistication typical of most Western art. An underlying suavity tempers Gauguin's work and gives it a quality reminiscent of the old masters' paintings in spite of its barbarity of color and freedom of pattern. The decorative style of the French Fauves in the early twentieth century stems primarily from the work of Paul Gauguin.

The work of Vincent van Gogh, the third pioneer Post-Impressionist, represents the beginning of the new, highly charged, *subjective expression* which we find in many forms of contemporary painting. The character of twentieth-century Expressionism owes a great deal to the impetuous brush strokes and the dramatic distortions of color and object forms first found in the work of Van Gogh (plate 78; *see also* plates 1, 4, 35, and 48).

Twentieth-Century Forms of Expression 1900–1950

Expressionism

French and German Expressionism, perhaps the most significant phase in the evolution of newer art forms, began as the first decade of the twentieth century was almost over. The young artists of this movement were the first to declare on a large scale the complete freedom of the artist to work in a manner consonant with his feeling about a subject. In a sense, we see these artists as merely being more liberal Romantics; however, it was possible to be more liberal only after those intervening years of change which had introduced new ways of seeing and feeling.

The twentieth century saw the growth of a new awareness or consciousness which was related to the many changes taking place, or about to take place, in the whole order of existence. Cézanne, Gauguin, and Van Gogh had opened the door through which hosts of young artists were now eager to plunge, anxious to explore this new world of previously unknown artistic sensations, diversions, and mysteries. The shape of this new artistic world was signaled by an explosion of color and an exciting style of drawing which ran the gamut from the graceful curves of Matisse to the bold slashings of Kokoschka.

The Fauves.   The members of the earliest Expressionist group were called the *Fauves.* This title was attached to them because of the "wild" appearance of their paintings in comparison to the academic formalism which was accepted and expected by the general public of the period. The term, literally translated, means "wild beasts." Whereas the public had been only dimly aware of Cézanne and Van Gogh as revolutionaries, they could not ignore this host of young painters who threw Paris into a turmoil with group exhibitions, pamphleteering, and other forms of personal publicity. In fact, the Fauves seemed to be trying to live up to their name. However, within a period of only seven years, they had lost their original vigor and were considered rather calm compared to the newer movements which were evolving. Fauvism is a form of expression which tries to arrive at the emotional essence of a subject rather than to show its external appearance; its characteristic style is decorative, colorful, spontaneous, and intuitional. When the emotional excitement of the artist about his subject is communicated to the spectator, his work of art may be called successful.

The color, brilliance, and persuading sophistication found in the work of Henri Matisse, nominal leader of the group, was largely influenced by Persian and Near Eastern art *(see* figs. 84 and 120 and plate 22). The group as a whole felt similar influences, often searching for "patterns" in the areas of the museums dedicated to older and more remote group expressions; they received inspiration from the work of the Byzantines, the Coptic Christians, the Greek artists of the archaic age, as well as the primitive tribal arts of Africa, Oceania, and the American Indian. The use of African masks and sculpture as sources of Matisse's style can be detected in the mask-like, impersonal quality of the human faces found in his paintings. Back of this impersonal effect there also seems to lie a sense of mystery or threat engendered by the enigmatic quality of an alien style of expression (plate 79).

Despite the rather strong, vibrant color generally preferred by the Expressionists, Matisse, Utrillo, Vlaminck, and Modigliani often built charming, decorative structures which continued

the long tradition of classical restraint found in French and Italian art (plate 80; *see also* fig. 122 and plate 53 and fig. 57). Georges Roualt, on the other hand, is an exception in French Expressionism, his work being more dramatic like that of the German artists. His painting expresses a violent reaction to the hypocracy and materialism of his time through a favorite use of thick, crumbling reds and blacks. His images of Christ are symbols of man's inhumanity to man; his portrayal of judges reveals the crime and corruption that can reach even into those areas where justice should prevail (plate 81; *see also* plate 58). Roualt's comment through his painting on the French leaders of the day was anything but complimentary.

German Expressionism.   Paralleling the movement in France, the artists of Germany felt that they as prophets of new, unknown artistic values must destroy the conventions which bound the art of their time. The foundation of painting in Europe for the next fifty years was provided in the aims of three groups of German artists: *Die Brucke* (The Bridge), the *Blaue Reiter* (Blue Knights), and *Die Neu Sachlichkeit* (The New Objectivity). The Expressionism of these artists, drawn from an environment that seemed complacent toward social and political injustices, was ultimately an art of protest. While producing work which protested against the outrages of the period, the artists attempted to create in as direct a fashion as possible work which represented their basic urge for expression. The combination of this driving creative urge and the desire to protest became the foundation for a number of varied movements in German art. The resulting art forms took on a quality of vehemence, drama, gruesomeness, and fanaticism never completely achieved by the *raison* (reason) of French art.

The young artists of this style identified with the religious mysticism of the Middle Ages as well as with the tribal arts of primitive peoples. Many followed the manner of children with their naive but direct expression of emotional identification with environment. For example, the art of Emil Nolde is similar in feeling to the mystic art of the Middle Ages, while Edward Munch based many of his creations on medieval and primitive folk art traditions (fig. 188; *see also* plate 50). Franz Marc was an artist who used the emotional reality of caveman art as a basis for his inspiration. Protests against Prussian *jingoism* became the subject matter of the paint-

Fig. 188. ANXIETY (1896) by Edvard Munch. Some of the unhappy experiences in the life of this artist are presented with the characteristic exaggeration of emotional content. Childish terrors and medieval superstitions are interwoven into a form expressive of frightful conditions seen in their time.

Collection, the Museum of Modern Art, New York. Abby Aldrich Rockefeller Fund

ing of George Grosz and Otto Dix (fig. 189). This characteristic aspect of Prussian culture led to World War I and ultimately to Hitlerism and World War II.

Max Beckmann, although not a part of any organized group of Expressionists, followed a path somewhat kindred in spirit to the work of Otto Dix. Following World War I, Dix had worked in a style which satirized the swampy, degraded underworld of political society. Beckmann cultivated a similar style of frank, satirical veracity but modified the emotional intensity of

his expression with the calm, geometric arrangement which he had learned from Cubism. This latter quality gives a certainty of execution to his manner of painting quite reminiscent of the work of the old masters (plate 82).

Expressionism in United States and Mexico. The Expressionistic style had adherents in the Americas as well as in the European countries. The great depression of the thirties influenced such artists as Max Weber and Ben Shahn to make mournful and satiric comment on American society of the period (*see* fig. 17). Evergood and Levine are more recent artists making similar commentary on the political and social confusion of the cold war years (fig. 190).

Mexico during the twenties and thirties underwent an artistic renaissance which many artists found fruitful ground for an Expression-istic style—a style based on identification with problems inherent in the growth of freedom for the Indian and mestizo classes. José Orozco, whose art evolved during this period, became the greatest exponent of Expressionism in the Western Hemisphere. Inspired by the rapidly chang-

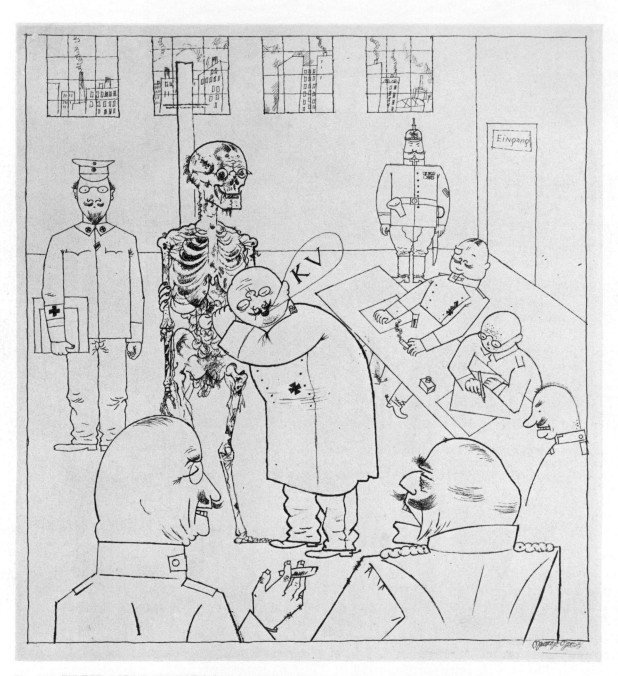

Fig. 189. FIT FOR ACTIVE SERVICE (1918) by George Grosz. In this work, characteristic German emotionalism is forced to new limits of satire as a result of the artist's personal experiences during World War I. Expressionism, which shows moral indignation at its peak, now becomes an instrument of social protest. Niceties of color are ignored in favor of harsh, biting black lines.

Collection, the Museum of Modern Art, New York. A. Conger Goodyear Fund

Fig. 190. ELECTION NIGHT (1954) by Jack Levine. Influenced by the social and political problems of the post-World War II period, the artist arrived at a distinctive manner which combines a complicated and glowing technique with an expressionist pungency of feeling.

Collection, the Museum of Modern Art, New York. Gift of Joseph H. Hirshhorn

ing social order in Mexico, he produced work which had a quality of expression similar to that of Roualt in Europe. There is something of the same black tragedy in the work of both artists, although at the same time the style of each was different in form and meaning (fig. 191; *see also* plate 11).

Post-Impressionist and Expressionist Sculpture

New concepts in painting remained in advance of those in sculpture until about the 1950s, but there was a continuous interchange of ideas so that, even though sculptors did not follow the movements in painting, similar lines of development were parallel in the two groups.

Fig. 191. BARRICADE (1931) by José Clemente Orozco. Slashing diagonals of line combine with agitated hues and values to express the feeling of this artist concerning the furor of the Mexican social revolution in the early twentieth century.

Collection, the Museum of Modern Art, New York. Given anonymously

By 1900, revolutionary changes can be detected as sculptors began to express their reaction to contemporary thought and experience rather than to ancient myth or legend. Sculpture then took three general directions: (1) the human figure was retained, but simplified to express only the essential structure and material, (2) forms were abstracted from nature or new forms of a highly formal or structured character were invented, and (3) experimentation with new materials produced new shapes and new techniques.

There was no Post-Impressionist movement as such in sculpture, but the concern of some artists such as Aristide Maillol, Gaston Lachaise, and Wilhelm Lehmbruck suggest new interest in the totality of form and accent on the intrinsic beauty of materials that is similar to the new synthesis of form from nature in Post-Impressionist painting.

Maillol pioneered simplification of figural form to recover the sense of sculptural monumentality that reasserts the essential blockiness of stone and the agelessness of bronze and lead. He not only shook up academic stagnation of representation of the human figure by using slightly exaggerated proportion, but also achieved a classical sense of serenity and repose suggesting Cézanne and Seurat (fig. 192).

Fig. 192. MONUMENT TO DEBUSSY (1931, bronze) by Aristide Maillol. Maillol combined classical concepts with a sense of contemporary monumental form.
Courtesy the Toledo Museum of Art. Gift of Edmund Dummond Libby

Gaston Lachaise, a Franco-American sculptor, created weighty, voluminous female figures that evoked the sensuous through exaggerated proportions that were rhythmically balanced. At times, his sense of poise gave figures a feeling of aerial suspension seemingly at odds with the amplitude of his forms, but reconciled by his exquisite sense of balance and the finish he gave to metal (fig. 193).

Fig. 193. STANDING WOMAN (1927, bronze) by Gaston Lachaise. Ponderous figures were somehow given a feeling of lightly balanced poise.
Courtesy the Art Institute of Chicago

Lachaise and Lehmbruck both worked in a manner similar to the more emotional aspects of Post-Impressionism, comparable in some ways to a Gauguin or Van Gogh painting. Lehmbruck evolved a style of elongated figures that were suavely charming or nostalgic and melancholy. Like Lachaise, he distributed the masses of his figural forms rhythmically, but used a strong vertical axis, unlike Lachaise's variable axis. Where Lachaise used rounded masses, Lehmbruck created leaned-down forms which were almost stripped of fleshy connotation (fig. 194).

Just as there was not a clearly defined Post-Impressionist movement in sculpture, neither was there a clearly perceivable expressionist sculptural school.

Several sculptors worked in a manner related to the ideal which the *Blaue Reiters* in Germany had expressed as "stripping away surface reality to arrive at underlying truths." Generally speaking, however, those artists who may be called expressionist were less disposed than the painters toward violent distortion of form to reveal the psyche. For this reason Lachaise and Lehmbruck are sometimes also called Expressionist because of their moderate distortion of human form.

Jacob Epstein, the Anglo-American sculptor, developed an expressionist, as well as an abstract, manner during his lifetime. His expressionist works, usually cast in bronze, were based on an exaggerated clay-pellet technique. These works seem distantly related to the late style of Rodin in emotional impact and technique. When Epstein carved in stone, his approach was more often formal and semiabstract, rather than the emotional abandon of Expressionism (fig. 195).

There are more recent sculptors whose work is reminiscent of this mildly expressionist idiom of early twentieth-century sculpture. Among these we might mention the American graphic artist and sculptor Leonard Baskin. He seem concerned with the tragic tension between man and environment as expressed through figures of men and birds and more recently through studies of figures and heads of cultural heroes and heroines. It is as if in the great of the past Baskin finds hope for solution of present-day problems.

The Italian artist Marino Marini also works in a manner of slight distortion in his best known works, equestrian figures produced in the late 1940s and early 1950s. The slightly abstract shape of horse and rider may be related to Kandinsky's rider series of 1909–10 and seem to imply Ma-

Fig. 194. SEATED GIRL (1913–14, bronze) by Wilhelm Lehmbruck. This work is an example of the mildly Expressionist sculpture which dominated the early twentieth-century pioneering phase of contemporary sculpture.

Courtesy the Detroit Institute of Arts. Bequest of Robert H. Tannahill

Fig. 195. SOCIAL CONSCIOUSNESS (ca. 1954-55, bronze) by Jacob Epstein. Multiple figures may be used to express human as well as formal relationships.

The Ellen Philips Samuel Memorial; Courtesy the Fairmount Park Art Association

Fig. 196. MAN ON A HORSE (1947, bronze) by Marino Marini. The tradition of equestrian sculpture joined to twentieth-century abstraction and formal tension.
Courtesy the Art Institute of Chicago

rini's concern with the impersonality of modern life (fig 196). Marini's sculpture has become increasingly abstract.

Abstract Art

Cubism—the beginning of Abstraction. Beginning about 1906 in Paris, a new attitude toward nature was observed in the work of certain artists. Before Cézanne, the artists of Europe tended to see nature in terms of material surfaces. Cézanne began the trend toward the search for reality (the universal unvariables) beneath these material surfaces by observing and emphasizing the basic structure of nature. This new way of seeing developed gradually over a period of twenty-five years, paralleling the changing concepts of reality in science. Cézanne had stated his concept that the artist should seek the universal forms of nature in the cube, the cone, and the sphere. Artistic exploration founded directly on this concept developed gradually in the work of the Fauves and finally resulted in a style labeled Cubism.

One of the most active young artists of the Fauve movement in Paris from 1903 to 1906 was the Spaniard Pablo Picasso (*see* fig. 86 and plates 14 and 47). Possibly because of his admiration for the work of Cézanne or because of a desire to challenge the leadership of the Fauves by Matisse, Picasso began to look for new possibilities of form expression in his painting. He based his exploration on analysis of volume and space structure. With much of the same attitude as Cézanne, Picasso became dissatisfied with the emphasis on the external characteristics of objects and sought for a method of expressing their internal structure. He eventually developed paintings which displayed many facets of the same object at the same time on the same canvas. Many of Picasso's ideas may be traced back not only to Cézanne, but also to characteristic styles of primitive art forms—archaic Greek sculpture as well as African negro sculpture (fig. 197; *see also* fig. 85 and plate 28).

Fig. 197. MAN WITH VIOLIN (1911) by Pablo Picasso. The shapes in Picasso's Facet-Cubist style are component planes coaxed forth from subject forms and freely rearranged to suit the artist's design concept. Some facets are retained in their original position, and certain elements of the figure are fleetingly recognizable.
Courtesy Philadelphia Museum of Art. The Louise and Walter Arensberg Collection

The most noticeable aspect of cubist form as evolved by Picasso, his colleagues, and their followers was geometric crystallization of shapes. By this means the artists tried to arrive at a more permanent type of order than that found in natural form. At the same time, the traditional illusionistic rendering of space was reordered into what the artists felt was a more stable form of spatial relationship, independent of the vagaries of light and the distortions of shape caused by the use of linear perspective.

In his concern with arriving at a new statement of the structure of matter seen from an aesthetic point of view, Picasso often stripped away many aids to expression, for example, richness of color. However, in this process of reduction he formulated a new artistic language that put an end to the respect for surface appearance observable in all art since the time of the Renaissance. Paintings were now made with the intention of primarily emphasizing the artistic devices *for their own sake* rather than of merely adapting these devices to the *imitation of nature*; traditionally accepted object forms began to give way to pure or maximum form. With the new emphasis on the intrinsic quality of the artistic elements (line, shape, value, texture, and color) a new set of terms had to be invented in order to make a more convenient explanation of what the artist was trying to do—especially for those who were not prepared to accept complete purity of form. The term *abstraction,* which had had only a general meaning up to the 1900s, was now applied to this form of expression which was considered no longer associational with observed objects. Cubism, which is a semiabstract art form, can now be seen as the forerunner for all the later forms of *Abstraction* in art. In semiabstract art, we can generally still recognize certain objects from nature; the transformation of such forms in the process of abstraction is meant to express the artist's convictions about life and matter. Transformation of forms is a matter of degree and may vary from the semiabstract styles of Cubism and Futurism to the pure abstraction of Wassily Kandinsky and Piet Mondrian.

Cubism as the beginning of abstract art was of major importance. It was introduced to the world not only in the works of Picasso, but also in those of Georges Braque, a French artist who collaborated with him. The two artists occupied the same studio for a number of years. Braque added an uniquely expressive quality to the usual Cubist approach by the use of foreign, textured materials which he attached to the canvas surface—a technique called *papier collé* or just *collage* (fig. 198; *see also* fig. 97). On the whole, he remained true to the typical French art tradition of quietness of expression in spite of his use of new forms; this was a contrast to the more forceful, explosive quality of the work of Picasso. In all of Braque's work produced during the peak years of Cubist expression (1911 to 1914) is a sense of charm engendered by his restrained manipulation of color and value patterns; these patterns were developed in terms of the finite volume of space, one of the chief Cubist idioms (*see* plate 49).

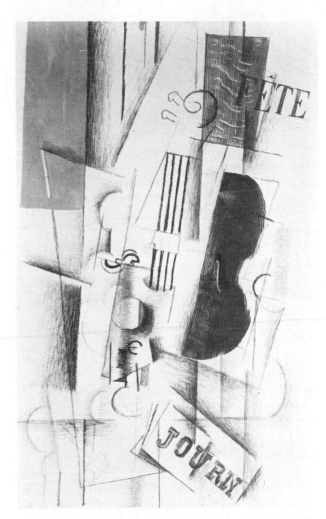

Fig. 198. MUSICAL FORMS (1913) by Georges Braque. Braque varies the usually Cubist handling of form by the inventive inclusion of textured foreign materials. Such textures added a new beauty of surface manipulation to the repertoire of contemporary art.

Courtesy Philadelphia Museum of Art. The Louise and Walter Arensberg Collection

Fig. 199. THE CITY (1919) by Fernand Léger. The rigidity and simple geometric character of industrial structures were subjects ideally suited to the Cubist style. The paintings of Léger follow this principle and become true products of a "machine-age aesthetic." Courtesy Philadelphia Museum of Art. A. E. Gallatin Collection

Two other Cubists of note were Fernand Léger, another French artist, and Juan Gris, a fellow countryman of Picasso. These two preferred the more austere expressionism of Picasso, but not the violence which was the other side of that artist's personality. Léger and Gris developed individual form qualities within the Cubist pattern which set them apart as important creators in their own right. Because of the impact of industry on society, Léger accepted the machine as a styling motif for cubist form (fig. 199; *see also* fig. 28 and plates 26 and 52). Instead of abstracting away from nature, Gris dealt with volumes or decorative patterns which suggested recognizable objects. He would then develop these shapes in the direction of object recognition without resort to mere imitation of superficial appearance (*see* figs. 55 and 138 and plate 34).

Futurism—the second phase of Abstract art. Futurism, like Cubism, remained a submovement within the overall abstract category. Futurism was actually a form of Cubism remodeled by certain Italian artists who had been to Paris during the excitement caused by the new artistic ventures of Picasso and Braque. Among the more important artists in this movement were Umberto Boccioni and Giacomo Balla (*see* fig. 140 and plate 83). These artists studied in France,

and on their return to Italy were much intrigued by the rapid advances that had been made in domestic industry. Together with the poet Marino Marinetti they formed a union of ideas. Their expression was formulated on the basis of the modern machine, the speed and violence of contemporary life, and the psychological effects of this ferment on human mentality and activity. Boccioni, Severini, and their followers attempted to show the beauty of modern machines through sheaves of lines and planes which created an effect of dynamic movement and tension within the canvas. The translation of rapid motion into artistic terms was a constant preoccupation. The Futurists also attempted to interpret contemporary incidents of violence such as riots, strikes, and war which presumably would affect future events.

The fervor of this group was not matched by its artistic contributions as the artists merely energized the somewhat static geometry of Cubism and brought back richer coloring. Perhaps its attention to the new subject matter of the machine was the most important contribution, for other artists and the public became more aware of the nature of their time. Following the traditional mission of art, the art of this group expressed the age in which it was created.

Fig. 200. IMPROVISATION No. 30 (1913) by Wassily Kandinsky. About 1910, the Russian Wassily Kandinsky began to paint freely moving, biomorphic shapes in rich combinations of hues. The characteristic early style which the artist evolved can be seen in this illustration. Such an abstract form of expression was an attempt to show the artist's feelings about object surfaces rather than to describe their outward appearance.
Courtesy the Art Institute of Chicago. Arthur Jerome Eddy Memorial Collection

Pure Abstract art—the elimination of nature. During the period from 1910 to 1918, the chief motivation of artists throughout Europe was complete elimination of nature from art. Deriving inspiration primarily from the experiments of Picasso, artists explored pure abstraction in two main directions. Some, like the Russian Wassily Kandinsky, preferred an emotional, sensuous expressionism which later influenced American abstract painting. Other artists such as Mondrian were more interested in the cold precision of geometric arrangement. Kandinsky's best known work featured powerful rhythms and loose biomorphic shapes which had a feeling of great spontaneity (fig. 200; *see also* plate 3). Although it was rarely evident, Kandinsky's paintings usually originated from specific conditions or circumstances. The artist always attempted to interpret his response in terms of pure visual language without reference to outward appearance. Kandinsky's loose, direct manner is essentially that of a Romantic. His appeal is directed at pure emotion, and in order to assess

his works, the observer must have had similar experiences to those motivating the artist. Later, while working at the German Bauhaus (an architectural school which stressed the unity of all art in terms of design), Kandinsky's work began to be influenced by the geometric abstraction practiced by some of its artists.

The most representative exponent of geometric abstraction was Piet Mondrian of Holland. Like Kandinsky, Mondrian dealt with the pure elements of form, but unlike Kandinsky, purged them of the emotional extremes of romanticism. Mondrian's art is the unemotional rationalization of line, shape, value, and color pushed to maximum optical purity (fig. 201). In such work meaning or *content* is inherent in the precise relationships established. This direction seemed sterile and shallow to artists and critics alike when it first appeared; that it was, instead, momentous and rich in possibilities seems proved by its tremendous impact on thousands of artists. The dissidents taking verbal slaps at geometric abstraction were soon in the minority.

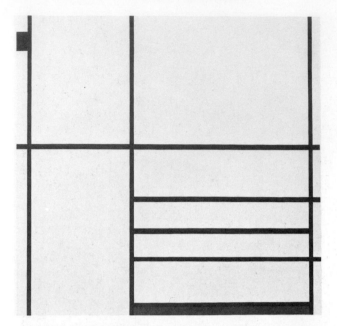

Fig. 201. COMPOSITION IN WHITE, BLACK, AND RED (1936) by Piet Mondrian. Mondrian created a "pure" art purged of all but the elements of art structure. His simple, bold style, evolved from study of the subtle relationships of these elements, has been readily assimilated into many forms of contemporary expression. Its influence on present-day commercial and industrial design is obvious.

Collection, the Museum of Modern Art, New York. Gift of the Advisory Committee

Nonobjective Variants of Abstract Art

Heretofore, the abstract art discussed originated from nature; the next development was so-called Nonobjective painting which presumed to divorce itself from nature altogether and to originate entirely (insofar as this can be determined) within the mind of the artist. The differences in Pure Abstraction and Nonobjective works of art are not readily apparent; perhaps an attempt to differentiate is of theoretical interest only. Both concepts opened up a new realm of aesthetic endeavor, and exploration in this area continues to the present time. Obviously, the term *Nonobjective* does *not* mean that the artist has no objective. The artist definitely communicates but without resort to *objective* reporting. A certain amount of pure abstract and nonobjective work is more imitative than original. It is easy to produce synthetic abstract art that is an end in itself. However, it is as a creative process that abstraction is more properly employed, and this calls for the maximum power of the artist.

A great part of what we see in our world today derived its personality from the continuing influence of the abstract concept. Modern designers readily assimilated the theories of form underlying this concept. Buildings, furniture, textiles, advertising, machines, and costuming are only a few of the areas which bear witness to the tremendous impact of abstract art. Stylistically, the gap has constantly narrowed between fine art and art of a commercial or industrial nature. This may be in part due to the fact that abstract art developed out of an environment in which the practical function of the machine had become an unconscious, as well as a conscious, part of life. In a sense the abstract artist created a machine-age aesthetic.

Abstract Art in the United States

Abstract art was slow in coming to America but shortly after World War II the movement quickly gathered momentum. The influence of European expatriate artists was an important factor. Actually, during the period between the two world wars many American artists had been affected by the structural order of Cubism. Arthur Dove (who actually began pure abstraction in 1912), John Marin, Lyonel Feininger, Georgia O'Keefe, Stuart Davis, and Marsden Hartley were among the early pioneers of abstraction in the United States (fig. 202; *see also* figs. 18, 59, and 119 and plate 24). In a peculiarly American way, however, they seem to have refrained from going completely over to pure abstraction and retained a strongly personalized vision. After World War II, a new generation of younger American artists renounced the last ties with nature. Some of the leaders in this movement of the mid-1940s were Irene Rice Pereira and Loren Mac Iver among the women (fig. 203) and Bradley Walker Tomlin and Mark Rothko among the men (plate 84). Toward the end of the forties a new impulse, stemming from a mixture of Abstraction, Surrealism, and Expressionism, began to be manifest. Pure geometric abstraction slipped almost indistinguishably in this new direction. We must now go back in time to see how this came about.

Abstract Sculpture, 1900–1950

Picasso's collages and constructions in the Cubism of 1912–14 opened the way toward a wide range of new sculptural forms in the abstract which sculptors soon explored. Perhaps

Fig. 202. BRIDGE V (1919) by Lyonel Feininger. American artists inheriting a tradition of native Romantic Realism seemed to have been reluctant to accept pure Abstract Expression. Inspired by the dramatic shapes found in man-made structures, but informed by the careful designs of Cubism, Feininger eventually merged these two forms of expression in a semiabstract style.

Courtesy Philadelphia Museum of Art. Purchased: The Bloomfield Moore Fund

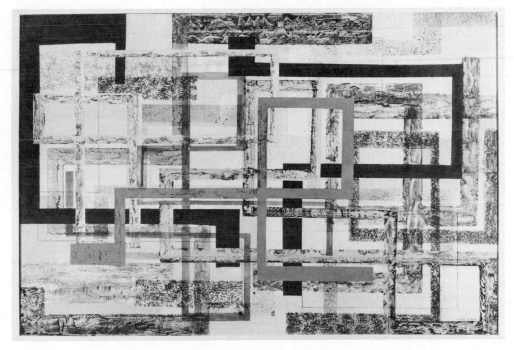

Fig. 203. DAYBREAK by I. Rice Pereira. This painter developed a style of abstraction which investigated space, light, and dimensions—all of which are inherent in the structure of the painting itself. Her work is one of the unique variations that the general concept of abstraction has followed in this country.

Courtesy the Metropolitan Museum of Art. The Edward Joseph Gallagher III Memorial Collection

the most important early abstract sculptor was the Franco-Rumanian Constantin Brancusi. He was an artist who as early as 1913 chose to free sculpture of representation. His works such as the *White Negress* (1928) (fig. 204) and the even more famous *Bird in Space* (1919) reveal an effective and sensuous charm due to their flowing, geometrical poise and the artist's emphasis on beautifully finished materials. Brancusi usually preferred to work in the near-abstract, but always considered the quality of shape and the texture and handling of materials to be more significant than the representation of the subject.

Another pioneer abstract sculptor was the Russian-born artist Alexander Archipenko. Archipenko belonged to the so-called School of Paris during the Cubist period of Picasso and Braque. His significant contribution was use of negative space or the void in sculpture, as in his *Woman Doing her Hair* (1916) (*see* fig. 158) in which

hollow replaces the face. Archipenko also explored the use of new materials and technology, occasionally incorporating machine-made parts into a work.

The same Cubist intellectual and artistic ferment that led Archipenko to explore manmade materials and Brancusi to pioneer in use of power tools also led the Russian brothers Naum Gabo and Antoine Pevsner to their very important *Constructivist* concepts of *pure form*. This movement was founded by Vladimir Tatlin, but it is usually associated with Gabo and Pevsner because they issued the definitive manifesto in 1920, which proclaimed *pure form* to be the new realism in art. Gabo was the more exciting, being the inventor of nonobective and nonvolumetric forms (three-dimensional forms that do not enclose space but interact with it). Pevsner worked more in solid masses, nearer to sculpture of a traditional kind (fig. 205). Many artists were

Fig. 204. WHITE NEGRESS (1928, marble) by Constantin Brancusi. Brancusi abstracted down to essential forms, with infinite concern for the properties of his medium.
Courtesy the Art Institute of Chicago. Grant J. Pick Collection.

Fig. 205. LINEAR CONSTRUCTION #4 (plastic and nylon) by Naum Gabo. Gabo, with his brother Pevsner, pioneered in the use of new materials, the use of voids, and the use of nonobjective structure.
Courtesy the Art Institute of Chicago. Florence M. Schoenborn Gift

Plate 72. ARABS SKIRMISHING IN THE MOUNTAINS (1869) by Eugene Delacroix. A subject matter offering violent action located in exotic foreign settings was often found in paintings of the Romantic movement. Although relaxed in style, interpretation was generally bold in technique with an emphasis on the selection of bright colors.

Courtesy The National Gallery of Art, Washington, D.C. Chester Dale Fund.

Plate 73. KEELMEN HEAVING COALS BY MOONLIGHT by Joseph Turner. The historical origin of theme and semi-narrative presentation of subject represent qualities found in many works of the Romantic movement. In his manner of using color to produce atmospheric effects, Turner anticipated the techniques of the later Impressionists. Like these artists, he placed less emphasis on formal organization.

Plate 74. MAX SCHMITT IN A SINGLE SCULL (1871) by Thomas Eakins. The Naturalist artists were Realists who became more interested in particularizing people and events by a carefully descriptive style of expression. The oarsmen are here minutely described by the artist in terms of specific people taking part in a particular activity and in a particular setting.

Plate 75. BANKS OF THE SEINE, VETHEUIL (c. 1880) by Claude Monet. The selection of subject in this painting is typical of the Impressionist movement. The bright scene and the shimmering water offered opportunity for the expression of light and atmosphere through a scientific approach to the use of colors.

Plate 76. FOUR DANCERS (c. 1899) by Edgar Degas. Two aspects of the Impressionist artist's recording of natural form may be found in the painting of four dancers. First, it demonstrates the customary interest in the effects of light (although in this case we find an interior lighting rather than sunlight in the out-of-doors); in addition, it shows a high angle viewpoint of composition derived from Japanese prints or from the accidental effects characteristic of photography.

Courtesy The National Gallery of Art, Washington, D.C. Chester Dale Collection.

Plate 77. THE MOON AND THE EARTH (1893) by Paul Gauguin. Color and form are here freely interpreted to suggest the naive qualities of an uncivilized people; the relationships of these elements are expressed in terms of an over-all decorative structure which adds to the general effect of tranquility.

Collection, The Museum of Modern Art, New York. Lillie P. Bliss Collection.

Plate 78. CYPRESSES (1889) by Vincent van Gogh. This highly personal style exaggerates the organic forces of nature and makes them dramatically expressive. The heavy, swirling applications of paint enhance the movements extracted from the natural form.

Courtesy The Metropolitan Museum of Art, New York, Rogers Fund, 1949.

Plate 79. COFFEE (1916) by Henri Matisse. The Fauve Expressionists, led by Matisse, tried to arrive at the emotional "essence" of a subject rather than its external appearance. Matisse also reveals the characteristic decorative, colorful spontaneous, and intuitional qualities of this French Expressionist style.

Courtesy The Detroit Institute of the Arts. Bequest of Robert H. Tannehill.

Plate 80. GYPSY WOMAN WITH BABY by Amedeo Modigliani. The artist's painting stresses sensitive shape arrangement and subtle modeling of form within a shallow space concept. His interpretation of the figure is a personal mannerism suggesting the influence of Gothic and African negro sculpture.

Courtesy The National Gallery of Art. Washington. D.C. Chester Dale Collection.

Plate 81. THE THREE JUDGES (1913) by Georges Rouault. This Expressionist's intensity of feeling is accomplished in terms of color by the use of somber recs framed in black and nocturnal blue. Rouault's work lacks the ingratiating character usualy found in that of the other French artists of the movement.

Plate 82. DEPARTURE (1932-35) by Max Beckmann. Here style is emotionally intensified through strong contrasts of value and the impasto with which the artist has applied his pigment. However, this intensity of expression is partially modified by the cool, orderly arrangement derived from Cubism.

Collection, The Museum of Modern Art. New York Given anonymously.

**Plate 83. SPEEDING AUTOMOBILE (1912)
by Giacomo Balla.** This artist's handling of
the image of a speeding machine is characteristic of the Futurist idiom. Incorporated into the dynamic form is a sense of
the hysterical approach to violence and the
psychological impact of tensions in modern
times.

Collection, The Museum of Modern Art, New York.
Purchase.

Plate 84. NO. 10 (1950) by Mark Rothko.
Using apparent simple masses of color on
a large scale, the artist is able to evoke
emotional sensations in the observer. Mark
Rothko was one of the American artists
who worked in the Pure Abstract idiom.

Collection, The Museum of Modern Art, New York.
Gift of Philip C. Johnson.

Plate 85. VILLAGE IN THE FIELDS (1922) by Paul Klee. Many artists developed fusions of twentieth-century concepts which defy classification insofar as any one category of expression is concerned. This reproduction illustrates a refined synthesis of relaxed Cubistic forms and the naive charm of children's art.

Collection, The Museum of Modern Art, New York. Katherine S. Dreier Bequest.

Plate 86. PERSON THROWING A STONE AT A BIRD (1926) by Joan Miro. In this painting, Miro shows sophisticated color and bio-morphic shapes combined with simple child-like images. In many respects, it is similar to the Klee painting illustrated earlier in the book. The Abstract Surrealism of Miro is, in general, semi-representational in character.

Collection, The Museum of Modern Art, New York. Purchase.

Plate 87. WOMAN, I (1950-52) by Willem de Kooning. The
artist summarizes most aspects of the "Romantic" or
"Action" group of abstract expressionism: revelation of
the ego through the act of painting, neglect of academic
or formal organization in favor of bold, direct, free gestures that are instinctively organized, and willingness to
explore unknown and undescribable effects and experiences. Even though he seems to use the figure, its representational value is subordinated by the motivating "activity" of pure painting.

Collection. The Museum of Modern Art. New York. Purchase.

Plate 88. EMMA (1966) by Jules Olitsky. Characteristics of
minimal are shown in this painting art the relatively insig-
nificant changes in hue and value. One has to make an
intensely concentrated effort to determine that the field is
differentiated in any manner at all from the dominantly
dark value of the color.

Courtesy of Mr. and Mrs. S. Brooks Barron, Detroit, Michigan.

Plate 89. NUMBER 99 (1959) by Morris Louis. Louis was of an older generation of artists related to Abstract Expressionism, such as Kline and Rothko, he became identified with the Post-Painterly Abstractionists. As a "Field Painter" he was among the pioneers who flooded canvas surfaces with stains of pigment, which calmed the impetuosity of action paintings, and created a new emphasis on the detached objectivity of the work of art. As opposed to hard-edge painters like Kelly, Newman, or Noland, his stripes and shapes become softly focused and sometimes almost intangible, thus influencing Minimal Art. He was also among the earliest painters of the mid twentieth century to explore the technique of spray painting.

The Cleveland Museum of Art. Contemporary Collection.

Plate 90. DOUBLE METAMORPHOSIS II (1964) by Agam (Yaacov Gipstein). The "Op" Artist explores not only the psychology of sight but the physical effect which viewing his forms of art may generate. In some ways, the forms of "Op" Art seem an extension of earlier twentieth-century geometric abstract art.

Collection, The Museum of Modern Art, New York. Gift of Mr. and Mrs. George M. Jaffin.

connected with the *Constructivist* movement: Rodchenko, Albers, and Moholy-Nagy are a few of them.

The common denominator discernible in the work of all Abstract sculptors during the period of 1900–1930 was expressionism which emphasized materials and de-emphasized the division between the fine arts and the functional arts. This was essentially the point of view held also by the *Constructivists* and the *Bauhaus*.

Fantastic Art: Background of Fantasy and Dadaism

The third major direction for twentieth-century art began to be recognizable about 1914, the first year of World War I. The war had evidently begun to raise questions about the individual's ability to master the machine, suggesting that individual freedoms might actually be destroyed in an age of technology. As a kind of antidote to the machine cult in abstract art, certain writers, poets, and artists began to extol artistic forms which reemphasized the emotional, subconscious side of creativity. During the period, for instance, Picasso's art moved away from the ennobled, monumental structures of early Cubism and began to take on structural perversions which eventually were to be the basis for Dadaism's destructive, cynical and absurd puns on the cult of materialism in society (*see* figs. 100 and 134).

A certain element of artistic endeavor in the past had been devoted to the creative invention of images that seemed manifestations of weird and fantastic imaginings. The centaurs of the ancient Greeks, the strange beast-symbols of human sin in medieval manuscripts and sculpture, the superstitions and alchemist's nightmares of Jerome Bosch in the early sixteenth century, and the fantasies of Goya in the late eighteenth and early nineteenth centuries may be cited as a few of the prototypes of twentieth-century fantasy.

The years of World War I nurtured the growth of an art that emphasized the irrational side of human behavior. Neutral Switzerland had become the mecca for poets, writers, artists, liberals, and political exiles who sought refuge there from persecution or the terrors of modern warfare. Out of the intellectual ferment motivated largely by disillusionment arose Dada, a semiphilosophic creed for protestation of the moral and social degeneracy responsible, it was felt, for the war. According to Dada, complete erasure of accepted institutions and conventions was needed; only on completely virgin soil could mankind rebuild a more desirable society. The Dadaists, therefore, embarked on programmatic undermining of traditional civilized mores by cynical and sardonic derision of all its manifestations.

Duchamp, Picabia, Ernst, and others began to fashion machinelike humanized forms which suggested the robotizing of man. Later, with even more remarkable ingenuity, they created biomorphic images which discredited the semi-organic qualities of Kandinsky's romanticised abstract art (fig. 206; *see also* fig. 13). These inventions were meant to show disrespect for the experimental forms of the art leaders of the new century and shock a public already disturbed by a visual revolution.

The basic premise of this bizarre movement was that every Dadaist had complete expressive freedom in his attack on the old order. In principle, there was no limit to the disorder which might be projected in painting, poetry, and general social behavior. All of this left a bad taste in the mouth of the general layman, who now usually classifies all of modern art with the outlandish forms excuted by the Dadaists. Actually, the disorder of the movement eventually led to its demise. Dada was pure negativism, an exhibitionism of the absurd. Being against art, its only medium was nonsense publicly displayed to discredit all forms of sense. Its main value today is historical as the principal source of Surrealism and the liberator of expressive freedom.

Individual Fantasists

The inclination toward private fantasy seemed to be a general tendency in Western Europe during the period of Dada satire .This fantasy took individual, but quite influential, direction in the hands of certain artists who were not a part of the Dada movement. Giorgio de Chirico, an Italian, placed incongruous modern machines in ancient shadowed plazas (fig. 207; *see also* fig. 78). The decadence of the modern world seems implied by the image of a classical world of silent squares inhabited by statuelike remnants of an unknown people. The frozen, unprogressive, and even trancelike expression seems to suggest a wistful desire to recover the past.

Paul Klee, a Swiss, created an art of witty, abstract imagery based on Expressionism and

Cubism. His work seems to poke gentle but penetrating fun at the cult of the machine and to smile shyly at human pretensions. The implication seems to be that there is more to extrasensorial perception than modern man's addiction to practicality will allow (plate 85; *see also* plate 9).

Marc Chagall, Russian born but a resident of France and the United States, originally worked in an Expressionist manner. His stay in France brought him under the discipline of Cubism. Eventually, he joined the two styles in his own brand of romanticized poetic art which has an Alice-in-Wonderland quality. Chagall freely x-rays people and floats them about in a gravity-free world. The first contact with Chagall usually brings a chuckle to the spectator. On better acquaintance, his underlying humanitarianism is revealed (fig. 208).

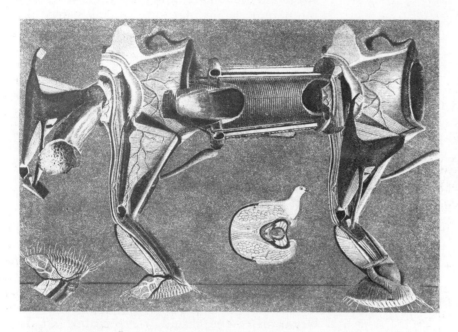

Fig. 206. THE HORSE, HE'S SICK (1920) by Max Ernst. As a part of the Dadaist's debunking of all twentieth-century art forms, a natural organism is here turned into a mechanical absurdity. At the same time, the use of pasted photoengravings is a nonsensical twist of the collage technique first invented by the Cubist Braque.

Collection, the Museum of Modern Art, New York. Purchase

Fig. 207. THE SOOTHSAYER'S RECOMPENSE (1913) by Giorgio de Chirico. This picture combines with poetic fullness symbols of the past (classical statue and Renaissance architecture) with forms of the modern world (railroad train) to create a feeling of vast timelessness and universality. In this way, de Chirico was able to emphasize the "reality of a personal symbolism."

Courtesy Philadelphia Museum of Art. The Louise and Walter Arensberg Collection

Fig. 208. I AND THE VILLAGE (1911) by Marc Chagall. The fairy-tale world of the Imagination is found in this example by another artist who evades fixed classification. Recent technological concepts are reflected in the freely interpreted transparency of object forms and the disregard for gravity.

Collection, the Museum of Modern Art, New York. Mrs. Simon Guggenheim Fund

Surrealism

Surrealism came into being about 1924 out of the work of individual fantasists and Dadaists. With World War I over, there was once again a semblance of stability and the public tended to become complacent about the ills of modern society. The Surrealists reacted to this by attempting to reassert "the importance of the individual's psychic life, and intended to preserve the life of the imagination against the threatening pressures and tensions of the contemporary world."[3]

According to Dr. Lester Longman, "Surrealism was Dada reborn with a program."[4] Both were a continuation of the counterattack (first instigated by the Romantics of the nineteenth century) against mechanistic materialism. The Romantics often created the hallucinatory imagery in which the Surrealist delights and in so doing gave evidence of the growing belief that man could not solve every problem by the right application of science and that little-known, often seemingly unsolvable, problems existed within the human mind. Sigmund Freud's theories of dreams and their meanings lent strong credence to this belief. Operating on this thesis, Surrealist artists created a new pantheon of subconscious imagery which was claimed to be more real than activities and behaviour on the conscious level. The Surrealists believed that only in dreams, which arise from the mind below the conscious level (nightmares or daydreams), had man retained his personal liberties. In their art, the Surrealists cultivated images which arose unbidden from the mind. These were recorded through automatic techniques of drawing and painting. Such images bring to attention the heretofore unrecognized arbitrariness of our senses concerning reality by exploring incongruous relationships of normal objects in abnormal settings. The Surrealists juxtaposed commonsense notions of space, time, and scale in unfamiliar ways.

Max Ernst's "frottages" (invented about 1925) was one technique used by the Surrealists to shut off the conscious mind. Frottages were rubbings made on rough surfaces with crayon, pencil, or similar media. In the resulting impressions, the artist would search for a variety of incarnations while in a state of feverish mental intoxication. A process bordering on self-hypnosis was practiced to arrive at this state. Some artists such as Salvador Dali affected a similar creative fever, but used a meticulous, naturalistic technique to give authenticity to their improbable, weird, and shocking images (fig. 209). Yves Tanguy used a method similar to Ernst's. Allowing his hand to wander in free and unconscious doodlings, he used his creative visualization to bring on nonfigurative objects which suggested life. Tanguy's pictorial shapes have the appearance of sentient, alien organisms living in a mystical twilight land (fig. 210; *see also* fig. 54).

There have been many Surrealist artists, but Ernst, Dali, and Tanguy have been most influential, thanks to their unflagging invention of arresting images. The influence of these outstanding artists extended to the great number of other artists who did not hold to the restrictions of the orthodox Surrealist brotherhood as

3. Charles McCurdy, ed., *Modern Art: A Pictorial Anthology* (New York: Macmillan Co., 1958), pp. 40–41.

4. Lester Longman, Notes from Longman's Lectures on Modern Art.

set forth in Andre Breton's manifesto of 1924. Many of these artists used some of the methods of the group while designing in a formal manner (an approach disdained by orthodox Surrealists), thus combining the methods of the Abstractionists, the Surrealists, and the Expressionists.

Surrealist Sculpture

There are not many twentieth-century sculptors who were purely Surrealist when we consider the character of their work. The effect of Surrealism on the work of many painters and sculptors was variable. However, the general trend was to merge the innovations of the first two decades to such an extent that classification into specific categories is not possible. The intensity of this trend has increased since mid-century and has led to the complex, interwoven movements of the last decade and a half.

Alberto Giacometti, a Swiss sculptor who spent much of his career in France, was perhaps

Fig. 209. THE PERSISTENCE OF MEMORY (1931) by Salvador Dali. Here we find a naturalistic technique of representation to give authenticity to improbable Surrealist images. Dali bends watches as if they were made of a soft, rubbery substance and otherwise adjusts natural objects to suit the fantastic world of his imagination.

Collection, the Museum of Modern Art, New York. Given Anonymously

Fig. 210. MULTIPLICATION DES ARCS (1954) by Yves Tanguy. Commonly working with nonfigurative objects in a polished technique, the Surealist Tanguy invents a new world that gives the appearance of being peopled by lifelike gems.

Collection, the Museum of Modern Art, New York. Mrs. Simon Guggenheim Fund

Fig. 211. GROUP OF THREE MEN (1949, bronze) by Alberto Giacometti. Giacometti emphasizes the lonely vulnerability of man by reducing him to a point of near-invisibility and by emphasizing the great spaces between the figures.
Courtesy the Art Institute of Chicago. Ayer Fund

Fig. 212. CACTUS MAN #1 (1934, bronze) by Julio Gonzalez. Expressively textured surfaces appealed greatly to this Spanish sculptor who was the earliest modern sculptor to introduce welding as part of the repertoire of artists. He also used suggestive qualities in his sometimes surreal approach to form.

one of the greatest Surrealist sculptors of this century. Involvement of his personal style was affected by such diverse influences as Lehmbruck's mild Expressionism, by Cubism, and by Constructivism. Like other twentieth-century sculptors, Giacometti was fascinated not only by the effects of new materials, but also by the effect of light and space on form. By 1934 he had evolved his nature style of elongated, slender figures pared away until almost nothing remained of substantial form. These figures (fig. 211) suggest arrested motion, poignant sadness, and isolation. His indirect method of approaching meaning stemmed from Surrealism and was related to the "stream of consciousness" theory supported by early twentieth-century psychologists.

The first sculptor to explore direct metal sculpture (welding) was the Spanish artist Julio Gonzalez. In the late 1920s Gonzalez began to substitute outlines for masses and planes and even allowed the tendrils of metal to stop short of completion so that they were completed by implication. His sense of the dematerialization of form is similar to Giacometti's, but is more often infected by a humorous quality of suggestivity that hinges on the edge of consciousness. He was an influence on Picasso's experiments with sculpture in the 1930s and was in turn influenced by Picasso himself (fig. 212).

The French artist Jean Hans Arp was another explorer of Surrealist preconscious suggestion and of the effect of the unexpected, or surprising, form. Before Arp's Surrealist direction, he explored most of the avant garde movements of the early twentieth century: Cubism, Blue Rider, Dada, Constructivism, and the like. Arp was a cofounder of the Zurich Dada movement in 1916. He was well known for his abstract collages and reliefs such as *The Mountain, Table,* and *Anchor and Navel* of 1925 before he turned to ovoidal sculptural forms in the 1930s. These later works reveal the influence of Brancusi and prehistoric Cycladic island sculpture (fig. 213). In fact, his ovoidal shapes became so famous that almost all kinds of rounded, biomorphoric shapes were called "Arp shapes."

Fig. 213. GROWTH (1960, white marble) by Jean Hans Arp.
The supple biomorphic "Arp shapes" contrast sharply with
the rigidity of the works of Cubist-inspired sculptors such
as Archipenko.

Courtesy the Art Institute of Chicago. Grant J. Pick Purchase Fund

Abstract Surrealism

Since about 1925 there have been a host of
artists who mix certain aspects of the three
major movements of early twentieth-century art.
Generally speaking, these artists found pure abstraction too impersonal, machinelike, and de-
humanized. On the other hand, Surrealism
seemed to disregard a desire for order that had
traditionally been held fundamental to art.

Among the artists who chose a harmony of
shape relationship stemming from Abstraction
mixed with Surrealism's unbidden imagery are:
Joan Miró of Spain, Rufino Tamayo of Mexico,
Matta Echaurren of Chile, Marx Tobey of the
United States, and some ex-Europeans such as
Willem de Kooning, Arshile Gorky, and Hans
Hofmann. The latter three artists, who lived in
the United States after World War II (some came
to the United States in the decade previous;
others, during the war), helped pioneer the first

American art movement called Abstract Expressionism (figs. 214 and 215 and plates 86 and 87;
see also figs. 47 and 60 and plates 20 and 51).

Abstract Expressionism

As a movement, Abstract Expressionism came
into being in the late 1940s. It is divided into two
basic groups: a generally romantic group (often
called "Action painting"), and a more classical
group closely allied to the geometric branch of
pre-World War II Abstraction. In the first group
were such artists as Jackson Pollock, Franz Kline,
and Clifford Still. These artists turned to an
artistic manner that reminds one of the emo-

Fig. 214. THREADING LIGHT (1942) by Mark Tobey. Tobey
was not directly a member of the small group of young
Americans who originally founded the Abstract Expressionist movement in the immediate post-World War II years, but
seems to be formally related. He originated his own personal method of linear expression in painting (called "white
writing") which causes accretions of line to waver on the
edge of shape recognition only to slip off into abstract con-
trolled-tension between surface and space.

Collection, the Museum of Modern Art, New York. Purchase

Fig. 215. AGONY (1947) by Arshile Gorky. An engineering, as well as artistic, background in his student days, plus the stimulation of Surrealism's unbidden imagery led this artist into the emotionalized phase of Abstract Expressionism. A peculiar quality in his work is the precision and stability that becomes unsettled and unsettling, marking a personal life of inevitable change and tragedy. Gorky was an important influence on the younger generation of American Abstract Expressionists in the 1940s.

Collection, the Museum of Modern Art, New York. A. Conger Goodyear Fund

Fig. 216. NUMBER 1 (1948) by Jackson Pollock. This artist is considered the prime example among the youthful exponents of Abstract Expressionist Action painting in the late 1940s. He is noted primarily for the creation of swirling nonrepresentational images in linear-skeins of fast drying paint applied by dripping directly onto canvases through controlled gestures of his tools.

Collection, the Museum of Modern Art, New York. Purchase

tional content of the early works of Kandinsky (before 1921). Some acknowledge that even so unlikely a source as Monet suggested a kindred technical method. Confusion, fear, and uncertainty about man's place in a world threatened by thermonuclear holocaust may have led others to reject most of the forms of previous twentieth-century art and, as a kind of personal catharsis, to express their belief in the "value of doing" at the expense of disciplined design. Thus, Jackson

Pollock, frequently cited as the chief exponent of the "Action" painting trend in Abstract Expressionism, created swirling images of a nonrepresentational kind out of linear skeins of fast-drying paint dripped directly onto large canvases, expressing the reality of self in the act of creation (fig. 216).

Franz Kline, another member of the Action group, took a slightly different direction, but with a similar intention of expressing self through direct contact with the forms created. He utilized drawings made with gestures of a brush on newsprint which were cut up and reassembled to provide a sense of power and intensified personal rapport. Kline utilized these "sketches" as guides to their enlargement on big canvases without actually copying them. House painters' brushes and savage slashings in black and white or sometimes in color became monumental projections of inward experience. A similar kind of daring and willingness to explore the unknown which such artists displayed in revealing their ego is expected of the viewer to renew the experience of creativity. This conscious attempt to involve the spectator in art is, perhaps, the leitmotif of direction in the second half of this century. Involvement of the viewer goes far beyond a similar endeavour attempted in seventeenth-century European religious art. Perhaps the reason is that artists foresee that urban sprawl with its pressure and tension, causes man to seek isolation, and involvement in art has to be forced upon him, somewhat like a tonic, for his own good.

The second group of artists within Abstract Expressionism, given to a more restrained manner allied to the geometric branch of prewar Abstraction, includes Mark Rothko, Carl Holty, Ad Reinhardt, and Robert Motherwell, to name a few (see plates 12 and 84). Many of these artists were motivated by the subtle color relationships of Joseph Albers, a former teacher at the Bauhaus and émigré to the United States during World War II (Plate 27). Hans Hofmann was another influence. All these artists appear concerned with reducing form to the sensation of color or value alone. They tend to create broad areas of color or of shapes so closely related in value and/or color that they are not immediately detectable. Both types of painting seem to enwrap the spectator and make him a part of the painting as an experienced sensation. The intention seems akin in final analysis to the Action painter group discussed previously, but these paintings are not violent recollections of the emotional fervor of painting; rather they are quiet insinuations on the viewer's being.

Abstract Surrealist and Abstract Expressionist Sculpture

There are many sculptors who work in forms allied to Abstract Surrealism, ranging from the organically sleek figures of the Englishman Henry Moore to the open wire sculptures of Gonzalez and Picasso in the 1930s from whom Alexander Calder was influenced in creating the mobile. Gonzalez, as the pioneer of welded sculpture, must also be credited with instigating the attitude of a younger generation of sculptors like Theodore Roszak and David Smith who in using his technique came as close as their medium of bronze, iron, and steel permitted to the Action painting of the Abstract Expressionist painters of the late 1940s and early 1950s. Dadaism and Surrealism influenced some of the "junk" sculpture of men like John Chamberlain, Richard Stankiewicz, and Robert Mallary.

Henry Moore merged the vitality and expressive potential of Gonzalez and Arp with older traditions such as Egyptian, primitive, and Pre-Columbian sculpture which he had discovered as a student. Moore's objective over the years was to create lively forms, not lifelike forms. All of his forms grew out of the selected material used in a way natural to it. Only secondarily do they resemble human forms. In this respect, his frequently repeated theme of the reclining nude seems in stone to retain a geologically inspired character and in wood to have a feeling of organic growth and grain (fig. 217). Moore was primarily responsible for re-establishing British art on the international scene and laid the basis for the great vitality English sculpture and painting have shown in the twentieth century.

The Lithuanian sculptor Jacques Lipchitz, who worked in France before World War I and was at that time strongly influenced by Cubism, began to be concerned with the Surrealist idiom in the 1930s. He developed a highly robust configuration of freely flowing, knotted, and twisted masses that suggest at times the agonies of birth and death, at others the suffering of psychic torture, and at others the creation of nameless new species of mythological monsters. From Surrealism he learned to exploit the semiautomatic principle, kneading his favorite sketching medium of clay into shapeless blobs without forethought and then through the accident of suggested form devising his final form (fig. 218). Lipchitz came to the United States in 1941 and was not only a strong influence on a younger generation of American Abstract Surreal sculptors, but also a significant influence internationally.

The most influential American pioneer of

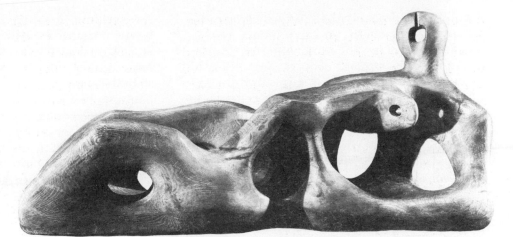

Fig. 217. RECLINING FIGURE (1939, wood) by Henry Moore. Moore's work is a synthesis of influences from primitive sculpture with a lifelong study of the forms of Nature.

Fig. 218. RAPE OF EUROPA (bronze) by Jacques Lipchitz. After an early exposure to Cubism, Lipchitz developed his unique sculptural shapes and personal symbolism, but his Cubist background always served as a disciplinary force.

Abstract Surreal sculpture was the Philadelphia-born artist Alexander Calder. Calder's parents were sculptors in a conservative nineteenth-century realist style. Calder reacted at first to this academic conservatism by studying engineering. He also studied for a time at the Art Student's League in New York and then went to Paris in 1926 where he began to create the animal wire sculpture that won him almost immediate recognition. In the late 1920s he was mingling in Dada, Surrealist, and Neo-Plasticist circles, meeting people like Miró, Mondrian, Gonzalez, and Arp. This apparently caused him to break with figurative forms for free-form abstract shapes of sheet metal and wire. By 1930 he had created the first of his mobiles after previously employing motors and pulleys to move his kinetic assemblages. The delicate balance and perfect engineering of the mobiles needed only air current to create rhythmic, varied motion that constantly produced new compositions and relationships of shapes in space (*see* fig. 167). Thus, Calder achieved the fourth dimension of time and movement in space for which artists, with their implied kinetics, had searched since the beginnings of Impressionism.

Calder finally evolved three basic types of assemblies:

1. *The stabile*—usually attached to a base, can rest on the ground, and does not move. However, some later works of this kind were made with moving parts.
2. *The mobile*—hangs in the air, usually from a ceiling.
3. *The constellation*—a form of mobile, but usually suspended on one or more arms from a wall.

Mobiles are probably the most widely appreciated form of modern art, and Calder is thus considered by many the most important American artist of the present century. Since 1933 he has divided his time between farms in Connecticut and France. His best known recent works consist of monumental stabiles in welded iron, some of which are architectural in size (fig. 219).

Some of the most interesting new shapes and techniques in sculpture of the late 1940s and 1950s suggested affinity with Abstract Expressionist painting. Among artists whose creations favor contact with this kind of painting is the Polish-born American sculptor Theodore Roszak. Roszak began his career before World War II as a Constructivist of severely geometric shapes, but later underwent a complete change. He became engrossed in portraying the conflict inherent between natural phenomena as a reflection of man's potential to destroy himself. Roszak employed coarse, eroded, scarred, and pitted textures as in *Mandrake* (1972) which, with its spiked and anguished skeletal angularities, expresses with controlled violence some of the terror of the nuclear age (fig. 220).

The promising career of David Smith, who was born in Indiana and a student at the Art Student's League in New York during the 1930s, was cut short by a fatal automobile accident in 1965. He was the earliest American sculptor to use welding, creating powerful statements in wrought iron and steel which at first held organic and Surreal elements. His later works showed more Cubist-Constructivist use of volumetric shape systems strongly reminiscent of Action painters like Clifford Still and Franz Kline. Smith's ruggedness and the slashing diagonals of his metal cubes on tall poles and stands remind one particularly of the black diagonals of Kline against their flat-white canvas surfaces. Smith's last cubic style before his death also influenced the following generation of young sculptors who got away from the open, flowing sculptural trend of the 1950s (*see* fig. 5).

Other artists who often used biomorphics with varying degree of openness or closedness suggesting involvement with Surrealist preconscious imagery resolved by Cubist, Constructivist, or Abstract formality are: Egyptian-born Ibram Lassaw, Seymour Lipton (fig. 221), and Richard Lippold (*see* fig. 164), to name a few. Reuben Nakian appears to be a product more of the free-form manner expressed by earlier twentieth-century artists such as Gaston Lachaise and Jacques Lipchitz. However, Nakian prefers the porous surfaces used by his peers of the 1950s rather than the smoothly refined surfaces used by his teacher Lachaise or those used by the Primary Structurists of the 1960s (fig. 222).

Fig. 219. CLOUDS OVER MOUNTAINS (1962, steel plate) by Alexander Calder. A recent work by this famous inventor of movable sculpture, which combines portions of moving (Mobile) and static forms (Stabile).
Courtesy the Art Institute of Chicago. Kate Maremont Foundation

Fig. 220. MANDRAKE (1951, steel brazed with copper) by Theodore Roszak. In sculptural forms which paralleled the Action painting of the late 1940s and early 1950s, artists like Roszak employed welding techniques to capture through spiked angular shapes and corroded porous surfaces some of the anxieties of the nuclear age.

Courtesy the Cleveland Museum of Art. Gift of the Cleveland Society for Contemporary Art

Fig. 221. EARTH LOOM (ca. 1958, bronze) by Seymour Lipton. In this Surreal Abstract sculpture are combined life-suggestive shapes and tenser rectilinear thrust—an influence, perhaps, from earlier Constructivist tendencies.

Courtesy the Detroit Institute of Arts. Gift of the Friends of Modern Art

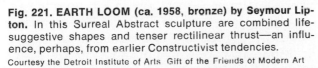

Fig. 222. GODDESS OF THE GOLDEN THIGHS (bronze) by Reuben Nakian. Although he studied under Gaston Lachaise, Nakian rough cast his sculptural forms to take full advantage of the emotion-evoking qualities of the resulting texture, rather than use the more smoothly finished forms employed by his teacher. His abstractions also suggest surreal-like inward forces that assert a life of their own.

Courtesy the Detroit Institute of Arts. Purchase, the W. Hawkins Ferry Fund

Directions in Art Since 1950

Post-Painterly Abstraction: Hard Edge Painters, Field Painters, and Minimalists

Throughout history a common occurrence has been for new generations of artists to become dissatisfied with the direction taken by their elders and to strike out in new directions. The feeling that inherited methods and media have reached a state of perfection, or have exhausted their possibilities, has been especially keen among artists of the twentieth century and increasingly so since midcentury. A strong motivation for change in the present century has been the development of motion pictures and other technological advances in machinery, electronics, and space flight.

Drawn by these technological innovations, artists have met the desire for change by no longer observing the separate categories of painting and sculpture, but instead merging the two in assemblages which partake a bit of both. This mixture of heretofore separate disciplines has its closest parallel in the Baroque art of the seventeenth century in which a similar intermingling of traditionally separate mediums and disciplines took place, bringing about synthesis of the two.

The first serious challenge to the dominance of Abstract Expressionism after World War II was among a group of painters known as the Post Painterly Abstractionists. This category of painting breaks down into Hard Edge painters, Field painters, and Minimalists. All owe source attributions to early twentieth-century geometric Abstraction, particularly to Joseph Albers. (See page 168.) After coming to the United States, Albers, who was a product of the Bauhaus tradition, did a series of paintings during the 1930s called *Homage to the Square* (see plate 27). In this series he showed interest in gestalt psychology as expressed through the effects of optical illusion. He created passive, free-floating square shapes that had just enough contrast of value, hue, and intensity with surrounding colors that they seemed to emerge slightly from the background.

Albers' successors, Hard Edge painters like Ellsworth Kelly, stress definition of edges which set off shapes in their canvas more explicitly than in the case of the Field painters. In this context are artists like Barnett Newmann, Morris Louis, Kenneth Noland (fig. 223, *Purple in the Shadow of Red*), Frank Stella (see plate 10), and Larry Poons. Newmann, who can be considered one of the originators of Field painting in the early

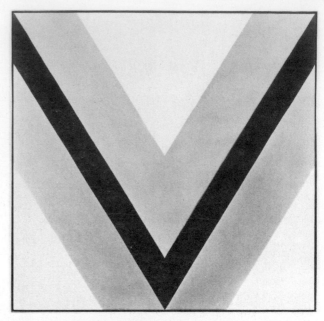

Fig. 223. PURPLE IN THE SHADOW OF RED by Kenneth Noland. Field painters of the late 1950s and early 1960s discovered the power of pure color surface that were differentiated only by hard-edged lines, or shapes, of intense hues which give a feeling that the art object is an extension of modern technology. They are based on early twentieth-century nonobjective forms like those of Malevich and Rodchenko. A similar idea was carried into sculpture by the Primary Structurists.

Courtesy the Detroit Institute of Arts. Purchase, the Dr. and Mrs. George Kamperman Fund

1950s, allowed the shape of the canvas to dictate the pictorial form. He divided the canvas either horizontally or vertically with a line or lines of intense color set off by slight changes in nuance in the resulting shape of the color field.

Minimalists, of whom the nonconformist New Yorker Ad Reinhardt was a chief exponent in the late 1950s, painted pictures in such close values that only after intense concentration could the spectator determine that any shapes or lines or other elements of form were present at all. Jules Olitsky was also an exponent of such Minimalist work in the 1960s, as seen in his *Emma*, 1966 (see plate 88). Another characteristic of Post-Painterly Abstraction was the tendency either to thin down the pigments to stain, to soak the canvas in color, or to lay color on in such thin layers as to make the work entirely without texture, except for that of the canvas support (ground) on which it was painted. Morris Louis *Number 99* (1959) is an example (plate 89).

Most present-day art is concerned with ways of seeing as much as it is with what is seen. To put it another way, artists are much more concerned with the processing of the art object than with form. This has tended to breakdown the

Fig. 224. GRACEHOPER (sheet steel, 23 x 22 x 46 feet) by Tony Smith. A primary sculptural structure is shown here which utilizes size and a simplified geometric volume to create impact on the visual senses of the observer.

Courtesy the Detroit Institute of Arts. Purchase, Donation from W. Hawkins Ferry and Founders Society Fund

Fig. 225. UP FRONT (1971, sheet metal and steel beams) by Anthony Caro. This work by the Primary Structurist Caro owes some of its bluntness of expression and direct simplicity of form to the later work of David Smith. Its quality of technological precision contrasts, however, with the haphazard, ready-made castoffs of present-day technological society as suggested by the ethos of Neo-Dadaism and Junk Art.

Courtesy the Detroit Institute of Arts. Purchase, Contributions from W. Hawkins Ferry and Mr. and Mrs. Richard Manoogian

former requirements for acquired skill, so much that "anyone can call himself an artist today and very few seem to be craftsmen any longer."

Primary Structurists

In sculpture, the Post-Painterly Abstractionists have a parallel in a group of artists that includes Robert Morris, Donald Judd, Tony Smith and (see back cover), Anthony Caro, (fig. 225), and others who carry the late mechanomorphic cubes of David Smith into blunt sculpture of simplified

geometric volume which seems stripped of all psychological or symbolic meaning. They are called Primary Structurists. Quite often they reject metal and welding for materials hitherto uncommon to sculpture. Cardboard, Masonite, plywood, and the like are used. In some cases hard sheet plastic is used to create transparent volumes that enclose space. Obliteration of the core seems to be another characteristic of this group. The objects they create express through the power of simple volume all that they want to say. Some are merely boxes of gigantic size; others are rectilinear, with beamlike arms or girderlike extensions. These sculptures sometimes manifest relationship to the wall, floor, or ceiling of a room and at other times seem only to comfortably inhabit exterior space. A few stress brightly colored surfaces, while others are neutral or void of color. Without doubt, many have impact, but the overview of these primary structures often leaves one with a feeling of sameness or monotony.

Again, the processing of these objects seems more important than form and its affect on the vision of the observer.

Neo-Dada Art, Pop Art, and Op Art

Another branch of Post-Painterly Abstraction, Neo-Dadism, led directly to a significant trend of the 1950s and 1960s, Pop Art. Robert Rauschenberg, using combinations of pure, fluid brush work in pigments and foreign materials like old mattresses, wireless sets, photographic images, animals, and the like attached to the canvas, was one of the first to indicate a drift away from pure Abstract Expressionism. From his combine-paintings also came much of the new art of Assemblage (fig. 226).

Jasper Johns, another American artist more satirical in his approach than Rauschenberg, was equally important in pointing the new direction away from Abstract Expressionism. He chose as his chief motif single images of commonplace objects that had lost their effectiveness, such as the United States flag, targets, and the like.

It was the strictly sculptural usage of the assemblage concept which had the greatest consequence on the sculptors of the 1960s and early 1970s. Louise Nevelson, for instance, began by using smooth abstract shapes in a way comparable almost to Henry Moore. Later she moved toward assemblage, fitting together ready-made wooden shapes such as knobs, bannisters, mold-

Fig. 226. MONOGRAM WITH RAM (1963) by Robert Rauschenberg. In this combine-painting, which merges into three dimensional assemblage, we have revealed the drift away from pure painting of the 1950's. Such a work provided precedents for the Pop Art movement shortly thereafter.

Courtesy the National Museum, Stockholm, Sweden and the Art Reference Bureau, Inc.

Fig. 227. "AMERICAN-DAWN" (1962–67, wood, painted white) by Louise Nevelson. An example of the assemblage concept in today's art by a well known sculptress. She utilizes separate, columnar-like, shapes which builds up to a unified, but dynamic verticalized accent, that contrasts with the more frequently used box-like screens enclosing smaller sculptural units in other works.

Courtesy the Art Institute of Chicago

ings, and posts gleaned from demolished houses and old furniture. These framents were associated in boxlike forms compartmented into various sized rectangles and squares which became large screens or freestanding walls. These complex pieces were usually painted a uniform color, which stressed the relationship of the parts as a unified total. Her relationships and complexities seem in keeping with the new trend toward processing rather than form. But her final results are more exciting than those of the Primary Structurists (fig. 227).

The popularity of *assemblage* and the enhancement of the Dadaist idea of the found-object also led to the junk ethos in metal and other material form combinations. In modern technological terms, the use of junk is often related to the scrapped fragments of man-made objects such as automobiles, farm machinery, factory parts, airplanes, bicycles, and the like. John Chamberlain's sculptures made from the parts of wrecked automobiles (fig. 228) and those of Richard Stankiewicz created from old boilers, sinks, or whatever welded together are a kind of comment on consumer culture which also occurs in Pop Art. The artists just mentioned are American, but Europeans like Cézar work along similar lines. Cézar's *Compressions Derigées* are objects made using the giant baling machines which compress junked automobiles and other scrap into small size.

Fig. 228. UNTITLED (1958, painted metal) by John Chamberlain. The popularity of *assemblage*, enhanced by the Dadaist idea of the "found object" led to the Junk ethos of metal and other material form combinations. During the 1950s and 1960s artists of this persuasion like Chamberlain, who works with bent and crushed metal from old automobiles, have also been called Neo-Dadaists.

Courtesy the Cleveland Museum of Art. Purchase, Andrew R., and Martha Holden Jennings Fund

Edward Keinholz' works, which he calls *Tableaus*, also fall into the category of junk or funk art assemblages. His combinations of a variety of materials have something of the shock value of Dada art, making satirical comment on the sickness, tawdriness, and "dopeyness" of modern society.

The trend away from Abstract Expressionism in the various forms just mentioned culminated in the early 1960s in two main international movements called Pop Art and Op Art. The term *Pop* stands for Popular Art or even for Pop Bottle Art, judging by the frequency with which such objects have appeared. The movement as a whole seems to have originated in England in the fifties and then became rather naturally acclimated to the United States. In it, images made popular by mass media advertising, comic strips, and other everyday objects such as pop bottles, beer cans, and supermarket products, are presented in bizarre combinations, distortions, or exaggerations of size, always rendered with fidelity to the original man-made object. The effect of these objects, as in the case of Andrew Warhol's *Campbell Soup Cans* or Roy Lichtenstein's grotesquely magnified comic strip heroes and villains, is to cause the viewer to react in a manner best described as a double take. As with Abstract Expressionism, the observer is again involved directly in the work of art, but now by the frequency with which he sees these commonplace items in everyday life and not only as an experienced sensation of the art form itself. The blurring between the realm of art and real life in Pop Art is more pronounced in the recent Pop-originated Happening.

Since similar experiences were promoted by the Dadaists in 1916, some Pop artists have also been called Neo-Dadaists. But whereas Dada was nihilistic, self-exterminating, and satirical, Pop Art seems to have little such purpose. Instead, there is more joyful enthusiasm for exploring the possibilities implied by the daily images and objects of a megalometropolitan society and culture. Significant artists of Pop persuasion besides Warhol and Lichtenstein are: Jim Dine, Robert Indiana, Tom Wesselman, Claes Oldenburg, and George Segal. Several, but especially Oldenburg and Segal, are sculptors or assemblers, fields in which Pop Art makes inroads as much as in painting (figs. 229 and 230).

Op Art stands for the term *Optical*, and, again, seems merely an extension and modification of earlier twentieth-century Geometric Abstraction and Nonobjectivity. Artists in the movement (many again influenced by Albers) such as Victor Varsarely, Richard Anuskiewicks, George Ortman Agam, and Bridget Riley, employ precise shapes and sometimes wriggly lines or concentric patterns having a direct impact on the physiology and psychology of sight (plate 90). They have explored moiré patterns and have formed groups which seem almost dedicated more to scientific investigation of vision than to its intuitive expression in art.

Fig. 229. FALLING SHOESTRING POTATOES (1965) by Claes Oldenburg. Pop artists generally disregard all consideration of form in the belief that they would create a barrier between the observer and the everyday objects which serve as subjects. Pop Art is an art of the "now" things.
Courtesy the Walker Art Center Minneapolis, Minnesota

Fig. 230. THE AMERICAN DREAM I (1911) by Robert Indiana. This is an example of Pop Art. Robert Indiana utilizes the Pop convention of commonly seen images of advertising. He mixes it with slogan-conscious idioms of daily American life to create new experiences in which the conventional becomes unconventional.

Collection, the Museum of Modern Art, New York. Larry Aldrich Foundation Fund

New Realism

A general trend in the 1960s was the extension of Pop Art into meticulously rendered images of reality and the movement was led by such artists as Wayne Thiebaud, Mel Ramos, Philip Pearlstein, and Richard Lindner. Artists of this persuasion are designated New Realists (fig. 231; *see also* fig. 77).

Kinetic Art—Environmentalist and Conceptualist

The terms *Environmentalist* and *Conceptualist* as used here are largely interchangeable. These forms of contemporary art are the result of response to the stimuli found in the idea that not only should the spectator's sense of vision be engaged in works of art, but also his physical body, his sense of touch, and his sense of smell. Pop Art gave rise to the Environmental form of art in which the work of art surrounds the spectator, forcing him to complete them by their stress on what is around them. And Kinetic forms of art derived from Op Art. Op Art used static forms to suggest movement, a throwback to the *time-and-space* concepts in some forms of Impressionism in the late nineteenth century and to Futurism in the early twentieth century. Dada also produced kinetics under the aegis of nonsense, as in Duchamp's swirling designs played on phonograph turntables, and later Calder introduced the ideal of *time and space* in the mobile.

Present-day artists use random movement as well as movement controlled by mechanical or

Fig. 231. CUT MERINGUES (1961) by Wayne Thiebaud. The Pop artist's concern with the New Reality of commonplace forms led some artists to concentrate on meticulously rendered nudes. Thiebaud is an artist who moved on to such figurative works after the Pop phase of his work demonstrated in this illustration.

Collection, the Museum of Modern Art, New York. Larry Aldrich Foundation Fund

electronic means to produce kinetic art. Jean Tinguely's mechanisms can be said to summarize this trend. He creates large, slack, junky-appearing contrivances that outdo the imaginary cartoons of Rube Goldberg of the 1920s and 1930s. Tinguely's creations sometimes move about, but more often merely stand and shake about as if they were going to throw away the gears and cogs that run them. In fact, Tinguely's most famous kinetic construction of this kind did just that, destroying itself in the garden of the Museum of Modern Art in New York City in 1960 (*Homage to New York*).

Other artists such as the Greek artist Takis and Pol Bury exploit similar possibilities in more elegant forms that sometimes seem almost immaterial. Takis, for example, has used small metal shapes suspended on rods whose movement can hardly be detected without close study, while Bury often uses biomorphic wood shapes that are motorized to make slight movement (fig. 232). Other artists explore the suggested movement in the work of Minimalist and Optical artists, and do achieve movement—but to a limited degree.

Some artists such as Chryssa, Dan Flavin, and Nicholas Schoeffer explore the combination of

Fig. 232. STAIRCASE (1965) by Pol Bury. Here is an example of an art form with actual movement that had precedent in both late nineteenth-century and early twentieth-century sculpture and painting. A growing number of technologically oriented artists exploit the possibilities of such *kinetic* art today.

Courtesy the Solomon R. Guggenheim Museum, New York

light, movement, and sound electronically produced to create kinetic fantasies. Chryssa uses the technology of the neon light in his fluorescent kinetics, as does Flavin. Schoeffer more frequently uses movement, electronic sounds, and lighting in his creations.

Environments in various materials emerged from the static assemblages of the 1950s and 1960s. Here again, Pop Art led the way. Making use of Pop-Art literal images built up in space and enwrapping the spectator, the Environmental specialists took the concept a step further. Among recent members of the Environmental movement are Chrysto, Oldenburg, and Lucas Samaris. Chrysto's great balloons, featured at the Whitney Gallery in 1968, gave way to colossal plastic sheets with which he wrapped a por-

tion of the Australian coast in 1969 and more recently tried to enclose a canyon in the western United States. Oldenburg is a well known Pop Art artist, but his monuments designed for the Thames River in London and his giant lipstick tube for Yale University are an extension of Pop Art into the more encompassing Environmental movement of the late 1960s and early 1970s. Lucas Samaris used mirrors in *Mirrored Room* (1966) to suggest expanded space which seemingly enclosed the spectator in the midst of the assemblage (fig. 233).

Happenings, popular in the late 1950s and early 1960s, were another form of Environmental Art linked to Pop Art. They were a form of theatricallike participatory art in which spectators as well as artists engaged. A Happening can be

Fig. 233. MIRRORED ROOM (1966, mirrors) by Lucas Samaris. This is an example of *environmental Art* which, using size and structure, seems to enclose, or actually encloses, the observer within the form of the work.

Courtesy the Albright-Knox Art Gallery, Buffalo, New York. Gift of Seymour H. Knox defined as an assemblage on the move. Happenings were based on the ancient ideal of drawing the spectator into the heart of a work of art (just as Environmental art) so that he would experience the work more directly—an ideal that first reached a climax in Baroque art in the seventeenth century when painting, architecture, sculpture, and music were often interwoven in an artistic fabric unified within itself, but dependent on the spectator's participation in the artistic experience for completion.

Environmental Art, Happenings, and Minimal Art all seem to cojoin in varying degrees in the movement called Conceptual Art during the last decade. Conceptual Art sometimes involves nature directly by changing its shape, as when Oldenburg dug a hole in Central Park in New York City (1967) which he called "invisible sculpture." Another example of "earth art" was produced by Michael Heizer in the Black Rock Desert of Nevada in 1969. It consisted of five 12-foot long trenches which he dug and then lined with wood. But perhaps the acme of Conceptual Art is the kind which presents no form whatsoever for the spectator's view and is present only in the artist's mind or at the very least in his assurance that he has *thought* of a piece of art. Close to these formless works are such concepts as releasing oxygen or steam vapor into the atmosphere and calling it "universal" art since it would presumably spread into the infinite void.

Happenings and Conceptual Art appear to be momentary phases or fads in the final third of the twentieth century and are the result of a desperate search by some people for a new direction in art. Since it is based on abstruse doctrine that appeals to very few and leaves nothing of permanent worth as an art form for future generations, it may be that this philosophy, wistfully called "Art" by its participants, is actually one manifestation of the growing decline of twentieth-century tradition. Perhaps twentieth-century art has already reached its peak and is passing into decline preparatory to giving way to another, more vital art movement not yet clearly perceived. Many feel that the new form of art may be kinetics. If this is true, students will have to have training which combines the practical side of science and technology with renewal of the artistic aesthetic of actual form before a monumental change such as this can come about. And schools for this kind of combined training would have to be generally available before a strong movement could be established.

Glossary

Abstract, abstraction. A term given to forms created by the artist but usually derived from objects actually observed or experienced. It usually involves simplification and/or rearrangement of natural objects to meet the needs of artistic organization or expression. Somtimes there is so little resemblance to the original object that the shape seems to have no relationship to anything ever experienced in natural environment.

Academic. A term applied to any kind of art which stresses the use of accepted rules for technique and form organization. It represents the exact opposite of the original approach which results in a vital, individual style of expression.

Accent. Any stress or emphasis given to elements of a composition which makes them attract more attention than other features which surround or are close to them. Accent may be created by brighter color, darker tone, greater size, or any other means by which expresses difference.

Achromatic. Relating to differences of lightness and darkness; the absence of color.

Aesthetics. The theory of the artistic or the "beautiful"; traditionally a branch of philosophy, but now a compound of the philosophy, psychology, and sociology of art. As a compound of the above, aesthetics is no longer solely confined to determining what is beautiful in art, but now attempts to discover the origins of sensitivity to art forms and the relationship of art to other phases of culture (such as science, industry, morality, philosophy, and religion).

Frequently used in this book to mean concern with artistic qualities of form as opposed to descriptive form or mere recording of facts in visual form (*see* Objective).

Amorphous. Without clarity of definition; formless; indistinct and of uncertain dimension.

Analagous colors. 1. Closely related colors, especially those in which we can see one common hue. 2. Colors which are neighbors on the color wheel.

Approximate symmetry. The use of forms which are similar on either side of a vertical axis. They may give a feeling of the exactness of equal relationship but should be sufficiently varied to prevent visual monotony.

Artificial texture. Textures of products created by man: i.e., glass, steel, plastic, etc.

Asymetrical balance. A form of balance attained when the visual units on either side of a vertical axis are not identical but are placed in position within the pictorial field so as to create a "felt" equilibrium of the total form concept .

Atectonic. The opposite of tectonic; a quality of three-dimensional complexity, involving fairly frequent and often considerable extension into space, producing a feeling of openness.

Atmospheric (aerial) perspective. The illusion of deep space produced in graphic works by lightening values, softening contours, reducing value contrasts, and neutralizing color in objects as they approach the horizon, while following the general principles of linear perspective.

Balance. A feeling of equality in weight, attention, or attraction of the various visual elements within the pictorial field as a means of accomplishing organic unity.

Biomorphic shapes. Shapes which are irregular in form and resemble the freely developed curves of organic life.

Calligraphy. The use of flowing rhythmical lines which intrigue the eye as they enrich a surface. Calligraphy is highly personal in nature similar to the individual quality of handwriting.

Cast shadow. The dark area created on a surface when another form is placed to prevent the light from falling on that surface.

Chiaroscuro. A technique of representation which concentrates on the effect of blending light and shade on objects to create the illusion of space or atmosphere.

Chromatic.   Relating to color.

Classical.   Art forms which are characterized by a rational, controlled, clear, and intellectual approach. The term derives from the Ancient art of Greece in the fourth and fifth centuries B.C. The term *classic* has an even more general connotation, meaning an example or model of first rank or highest class for any kind of form, literary, artistic, natural, or otherwise. *Classicism* is the application or adherence to the principles of Greek culture by later cultural systems such as Roman classicism, Renaissance classicism, or the art of the Neoclassic movements of the early nineteenth century (*see* Chapter 11, Forms of Expression).

Collage.   Similar to papier collé except that materials of all kinds are admissible to the picture. Painted and drawn passages are combined with scrap materials to create the desired effect.

Color.   The character of surface created by the response of vision to the wavelength of light reflection.

Color triad.   A group of three colors spaced an equal distance apart on the color wheel. There is a primary triad, a secondary triad, and two intermediate triads on the twelve-color wheel.

Complementary colors.   Two colors which are directly opposite each other on the color wheel. A primary color would be complementary to a secondary color which was a mixture of the two remaining primaries.

Composition.   The act of organizing all of the elements of a work of art into a harmoniously unified whole. Each element used may have intrinsic characteristics which create interest, but must function in such a way that "the whole is more important than its parts."

Concept.   A comprehensive idea or generalization which brings diverse elements into some basic relationship.

Content (meaning).   The essential meaning, significance, or aesthetic value of an art form. The psychological or sensory properties one tends to feel in art forms as opposed to the visual aspects of a work of art.

Contour.   A line which creates a boundary separating an area of space from its surrounding background.

Craftsmanship.   Aptitude, skill, and manual dexterity in the use of tools and materials.

Cubism.   A term given to the artistic style which uses mostly geometric shapes usually two-dimensional in nature.

Curvilinear.   Stressing the use of curved lines as opposed to *rectilinear* which stresses straight lines.

Dadaism.   A nihilistic, antiart, antieverything movement resulting from the social, political, and psychological dislocations of World War I. The movement is important historically as a generating force for surrealism.

Decorative.   The quality which emphasizes the two-dimensional nature of any of the visual elements.

Decoration enriches a surface without denying the essential flatness of its nature.

Decorative shapes.   Two-dimensional shapes which seem to lie next to each other on a picture surface; shapes which divide or break up the pictorial surface into smaller areas.

Decorative space.   A concept in which the visual elements have interval relationships in terms of a two-dimensional plane.

Decorative value.   A type of pattern dependent more on the standard or local value of shapes rather than on the representation of light and shadow; essentially a two-dimensional use of pattern.

Descriptive art.   A manner or attitude based upon adherence to visual appearances.

Design.   A framework or scheme of pictorial construction on which the artist bases the formal organization of his total work. In a broader sense, it may be considered synonymous with the term, *form*.

Distortion.   Any change made by an artist in the size, position, or general character of forms based on visual perception, when those forms are organized into a pictorial image. Any personal or subjective interpretation of natural forms must necessarily involve a degree of distortion.

Dominance.   The principle of visual organization which suggests that certain elements should assume more importance than others in the same composition. It contributes to organic unity by emphasizing the fact that there is one main feature and that other elements are subordinate to it.

Elements of art.   The basic visual signs as they are combined into optical units which are used by the artist to communicate or express his creative ideas. The combination of the basic elements of line, shape, value, texture, and color represent the visual language of the artist.

Expression.   A general term meaning the special characteristics of form which mark the work of an artist or group of artists. The style or manner in which artists attempt to say something about their time in terms of the artistic forms then considered to be of aesthetic merit.

When a work of art remains largely realistic in form but strongly emotional or intellectual in content, we call the work of art *expressive*. In a more general usage of the term, all art can be so characterized when the final goal is an intrinsic or self-sufficient aesthetic meaning. Opposed to this would be art with extrinsic, practical ends; commercial art with its easily read message, is intended to promote the product other than the work of art itself.

Expressionistic art is art in which there is a desire to express what is felt rather than perceived or reasoned. Expressionistic form is defined by an obvious exaggeration of natural objects for the purpose of emphasizing an emotion, mood, or concept. It may be better understood as a more vehement kind of *romanticism*. The term *expressionism* is best applied to a movement in art of the early twentieth century, although it may be used to describe all art of this character.

Fantasy (in art). Departure from accepted appearances or relationships for the sake of psychological expression—may exist within any art style, but usually thought of in connection with realism; unencumbered flights of pictorial fancy, freely interpreted or invented.

Fauvism. A name (meaning "wild beasts") for an art movement that began in Paris about 1905. It is expressionist art in a general sense but more decorative and with more of the French sense of orderliness and charm than in German expressionism (*see* Chapter 11, Forms of Expression).

Form. 1. The arbitrary organization or inventive arrangement of all of the visual elements according to principles which will develop an organic unity in the total work of art. 2. Three-dimensional: A portion of a three-dimensional work which has a certain degree of concavity or convexity.

Form-meaning. Another term for *Content,* the third component of a work of art as used in this book. Since artists create artistic forms which cause spectator reactions, form-meaning implies that such reaction is the associations and/or sensory experience which the observer finds in those forms.

Formal. An orderly system of organization as opposed to a less disciplined system.

Futurism. A submovement within the framework of abstract directions taken by many twentieth century artists. The expression of Futurist artists was based on an interest in time and rhythm which they felt were manifested in the machinery and human activities of modern times.

Genre. Painting that stresses subject matter of domestic trivia, homey scenes, sentimental family life, etc.

Geometric shapes. Those shapes created by the exact mathematical laws of geometry. They are usually simple in character such as the triangle, the rectangle, and the circle.

Graphic. As used in this book, the term refers to forms *physically* existing in a two-dimensional space relationship. For example, the graphic arts refers only to those arts whose elements are present on a two-dimensional surface although they might give the *illusion* of three-dimensions.

Harmony. The unity of all of the visual elements of a composition achieved by the repetition of the same characteristics or those which are similar in nature.

Highlight. The area of a represented shape which receives the greatest amount of direct light.

Hue. Used to designate the common name of a color and to indicate its position in the spectrum or in the color circle. Hue is determined by the specific wavelength of the color in the ray of light.

Illusionism. The imitation of visual reality created on the flat surface of the picture plane by the use of perspective, light-and-dark shading, etc.

Illustration(al). An art practice, usually commercial in character, which stresses anecdote or story situation, and subject in preference to serious considerations of aesthetic quality; noneloquent, nonformal, easily understood, and temporal rather sustained or universal.

Image. An arresting aspect; a mentally envisioned thing or plan given concrete appearance through the use of an art medium; the general appearance of a work (en toto).

Impression, and Impressionism. A strong immediate effect produced in the mind by an outward or inward agency. Artists may work in this general sense (as Impressionists) at any time in history. The specific movement known as *Impressionism* was a late nineteenth-century movement, primarily connected with painters such as Claude Monet and Camille Pissarro. (*see* Chapter 11, Forms of Expression).

Intensity. The saturation or strength of a color determined by the *quality* of light reflected from it. A vivid color is of high intensity; a dull color, of low intensity.

Intuitive. Knowing or recognizing by an instinctive sense rather than by the application of exact rules; sensing or feeling something without a specific reason.

Intuitive space. A pictorial spatial illusion which is not the product of any mechanical system but which relies, instead, on the physical properties of the elements and the instincts or feel of the artist.

Light pattern. The typical relationship of light and dark shapes appearing on a form as a result of its physical character and the kind and direction of light falling upon it.

Line. The path of a moving point, that is, a mark made by a tool or instrument as it is drawn across a surface. It is usually made visible by the fact that it contrasts in value with the surface on which it is drawn.

Local (objective) color. A tone which takes its color from the nature of the actual object portrayed (green grass, blue sky, etc.)

Local value. The characteristic tone quality of an area or surface which is determined by its particular pigmentation. For example, a shape painted with gray pigment will reflect only a *certain amount of light* even when that light strikes it directly.

Lyrical. A term borrowed from poetry which attempts to define a quality of a special aesthetic or sensory experience in the visual arts (as opposed to a dramatic experience, for example). A songlike outpouring of the artist's experience usually accomplished in form by graceful rhythms, light color tonalities, and spontaneous drawing or brushwork.

The term *poetic* is sometimes used in place of *lyrical*, for the same kind of meaning.

Mass. The physical bulk of a solid body of material.

Media, mediums. The materials and tools used by the artist to create the visual elements perceived by the viewer of the work of art.

Moments of force. Direction(s) and degree(s) of energy implied by art elements in specific pictorial situations; amounts of visual thrust produced by such matters as dimension, placement, and accent.

Motif. A visual element or a combination of elements which is repeated often enough in a composition to make it the dominating feature of the artist's expression.

Narrative art. A form of art which depends on subject matter to tell a story. At its best such art is more concerned with aesthetic qualities than with the story; at its worst, it is a documentary description of the facts of the story without regard for aesthetic form.

Natural texture. Texture existing as the result of natural processes.

Naturalism. The approach to art in which all forms used by the artist are essentially descriptive representation of things visually experienced. True naturalism contains no interpretation introduced by the artist for expressive purposes.

Negative areas. The unoccupied or empty space left after the positive shapes have been laid down by the artist. However, because these areas have boundaries, they also function as shapes in the total pictorial structure.

Neutralized color. A color which has been grayed or reduced in intensity by mixture with a neutral or a complementary color.

Neutrals. Tones which do not reflect any single wavelength of light. Neutrals create only effects of darkness and lightness as in black, white, or gray.

Nonobjective. An approach to art in which the visual signs are entirely imaginative and do not derive from anything ever seen by the artist. The shapes, their organization, and their treatment by the artist are entirely personalized and consequently not associated by the observer with any previously experienced natural form.

Objective. An impersonal statement of observed facts. In art, the exact rendering by the artist of surface characteristics without alteration or interpretation of the visual image.

Objective color (*see* Local color).

Optical perception. A way of seeing in which the mind seems to have no other function than the natural one of providing the physical sensation of recognition by sight.

Organizational control. Specific or planned relationships of the art elements in pictorial space.

Orthographic drawing. A two-dimensional graphic representation of an object showing a plan, a vertical elevation, and/or a section.

Paint quality. The use of the medium on a surface to give it enrichment through textural interest. Interest is created by the ingenuity in handling paint for its intrinsic character.

Papier collé. A technique of visual expression in which scraps of paper having various textures are actually pasted to the picture surface to enrich or embellish areas.

Patina. 1. A film, usually greenish in color, which results from oxidation of bronze or other metallic material. 2. Colored pigments, usually earthy, applied to a sculptural surface.

Pattern. The obvious emphasis on certain visual form relationships and certain directional movements within the visual field. It also refers to the repetition of elements or the combination of elements in a readily recognized systematic organization.

Perception. The act of taking notice; recognition of an object, quality, or idea through the use of the physical and/or mental faculties.

Perspective. A mechanical system of creating the illusion of a three-dimensional space on a two-dimensional surface. *Linear perspective* is primarily linear in treatment. *Aerial or atmospheric perspective* uses value and color modification to suggest or enhance the effect of space.

Pictorial area. The area within which the design exists; generally of measurable dimensions and bounded by mat, frame, or lines.

Picture frame. The outermost limits or the boundary of the picture plane.

Picture plane. The actual flat surface on which the artist executes his pictorial image. In some cases it acts merely as a transparent plane of reference to establish the illusion of forms existing in a three-dimensional space.

Pigments. Coloring matter or substances used by the artist to create the effect of color on a surface.

Plane. A shape which is essentially two-dimensional in nature but whose relationships with other shapes may give an illusion of third dimension.

Plastic. A quality which emphasizes the three-dimensional nature of shape or mass. On a two-dimensional surface, plasticity is always an illusion created by the use of the visual elements in special ways.

Plastic shapes. Shapes which are indicated by the artist as being "in the round" and surrounded by space. Shapes displaying the third dimension of depth.

Positive shapes. The enclosed areas which represent the initial selection of shapes planned by the artist. They may suggest recognizable objects or merely be planned nonrepresentational shapes.

Primary colors. The three colors in the spectrum which cannot be produced by a mixture of pigments: red, yellow, and blue.

Primitive art. The art of people with a tribal social order or a Neolithic stage of culture. This kind of art is characterized by heightened emphasis on form and a mysterious but vehement expression and content. A secondary meaning is found in the work of artists such as Henry Rousseau and Grandma Moses which shows a naivete of expression and form closely related to the untrained but often sensitive forms of folk art.

Proportion. The comparison of elements one to another in terms of their properties of size, quantity, and degree of emphasis. Proportion may be expressed in terms of a definite ratio such as "twice as big," or may be more loosely indicated in such expressions as "darker than," "more neutralized," or "more important than."

Radial balance. 1. Two or more identical forces distributed around a center point to create a repetitive equilibrium. 2. Rotating forces which create a visual circular movement.

Realism. A form of expression which retains the basic impression of visual reality but deviates only enough to relate and interpret universal meanings underneath surface appearances.

Reality. (*see* Visual reality)

Rectilinear shape. A shape which may be regular or irregular in character but is basically composed of straight lines.

Relief (sculptural). Partial projection from a main mass, the degree of projection determining the type of relief; limited three-dimensional masses bound to a parent surface.

Repetition. The use of the same visual element a number of times in the same composition. It may accomplish dominance of one visual idea, a feeling of harmonious relationship, or an obviously planned pattern.

Representation. A manner of expression by the artist in which the subject matter is naturalistically presented so that the visual elements seen by the observer are reminiscent of actual forms previously perceived.

Rhythm. A continuance, a flow, or a feeling of movement achieved by repetition of regulated visual units; the use of measured accents.

Romanticism. A philosophical attitude toward life which may occur at any time. In art, the *romantic* form is characterized by an experimental point of view which extols spontaneity of expression, intuitive imagination, and a picturesque rather than a carefully organized, rational approach. The *Romantic* movement of nineteenth century artists such as Delacroix, Gericault, Turner, and others is characterized by such an approach to form.

Saturation. (*see* Intensity)

Shadow, shade, shading. The area of a form which is dark in value because little or no light strikes it directly.

Shape. 1. An area having a specific character defined by an outline or by contrast of color, value, or texture with the surrounding area. 2. Three-dimensional: The silhouette (*see* definition) of an object, or a portion of that object, with an awareness of the forms (*see* definition) within.

Silhouette. The area existing between or bounded by the contours, or edges, of an object; the total shape.

Simultaneously. In art, use of separate views, representing different points in time and space, brought together to create one integrated image.

Simultaneous contrast. The direct contact between two colors tends to reduce the similarities and intensify the differences of the colors.

Space. 1. The interval between pre-established points. 2. Measurable distances. 3. "Denoting time or duration." (Oxford Universal Dictionary) *Two-dimensioned.* An extent (surface) possessing measurement as to length and breadth but lacking thickness or depth.

   Three-dimensioned. Possessing thickness or depth as well as length and breadth.

   Four-dimensioned. Possessing time as well as thickness or depth, length, and breadth.

   Decorative. In art terminology, limited to length and breadth.

   Plastic. Involving length, breadth, thickness or depth.

   Infinite. A pictorial concept in which the illusion of space has the quality of endlessness found in the natural environment. The picture frame has the quality of a window through which one can see the endless recession of forms into space.

   Shallow. This is sometimes called "limited depth" because the artist controls his use of the visual elements so that no point or form is so remote that it does not take its place in the pattern of the picture surface.

Spectrum. The band of individual colors which results when a beam of light is broken up into its component wavelengths of hues.

Style. The specific artistic character and dominant form trends noted in art movements or during specific periods of history. It also may mean the artist's expressive use of the media to give his work individual character.

Subject matter. In a descriptive style of art refers to the persons or things represented as well as the artist's experience which serve as his inspiration. In abstract or nonobjective forms of art it refers merely to the basic character of all the visual signs employed by the artist. In this case the subject matter has little to do with anything experienced in the natural environment.

Subjective. The personal as opposed to the impersonal; an individual attitude or bias through which the artist feels free to change or modify natural visual characteristics. In this approach, the artist is able to emphasize the emotions or feelings aroused within himself by the characteristics of the natural form.

Subjective colors.   Tones which are chosen by the artist without regard to the real color of the object. They have nothing to do with objective reality.

Surrealism.   A style of artistic expression which emphasizes fantasy and whose subjects are usually the experiences revealed by the subconscious mind.

Symbol.   Representation of a quality or situation through the use of an intermediate agent; the word is not the thing itself but a sign of the thing (for example, the owl represents blindness); indirect understanding as opposed to direct understanding through form-meaning.

Symmetrical balance.   A form of balance achieved by the use of identical compositional units on either side of a vertical axis within the confining pictorial space.

Tactile.   A quality which refers to the sense of touch.

Technique.   The manner and skill with which the artist employs his tools and materials to achieve a predetermined expressive effect. The ways of using the media can have an effect on the aesthetic quality of the artist's total concept.

Tectonic.   Pertaining to the quality of simple massiveness, lacking any significant extension.

Tenebrism.   A style of painting which exaggerates or emphasizes the effects of chiaroscuro. Larger amounts of dark value are placed close to smaller areas of highly contrasting lights in order to concentrate attention on certain important features.

Tension (pictorial).   Dynamic interrelationships of force as manifested by the moments of force inherent in art elements; semiarchitectural stresses affecting balance.

Texture.   The surface feel of an object or the representation of surface character. Texture is the actual and "visual feel" of surface areas as they are arranged and altered by man or nature.

   Actual.   A surface which stimulates a tactile response when actually touched.

   Simulated.   A representation of an actual texture created by a careful copying of the light and dark pattern characteristic of its surface.

   Invented.   Two-dimensional patterns sometimes derived from actual textures, frequently varied to fit pictorial needs, and often freely created without reference to any item.

Three-dimensional.   Possessing the measurements of length, width, and thickness; a solid surrounded by space.

Tonality.   An orderly planning in terms of selection and arangement of color schemes or color combinations. It is concerned not only with hue, but also with value and intensity relationship.

Tone.   The character of color or value of a surface determined by the amount or quality of light reflected from it. The kind of light reflected may be determined by the character of the medium which has been applied to the surface.

Trompe l'oeil.   A painting technique involving the copying of nature with such exactitude that the painted objects may be mistaken for the actual forms depicted.

Unity.   The whole or total effect of a work of art which results from the combination of all of its component parts.

Value.   1. The tone quality of lightness or darkness given to a surface or an area by the *amount of light* reflected from it. 2. (color) The characteristic of a color in terms of lightness and darkness. This is determined by the amount or quantity of light reflected by a color.

Value pattern.   The total effect of the relationship of light and dark given to areas within the pictorial field.

   Two-dimensional.   Value relationships in which the changes of light and dark seem to occur only on the surface of the picture plane.

   Three-dimensional.   The value relationships which are planned to create an illusion of objects existing in depth back of the picture plane.

Visual reality.   The objective (insofar as that is possible) optical image; obvious appearances; naturalism in the sense of the physically observed.

Void.   The penetration of an object to its other side, thus allowing for the passage of space through it. An enclosed negative shape.

Volume.   1. The space occupied by an object (preferred). 2. The object itself.

Wash.   A transparent layer or coating of color applied to a surface allowing underlying lines, shapes, or colors to show through. Any transparent medium may be lightly applied to previously painted shapes or areas in order to modify their appearance without completely hiding or covering them.

Bibliography

Arnason, H. H. *History of Modern Art.* Englewood Cliffs, N. J.: Prentice-Hall, Inc.; New York: Harry N. Abrams, Inc.

Barr, Alfred H., Jr. *Painting and Sculpture in the Museum of Modern Art.* New York: Simon & Schuster, Inc., 1946.

Bethers, Ray. *Composition in Pictures.* 2nd ed. New York: Pitman Publishing Corp., 1956.

Canaday, John. *Mainstreams of Modern Art.* New York: Henry Holt & Co., 1959.

Cheney, Sheldon. *Expressionism in Art.* New York: Liveright Publishing Corp., 1934.

Coleman, Ronald. *Sculpture: A Basic Handbook for Students.* Dubuque, Iowa: Wm. C. Brown Co., Publishers, 1968.

Compton, Michael. *Pop Art.* London: Hamlyn Publishing Group, Ltd., 1970.

Emerson, Sybil. *Design: A Creative Approach.* Scranton, Pa.: International Textbook Co., 1953.

Hunter, Sam. *American Art of the Twentieth Century.* New York: Harry N. Abrams, Inc.

Kepes, Gyorgy. *Language of Vision.* Chicago: Paul Theobald & Co., 1951.

Longman, Lester. *History and Appreciation of Art.* Dubuque, Iowa: Wm. C. Brown Co., Publishers, 1949.

Lucie-Smith, Edward. *Late Modern: The Visual Arts Since 1945.* New York: Frederick A. Praeger, Inc., 1969.

Mather, Frank J. *Concerning Beauty.* Princeton, N. J.: Princeton University Press, 1935.

McCurdy, Charles, ed. *Modern Art: A Pictorial Anthology.* New York: Macmillan Co., 1958.

Moholy-Nagy, L. *Vision in Motion.* 5th ed. Chicago: Paul Theobald & Co., 1956.

Onions, C. T., ed. *The Oxford Universal Dictionary.* 3rd ed. Oxford: Clarendon Press, 1955.

Rasmussen, Henry N. *Art Structure.* New York: McGraw-Hill Book Co., 1950.

Read, Herbert. *A Concise History of Modern Sculpture.* New York: Frederick A. Praeger, Inc., 1964.

Runes, Dagobert D., and Schrickel, Harry G. *Encyclopedia of the Arts.* New York: Philosophical Library, Inc., 1946.

Scott, Robert G. *Design Fundamentals.* New York: McGraw-Hill Book Co., 1951.

Seltman, Charles. *Approach to Greek Art.* New York: The Viking Press, Inc., Studio Books, 1948.

Seuphor, Michel. *The Sculpture of This Century.* New York: George Braziller, Inc., 1959, 1961.

Struppeck, Jules. *The Creation of Sculpture.* New York: Henry Holt & Co., 1952.

Wickiser, Ralph L. *An Introduction to Art Activities.* New York: Henry Holt & Co., 1947.

Chronological Outline of Western Art

200,000 B.C.	Prehistoric Art	Paleolithic Old Stone Age	
		Flint-tool industries	
25,000 B.C.		Art Beginnings cave painting, etc.	
10,000 B.C.		Neolithic New Stone Age	
		Beginning of architecture, pottery, weaving	

4000 B.C.	Ancient Art	Egyptian Old Kingdom	
3000 B.C.		Middle East Sumerian Babylonian	
2800 B.C.		Aegean Art Cretan (Minoan I)	
2200 B.C.		Cretan (Minoan II)	
2100 B.C.		Egyptian Mid-Kingdom	
1800 B.C.		Aegean Art Mycenaen Age (in Greece)	
1700 B.C.		Aegean Art Cretan (Minoan III)	
		Middle East Assyrian	
1580 B.C.		Egyptian New Empire	
1200 B.C.			
1100 B.C.		Aegean Art Homeric Age	ETRUSCAN ART, Italy
1090 B.C.		Egyptian Decadence and foreign influences	
750 B.C.		Greek Art Archaic Age	ETRUSCO-ROMAN, Italy
606 B.C.		Middle East Chaldean Babylonian	
530 B.C.		Middle East Persian (ca. 225 B.C.)	
470 B.C.		Greek Art *Classical Age*	
338 B.C.		Greek Art Hellenistic Age	
332 B.C.		Egypt Graeco-Egyptian or Ptolemaic	
280 B.C.			Graeco-ROMAN
146 B.C.		Greece Roman domination	ROMAN
30 B.C.		Egypt Roman domination	

300 A.D.	Medieval Art	EARLY CHRISTIAN ART in Italy
330 A.D.		EARLY BYZANTINE ART in Mid-East, Egypt (Coptic)
550 A.D.		MOHAMMEDAN or ISLAMIC ART, No. Africa, So. Spain (Moorish art)
768 A.D.		Carolingian Art, France, Germany, No. Italy
800 A.D.		DEVELOPED BYZANTINE ART, Mid-East, Greece, Russia, parts of Italy (Ravenna, Rome) (to 1453)
		Migratory, barbarian (Vikings, Huns, Goths), and Early Christian art in Western Europe
1000 A.D.		ROMANESQUE (Roman-like, or modified Roman art in France, England, No. Spain, Italy, and Germany)
1150 A.D.		GOTHIC ART in Europe

1300 A.D.	Renaissance Art	Proto-RENAISSANCE, Italy, Giotto, Duccio
1400 A.D.		EARLY Masaccio, Donatello, Francesca, Leonardo, etc.
		Renaissance in West modified by vestiges of Medievalism, Van Eycks, Weyden, Van der Goes
1500 A.D.		HIGH REN. Michelangelo, Raphael, Titian, Tintoretto; W. Europe influenced by Italy
1520 A.D.		Mannerism and Early Baroque, Italy

1600 A.D.	Baroque Art	BAROQUE ART in Europe. Age of Rubens, Rembrandt, Velasquez, etc. Early Colonial art, America
1700 A.D.		ROCOCO ART (primarily French, but spreads somewhat to other countries of Europe). Colonial art in the Americas

1800 A.D.	Modern Art	*Neoclassicism* David, Ingres, Canova (France)
1820 A.D.		*Romanticism* Gericault, Delacroix, Goya (Spain), Turner (England), Baryé (sculpture; France)
1850 A.D.		*Realism and Naturalism* Daumier, Courbet, Manet (France); Homer, Eakins (United States); Constable (England)
1870 A.D.		*Impressionism* Monet, Pissarro, Renoir, Degas (France); Sisley (England); Hassam, Twachtman (United States); Medardo-Rosso (sculpture; Italy); Rodin (sculpture; France)
1880 A.D.		*Post-Impressionism* Cezanne, Seurat, Gauguin, Van Gogh, Toulouse-Lautrec (France)
1900 A.D.	Twentieth-Century Art	*Sculptors working in a Post-Impressionist manner* Maillol (France); Lachaise (United States); Lehmbruck, Marcks, Kolbe (Germany)
1901 A.D.		*Expressionism* Picasso* Blue, Rose, and Negro Periods
		Les Fauves Matisse, Rouault, Vlaminck, Modigliani, Dufy, Utrillo (France)
		Recent French Expressionists (1930) Soutine, Fuffet, Balthus
		German Expressionists Nolde, Kirchner, Kokoschka, Schmidt-Rottluff, Marc, Jawlensky, Macke, Beckmann, Grosz, Dix
		Sculpture Marini (Italy); Epstein (England); Zorach (United States)
		Recent United States Expressionists (1930) Weber, Shahn, Levine, Avery, Baskin Orozco (Mexico)
1906 A.D.	Abstract Art (early)	*Cubism* Picasso,* Braque, Léger, Gris, Sculpture Laurens (French)
		Futurism Balla Boccioni, Severini, Carra (Italy)
ca. 1910 A.D.		*Abstraction and Nonobjective Art* Kandinsky, Albers (Germany); Moholy-Nagy (Hungary); Larionov, Malevich, Gabo, Pevsner, Tatlin (Russia); Delaunay (France); Sculpture Brancusi, Archipenko, Arp, Mondrian, VanDoesburg, Van Tongerloo (Holland); Nicholson, (England); Sculpture Epstein, Passmore
ca. 1912–15 A.D.		*Early United States Abstractionists* Dove, Marin, Feininger, Stella, O'Keefe, Mac-Donald-Wright, Stuart Davis, Demuth, Hartley, Knaths
		Later Abstractonists Diller, Pereira, MacIver, Tomlin; *Sculpture* Di Rivera, Nevelson, Hajdu (Rumania), Noguchi
ca. 1910 A.D.	Fantasy in Art	DeChirico (Italy); Chagall (France); Klee (Switzerland); Rousseau (French primitive)
1916 A.D.		*Dadaism* Tzara, Duchamp, Picabia (France); Ernst, Schwitters (Germany)
1924 A.D.		*Surrealism* Ernst (Germany); Tanguy (France, United States); Dali (Spain, United States); Magritte (Belgium); Masson (France); Bacon (England); *Sculpture* Giacometti (Switzerland); Gonzalez (Spain)
1925 A.D.		*Surrealistic Abstraction* Picasso* (France); Miró (Spain); Tamayo (Mexico); Matta (Chile, United States), Baziotes, Tobey, Gorky, Rothko, Hofmann, DeKooning (United States). Sculpture Moore, Hepworth (England); Lipchitz (Lithuania, United States, France); Calder (United States)
1930–1940 A.D.		*Traditional Realism* Regionalists: John Sloan, Grant Wood, Thomas Hart Benton; Andrew Wycth (United States)
1945 A.D.	Post-World War II Trends	*Abstract Expressionism and Action Painting* Pollock, Motherwell, Brooks, Francis, Frankenthaler, Tworkov, Rothko (United States); Mathiew, De Stael, Soulages, Manessier (France); Vieira da Silva (Portugal): Appel (Holland); Okada (Japan); Tapies (Spain)
1950 A.D.	Post-Painterly Abstraction	*Colorfield and Hard Edge Painters* (all United States) Newman, Morris Louis, Kelly, Noland, Stella, Poons
		Minimalists and Primary Structurists (sculpture); *Painters* Yves Klein (France); Olitsky, Reinhardt (United States); *Sculptors* Judd, Bontecou, Tony Smith, Di Suvero, Nevelson, Bill, Rosenthal, Bell (United States); Paolozzi, Caro, King (England)
ca. 1955 A.D.		*Neo-Dada and Funk Art* (collage-assemblage) Johns, Rauschenberg (United States); Dubuffet (France); *Sculptors* Keinholz, Stankiewicz, Mallory, Chamberlain (United States); César (France)
		Pop Art and Happenings Warhol, Lichtenstein, Dine, Indiana, Kaprow, Oldenburg, Segal, Grooms, Marisol, Wesselman, Rosenquist (United States); Hamilton, Kitaj, Smith (England)
1965–74 A.D.		*New Realism* Pearlstein, Ramos, Katz, Thiebaud, Lindner (United States)
		Op Art Vasarely (France); Anuskiewicz, Ortmann, Stanczak (United States); Agam (Israel); Riley, Denny (England)
		Environment, Land Art, or *Earthworks* Lansman, Andre, Chrysto, Smithson, Serra, Lewitt, Heizer, Oldenburg
		Technological Art (*Kinetics*) Wolfert (color organ, 1930–63); Tinguely (Swiss); Chryssa (Greece); Samaras, Sonnier, Riegack, Flavin (United States); Haese (Germany); Schoeffer (Hungary); Soto (Venezuela); Castro-Cid (Chile); Le Parc (Argentina); Takis (Greece)

*Artists frequently change their styles, hence the names appearing more than once under different categories of form-style. Most notable in this respect was Pablo Ruiz Picasso.

Index